P9-CRW-310

Also by Cynthia A. Branigan

Adopting the Racing Greyhound

The Reign of the Greyhound:
A Popular History of the Oldest Family of Dogs

THE LAST DIVING HORSE
IN AMERICA

THE LAST DIVING HORSE IN AMERICA

Rescuing Gamal and Other Animals—
Lessons in Living and Loving

Cynthia A. Branigan

Pantheon Books, New York

Copyright © 2021 by Cynthia A. Branigan

All rights reserved. Published in the United States by Pantheon Books,
a division of Penguin Random House LLC, New York, and distributed
in Canada by Penguin Random House Canada Limited, Toronto.

Pantheon Books and colophon are registered trademarks of
Penguin Random House LLC.

Library of Congress Cataloging-in-Publication Data
Names: Branigan, Cynthia A., author.
Title: The last diving horse in America : rescuing Gamal and other
animals—lessons in living and loving / Cynthia Branigan.
Description: New York : Pantheon Books, 2021. Includes index.
Identifiers: LCCN 2020055047 (print). LCCN 2020055048 (ebook).
ISBN 9781101871959 (hardcover). ISBN 9781101871966 (ebook).
Subjects: LCSH: Thoroughbred—New Jersey—Biography.
Horse adoption. Animal rescue. Human-animal relationships.
Seaside resorts—New Jersey—Atlantic City—History—20th century.
Classification: LCC SF293.T5 B73 2021 (print) |
LCC SF293.T5 (ebook) | DDC 636.1/3209749—dc23
LC record available at lccn.loc.gov/2020055047
LC ebook record available at lccn.loc.gov/2020055048

www.pantheonbooks.com

Jacket images: (top) courtesy of the author; (bottom) Postcard: Diving
Horse, Ocean End Steel Pier, Atlantic City, N.J.
Jacket design by Jennifer Carrow

Frontis: Vintage poster of Diving Horse show, Atlantic City
© Albatross/Alamy Stock Photo

Printed in the United States of America

2 4 6 8 9 7 5 3 1

To Gamal,

who inspired by example

THE LAST DIVING HORSE
IN AMERICA

Prologue

Gamal, the horse who would become mine, was born in the early 1950s, as was I. For all I know, we entered the world in the same year, month, and day.

He, a Texas native, went on to the more traditional horse pursuits of barrel racing and rodeos before being tapped for the unconventional career of diving. I was born in suburban New Jersey, and it was my father's fond hope that, after he invested in my education and travel, I enter a respectable profession of some sort. Instead, I became an inveterate rescuer of displaced animals. It was through our disparate occupations that Gamal and I wound up together.

We had help getting together, help that could be traced to two dissimilar yet equally headstrong men. "Doc" Carver, creator of the diving horse act, was born just before the Civil War, on the edge of America's fast-disappearing frontier. Carver was expected to follow in his father's footsteps, either as a doctor, or, as he did briefly, a dentist. Instead, he toured the world with diving horses while also showcasing his considerable sharpshooting skills. Cleveland Amory, scion of one of Boston's founding families, was born as America was entering World War I. His early life followed a prescribed route—prestigious boarding school followed by Harvard. But although he became a renowned writer, he devoted the last quarter of his life to advocating for animals.

There was a time when horses, flying through the air, could have been said to reflect the promise of America—the notion that anything, even the impossible, was possible. But as the decades wore on, people began to see the diving horse act as little more than animal cruelty. Eventually, diving horses became no more than a vacationer's distant memory.

That might have been the end of it, but there was one more chapter to be written in the diving horse saga: my relationship with the last of those horses.

Chapter One

In 1980 on West 57th Street in New York, you could set your watch by the chanting of the Hare Krishnas. Every afternoon at five o'clock the saffron- and claret- and tangerine-robed throng serenaded midtown with an ecstatic, impassioned, a cappella performance punctuated by a trembling tambourine. Actually, I heard them before I saw them, faintly when they rounded the corner of Seventh by Carnegie Hall, louder as they moved east toward the Russian Tea Room, and louder still as their spiritual conga line reached the office building of The Fund for Animals, where I was working. From a large bay window, I would gaze down at them as they snaked along the street, their daily devotional drifting from the gum-stained sidewalk, rising up the elegant but soot-covered building, and permeating the dingy windows.

Hare Krishna, Hare Krishna, Krishna Krishna, Hare Hare

Some of the other employees must have taken the song-and-dance routine as a sign from God that they should straighten their desks, pack their belongings, and call it a day. No one looked at me to see how long I was staying. By now they knew that I was more the ten-to-six type, or even the eleven-to-seven type, and no one was willing to stay at the office that late. And why should they? They arrived hours before I did. When they realized I was not watching them, they stopped watching me.

In fact, I barely noticed their departure. My interest was in the show on the street. It wasn't the Krishnas' bright swirling hues or

5

exotic sounds that caught my attention, although I could hardly be blamed if it was. Between New York's precarious financial footing and skyrocketing crime rate, these were bleak, even dangerous, times in the city. Any pop of color or hint of optimism was a welcome respite.

Neither was my interest in their ritual a result of my being shocked by every sight and sound in New York. I may not have been a native New Yorker, but I grew up little more than an hour away. It was vital to my father, if not always to me, that I be well traveled and well educated, someone who hailed from New Jersey, not Joisey. When we weren't traveling the world, we were visiting the crossroads of the world, New York.

Although I was affected by the Krishnas, surely it was not in the way they intended. I experienced no subsequent compulsion to bolt from the office, renounce my few worldly possessions, and join the devotees. My fascination was more practical than spiritual: they seemed not only to have discovered their calling, but knew what to do with it once they did. I could not say the same for myself.

My twin passions—wanting to write and wanting animals in my life—had been whispering in my ear for as long as I could remember. In Greyhound racing circles, they might have said I came out of the box with early speed. My mother unleashed a monster when, between music and art appreciation, she also taught me to read. By age three I had exhausted her homemade curricula and insisted on attending kindergarten. My parents enrolled me at the only school that would accept a child my age: a Victorian-era relic directed by its equally old-fashioned founder, Miss Ireland. By age five I grabbed my crayons, found some index cards, and wrote my first story, "The Book of a Kid's Life." The plot, thinly disguised propaganda: A girl refuses to take a nap unless her mother agrees to get both a cat and a dog from the local shelter. The mother relents, and both creatures become part of the family (using a writer's prerogative, I dropped the nap subplot).

In real life, my desire for animal companions was only partially fulfilled. We always had a cat or two, ragged males we found, or who found us. These scrawny, dirty, beat-up toms walked the thin line between feral and domesticated. With enormous scarred heads, and equally oversized testicles, their pleading eyes told a cautionary tale of what comes of being a slave to lust. If any stick-thin female cat tried to slither in our door, she would be whisked to an uncle's farm to live out her life as a mouser in an empty barn. Once there, I would never see her again; but I would never forget her, either.

I was given to understand that acquiring a dog was an impossibility. My father declared that they were too much trouble, had to be walked, had to be licensed, and, worst of all, held the potential to bite. He knew my proclivity for picking up and snuggling cats: I had the scars to prove it. But with a dog, the consequences of unwanted affection could be worse. So I made do with the old toms, and an assortment of short-lived creatures—birds and fish and hamsters—whose fragile bodies I carried home in flimsy containers from Woolworth's. Having no brothers or sisters, these animals became my de facto siblings.

Perhaps in the same way that I assumed the Krishnas were living out their dream, others might have assumed the same of me. After all, I was working side by side with author Cleveland Amory, the legendary founding father of the modern animal protection movement and president of The Fund for Animals. Yet I experienced my position as something of a double-edged sword. I had nearly free rein to choose and complete my own projects; and certainly by sitting at the feet of the master I was exposed to people and ideas I would otherwise have missed. But I had trouble finding my voice in the presence of such an august figure. None of the tasks I had tried—lobbying, picketing, or even working on the Fund's publications—had really been a good fit. It seemed that Cleveland was better at everything than I was, and I was left to wonder what, if anything, I really had to offer.

Cleveland Amory was the dominant figure in animal welfare. The towering Boston Brahmin with a booming voice and commanding presence had altered the public's consciousness about how we treat animals. Under his influence, the cause became more assertive, even aggressive. His goal, as he put it, was "to put cleats on the little old ladies in tennis shoes." After lending his name and his voice to other more established humane groups, he founded The Fund for Animals in 1967 with the motto "We Speak for Those Who Can't."

His thriving writing career, ranging from best-selling social commentaries such as *The Proper Bostonians* and *Who Killed Society?*, to being the well-known television critic for *TV Guide*, gave him access to like-minded celebrities and socialites who helped popularize his campaigns. His trademark wit ("I started out writing about Lady Astor and her horse, and later I just wrote about the horse"); his social standing; and his prominent career made the whole thing palatable to those who had never before considered the cause worthy. Besides, the times were ripe for social change. Only a few decades earlier, the civil rights movement had led the way, followed by the antiwar movement, and the feminist movement. Why not the liberation of animals?

I met Cleveland in 1974, after attending one of his lectures. I had never read a word he had written, barely knew who he was, but I was so galvanized by a pre-lecture radio interview that I pulled over my car to give the program my full attention. He had just published a book, *Man Kind? Our Incredible War on Wildlife,* that stirred a national debate on the subject of "sport" hunting. He and the interviewer discussed animal cruelty in a way I had never before heard it done—as a serious problem, one as worthy of people's attention as any other social ill. It signaled that concern for animals had reached the mainstream, that it was no longer the sole domain of fanatics, or softhearted women. When the radio host announced that Cleveland would be speaking that evening at the Art Alliance in Philadelphia, nothing could have kept me from attending. I had, even then, been seeking my place in the world, wondering how I could alleviate the suffering of animals. Fighting extinction was important; but the pain, the fear, the exploitation of animals was ubiquitous and urgent and spoke to me on many levels. I wanted to help, but how? I suspected Cleveland had the answer.

That evening, as the emcee joined the audience in applauding their guest, Cleveland rose to his full height of some six feet, four inches, strode to the podium, and slipped the emcee a familiar handshake. He stood for a moment, surveyed the audience while gathering

Cleveland Amory, 1974. We met after a speech he delivered in Philadelphia for his newly released book, *Man Kind? Our Incredible War on Wildlife.*

his thoughts, and ran his long slender fingers through his hair. This last move was a mistake. Hair that previously had been under some tenuous control now broke loose entirely. It seemed that a fine head of hair was the one gift he lacked. It wasn't thinning or receding, but it was an odd combination of wavy, straight, and wiry; and like the man himself, had a mind of its own. Adding to the catastrophe was the way it was styled, if you can call it that: it appeared to have been mowed, rather than cut. The unkempt hair drew my eyes to his overall appearance and the best I can say is that his hair matched the rest of him. Clearly, he was someone who had other things on his mind than sartorial splendor.

Cleveland's speech was not accompanied by photographs or charts, nor did he refer to any notes. In fact, his entire talk was off-the-cuff and conversational. But the moment his thunderous voice poured forth, the audience was his. I recognized a certain similarity between his tone and that of the evangelists my mother used to listen to on the radio as she washed the breakfast dishes. Cleveland was a preacher, too, but his gospel wasn't Jesus, it was kindness to animals. He gathered steam slowly, referring to his professional history, his books, his columns, his television appearances. But, he said, it was witnessing animal cruelty—a bullfight in Nogales, Mexico—that changed the course of his life. Some of what he said that night was recycled from his earlier radio interview, such as, "The mark of a civilized person

9

is how they treat those beneath them," but in the context of the evening, it didn't seem stale. These were points worth repeating.

While he told gruesome stories in graphic detail, he also found a way to lighten the mood by injecting humor, especially at the expense of the perpetrators of abuse. He said the best way to irritate a woman wearing fur is to say, loud enough so she can hear it, "But doesn't it make her look fat!" He repeated a remark he made in a review of the show *American Sportsman* that landed him in trouble with *TV Guide:* when a hunter pursuing his quarry was left hanging on the edge of a cliff, Cleveland said he was rooting for the cliff.

Half an hour passed in what seemed like minutes. Cleveland's last point was that he would be available afterward to speak to anyone in the audience who wanted to join him in his anticruelty crusade.

I was so stunned that he was actually asking for volunteers, that for a few seconds I hesitated. By the time I went forward, an eager if elderly throng of supplicants—the sort of women he wanted to equip with cleats—already had him surrounded. Some insiders called him Clip, or Clippy, his childhood nickname. Others wanted their books signed. Still others whispered in his ear as they discreetly pressed a check into his hand. Whenever I tried to move closer, there was always a shoulder or elbow in my way. I hovered on the fringe, resisting the urge to give up. I had no book for him to sign, and, in fact, had not even read his book. I didn't know him, barely knew who he was. Yet something told me that this was my chance. We made eye contact and he indicated nonverbally that he would get to me as soon as he could.

From the start, it was as if we were old friends. I told him I had been turned away while offering to volunteer with an endangered species program at the zoo because I was neither a scientist nor a veterinarian. Without missing a beat, Cleveland assured me that the lack of scientific credentials was no impediment to alleviating suffering, and that exactly the reverse might be true.

He took both of my hands in his and asked if I was free for breakfast the next morning. I had no idea what my schedule was like the following day, but I knew I'd make it work. He wrote the name of his

hotel and room number on a scrap of paper he dug out of his pocket
and told me he'd see me at eight sharp.

Cleveland was completely at ease as he leaned back in the suite's
sofa and lit a cigarette. He launched into a discussion of various
projects that the Fund had undertaken, the difficulties they were having, and their recent successes. "One of the problems in founding a
group called The Fund for Animals," he said, "is that everyone thinks
we're a bank and they want to make a withdrawal."

He stopped in mid-thought. "You say you're a reporter?"

I was surprised he had remembered from an offhand comment I
made the night before. Then again, the pad and pen I had taken from
my bag during his ramblings might have been a clue. I brought them
along in case I needed to take notes, but also as a prop. I didn't smoke,
but if I began to feel overwhelmed, I could at least hold on to a pen.

"Yes," I said, hoping to give the impression that I had my eye on
bigger things. "Reporting will be good training."

"Training for what?" he asked in the most skeptical of tones.

"Writing," I said with all the conviction I could muster. "I want
to be a writer."

Cleveland gave a knowing laugh. "Reporting is the worst training
there is for writing." This was delivered as a pronouncement with no
room for argument. Not that I wanted to argue. This distinctly was
not a meeting between equals.

He quizzed me about the kind of writing I wanted to do, what
books were on my nightstand, which writers I admired most. Then
he asked the question I had come to dread: where I had gone to college. This was something that, to me, seemed to require more than
simply the name of the place because, beyond counterculture insiders,
few had ever heard of it. But how much more to divulge? Certainly
I wasn't going to mention that a former president of the school had
delivered a one-sentence commencement address: "Don't shit on anyone's dream." Nor that the school had a dormitory named Xanadu.
Nor the call letters of its radio station, WOMB. I was not going

to delve into the goings-on at the co-ed dormitory, or the headline that blazed across the front page of the conservative *Manchester Union Leader:* "Bare Debauchery on the Hill." I also decided to leave out the fact that the school's current president, Leon Botstein, was a twenty-three-year-old doctoral student, even though he, like Cleveland, was a Harvard man.

Instead, I went for a generic description—Franconia was an experimental college that had abandoned the traditional grading system. He said nothing, but stared at me. He had, after all, the critical ear of a writer and I hadn't told a very compelling story. When I said it was located in the White Mountains, in Franconia, New Hampshire, there was a glimmer of interest. But when I added that it operated from the site of the former Forest Hills Hotel, Cleveland sat bolt upright.

"I know it well," he said. "In fact, I stayed there."

And we were off, with Cleveland telling stories of the way the exclusive and genteel place was then, while I countered with expurgated stories of its current incarnation. He asked about the elegant dining room, as if it held fond memories. I breezed over its new purpose as the school's shabby cafeteria, and instead raved about its spectacular view of the Presidential Range. He asked what I did with myself "up there," a strange question given that I had been a student. What else would I be doing?

Yet he sensed there was more going on than studying, and he was right. In fact, while I continued my lifelong habit of reading a wide variety of books at college, few had anything to do with coursework. Even at freewheeling Franconia, that wasn't exactly a recipe for academic success. Apart from reading, I spent much of my time rambling through the remote, snow-covered woods surrounding the school. I had no particular goal during these solo treks, just a desire to see what was out there. At a time when I was wondering who I was, and where my place was in the world, it is entirely possible that on some level I equated navigating my way through the wilderness with navigating my way through life.

I became adept at reading a compass and identifying animal tracks.

Looking for traces of animal life in the snow, mud, and sand became an obsession. While I was supposed to be bearing down on my college courses, perhaps even ones in a foreign language, I was instead reading the even more foreign languages of animals, ones that showed me how hard were their lives, and how magnificent their inventiveness and their triumphs.

Simple discoveries, such as differentiating between the paw prints of a raccoon and an opossum, or noticing that a thin, serpentine line in the snow was evidence of an animal dragging its tail, seemed miraculous. I became fluent in the language of wild creatures, yet was more astounded by the bond, the intimacy, that I was beginning to feel with these untamed beings.

In those broad expanses, I understood for the first time the difference between quiet and silence. Without a doubt, the alpine fields and forest were quiet. Except for the occasional cry of a circling hawk, or the sound of wind whistling through the trees, it was measurably quiet. But silence was another thing entirely. Silence was a palpable presence and became a soothing counterpoint to the everyday chatter inside my head. It was during one of my contemplative sojourns that I came across something that marked a turning point in my interest in helping animals.

I looked across at Cleveland, waiting for my answer about what I did at college, and wondered if I could trust him with what I considered a private matter. After all, we'd just met, and this was not something I had mentioned to anyone before. Somehow it was too personal, and too horrible. My fear was that he might not react with what I considered an appropriate degree of repulsion or sadness. Even worse would be if he accused me of that awful phrase I'd heard all of my life, that I was "too sensitive."

But just as in his way he was interviewing me, so, too, was I interviewing him. So I took a chance, and told him about the day, while following a trail of what I knew to be raccoon prints in the deep woods, I came across a raccoon's paw in a metal leg-hold trap. Just its paw, nothing else. Tiny frozen droplets of red blood, splattered against the white snow, told a terrifying and tragic tale of an animal so desperate to free itself that it had chewed off its own foot. That day, I knew I had to do something, somehow, to help other tortured, forgotten creatures.

Cleveland leaned forward, stared at the floor, and took a long draw on his cigarette. He was quiet.

Eventually he looked up and said, "This is just the kind of thing we have to do something about."

We. My heart leapt.

Before we were through, he informed me that I was the Fund's new volunteer eastern Pennsylvania coordinator. He offered no explanation of what that meant, nor did I ask; but I would have swept floors if that was what it took to help.

Four years later, after volunteering nearly full-time for the Fund by doing such things as picketing outside fur stores, leafleting at public events, giving media interviews, and, my favorite, chauffeuring Cleveland to his various appearances when he came to Philadelphia, finances forced me to take on a full-time job that was more lucrative, and more time-consuming, than what I had been doing— stringing for local newspapers. I was newly divorced and had half a dozen mouths to feed—cat mouths—and it was a responsibility I took seriously. My marriage had not been an absurd pairing. He had an interesting mind and was, after all, an animal lover; but our timing was off. The ignorance of youth took its toll, and we decided to explore what else and who else was out there, not realizing we would never meet either of our likes again.

Perhaps that's what it took, my unavailability, for Cleveland to reel me back in. For someone who abhorred hunting, he took a certain thrill in the chase. One deadly dull morning a few months into my new job, the phone rang in my office. It was Cleveland, asking me to come into the city so we could have a little chat.

I had been to the Fund's main office before, but this felt like the first time. As was typical when I came in for a meeting, Cleveland's first comment always concerned my welfare, if I made it in safely, whether the traffic was heavy. I would assure him I had arrived intact.

His long legs were often propped on his desk and crossed at the ankle. He would lean back in his padded blue leather, high-back chair and take a draw from his cigarette, an inch or two of ash hanging perilously from its tip. With one eyebrow arched as in his *TV Guide* sketch, he would look me over, make some flattering remarks about my appearance or my outfit, and then call in to his assistant, "Doesn't she look great, Marian?" She would mumble affirmative noises while I flushed with embarrassment.

That day, we spent an hour talking alternately about what I was doing for the Fund in Pennsylvania (not as much since I now had a full-time job), and what projects the Fund had undertaken elsewhere. In between, Cleveland took calls from the West Coast offices, phoned a friend about a chess match scheduled for the next day, or simply turned his chair sideways and stared out the window, presumably deep in thought. Anyone expecting a linear discussion with Cleveland would have been disappointed. There was no mention of a paying job for me, none at all, and I was beginning to think he really just wanted to have a chat. He seemed to enjoy my company, and our conversations were always as much about writing and reading, history and current events, as about animals.

Cleveland looked at his watch and, without explanation, stood up and asked Marian if she wanted to join us for dinner. Often she did, and was good company; but that night she did not. This was a small relief. If the subject of a job, or worse yet, money, was to be broached, I preferred it be done privately. We exited the building and turned left, which meant we would be going to what I thought of as our Italian restaurant, Fontana di Trevi, directly across from the Fund's office.

I don't know when Fontana was established, but I suspect that the decor had not changed much, if at all, in decades. It had the feeling of an old-fashioned supper club, minus the cabaret act. It was a narrow space with brass adornments on tan, stucco walls, and behind the bar, a hand-painted mural of the Trevi Fountain in Rome. A dining room captain, flanked by a fleet of Italian waiters, took orders by memory. Serving customers was not something these men did while waiting for their big break on Broadway. Serving customers was their break, their profession. Everyone knew "Mr. Amory" by name, he was a regular. A phalanx of servers gave him a half bow as he walked to his table.

We no sooner settled in when another of the Fund's field agents joined us. He would be attending a Billy Joel concert that night at Carnegie Hall and he, too, had arranged dinner with Cleveland. Whether it was before I was invited, or after, I didn't know. Although I liked the man well enough, I was not pleased with this turn of events. Maybe he wasn't, either.

Eventually, the agent left for his concert and Cleveland got down to business: a job offer. Its description, a grab bag of tasks: I was to keep close tabs on pending animal-related legislation in Trenton and Harrisburg, and write and edit the Fund's brochures and newsletter. Beyond that, it would be as when I was a volunteer: do whatever needed doing.

Eventually, he brought up a subject that, for wildly divergent reasons, neither of us wanted to discuss: money. He spoke from a deeply ingrained, perhaps even genetic script, one dictating that money was something to be held on to, not spent. Meanwhile, my own deeply ingrained script whispered that I should accept whatever was offered.

Cleveland began by reminding me that the Fund was not a bank, nor should anyone (presumably me) go into this sort of work for the money. I was insulted by the suggestion. Could he possibly think money had been my motivation? After I had volunteered nearly full-time for years? Then he pointed out that he himself did not take a salary, unlike the leaders of other, and by implication, lesser groups. When I heard him use the phrase "a living wage," I tuned out. Across the small dining room, I watched the captain's latest performance. With a pestle, he pounded a few cloves of garlic into the bottom of an oversized wooden salad bowl, cracked open a delicate white egg, and with theatrical flourish, whisked the two together.

At some point, I realized Cleveland had stopped speaking, and worse, seemed to have posed a question.

"Well?" he asked, for what I suspected was the second time.

"When would I begin?"

"As soon as you want," he said.

"Would my salary include health benefits?" I took a wild guess this hadn't been offered.

I could tell by the way he furrowed his brow that he was annoyed. "You can buy coverage as part of the group plan."

I reached across the table and extended my hand.

"So, we have a deal?" he asked.

I nodded and we shook on it.

I may not have known the amount I was to be paid, but with as many advance cautions as Cleveland had issued, I knew it would be meager. But I did know two other things about the job that were more important to me than money; and as shrewd as Cleveland was, he probably knew, too: I would be making a contribution toward the welfare of animals, and I would be doing so with near-total autonomy. He settled the tab and, slipping into grandfatherly mode, insisted on accompanying me to the parking garage.

"One more thing," Cleveland said as we skirted the stragglers rushing to Carnegie Hall to hear Billy Joel. "If I call one day and ask what you're doing, and you tell me you're writing, I'll consider that a very good thing."

I was twenty-five years old. I couldn't imagine how life could get any better than this.

A few years later, I was in charge, albeit temporarily, of The Fund for Animals. That may be a bit of an overstatement: I wasn't making policy, issuing directives, or mapping out the organization's future; but I would certainly be the one taken to task if everything fell apart in Cleveland's absence.

Cleveland was not the kind to go on vacation, ever. Along with watching every penny, another part of his DNA code compelled him to work almost nonstop, at least fifteen hours a day Monday through Friday and several hours a day on weekends. He had, after all, two full-time jobs: his writing career (for which he was paid) and his animal protection career (for which he was not).

But just because Cleveland did not take vacations did not mean

Cleveland Amory, with my cats Ramsey and Blanche, 1983.
Cleveland loved all animals, but felines held a special place in his
heart. The six-foot, four-inch man with a booming voice was not
at all shy about cuddling with cats. He became famous early in his
career with such social commentaries as *The Proper Bostonians,* but
later success came from animal-related books such as his anti-hunting
treatise *Man Kind?* and his best-seller *The Cat Who Came for Christmas,*
which detailed the exploits of his former stray cat, Polar Bear.

he never left the city, or that he was a slave to the office. One choice
opportunity required him to be away for a month: the Cunard Line
hired him to give talks and otherwise entertain the passengers aboard
the *QE2.* Two weeks would be spent at sea, one week going to England, and one week returning. Once abroad, he always managed to
dig up some additional work. In style and interests, Cleveland har-
kened to an earlier, and some might say more civilized, era. So, too,
did the Cunard Line and its passengers. Their clientele tended toward
the older, more affluent segment of society, the sort Cleveland would
persuade to contribute to the Fund's coffers.

The only downside to this busman's holiday was that such a long
absence required, and was enhanced by, the company of his longtime
assistant Marian Probst. Since it would have been impossible for both
of them to leave if the Fund were left unattended, I was asked to fill
in. I don't pretend to know why Cleveland chose me. Maybe I was
the only one available. Maybe it was just part of my amorphous job.
Or maybe I was the only one he could trust to take proper care of his

beloved cat Polar Bear, the feline who was about to become famous in Cleveland's best-seller *The Cat Who Came for Christmas*. Apparently I did not disgrace myself: I was brought back for several repeat performances.

In typical Cleveland fashion, he did not give any instructions, but it became clear within a day or two that prioritizing the incoming phone calls was, well, a priority. They came from one of three sources: other Fund agents, the media, and outsiders who wanted to make Cleveland aware of a particular problem facing animals.

Callers in need of money shot to the top of my list, and I would discuss their requests with Cleveland during his frequent, but not daily, calls. But if a project required an immediate decision, I used my best judgment. I knew that spending money on lawyers, or fundraising campaigns, was anathema to Cleveland. Conversely, if money for, say, a veterinarian, would save an animal's life, he would grumble, but eventually would agree. The first few times I loosened the purse strings on my own were daunting, but it became easier. Too easy, Cleveland might have said.

Long days at the office veered from incessant phone calls to extended quiet stretches when I read some of the books, galleys, and manuscripts that arrived daily by the dozen. For some, Cleveland was asked to write a review for publication. For others, he was asked to give a blurb for the book jacket, a complimentary phrase or two ("a must read," "compelling," "gripping"). Still others were unsolicited manuscripts sent by complete strangers, full of gall or naïveté, wanting either a critique or help in finding a publisher. Cleveland's fame as an author and an activist had its benefits, but also its price.

After work, I had little reason to rush back to Cleveland's apartment. Under other circumstances, say, with a friend or lover, staying in his apartment with its commanding view of Central Park might have been the biggest perk of baby-sitting the Fund, and Polar Bear. But when the workday was over, I was alone. I didn't relish the thought of solitary confinement, so I wandered the streets of Manhattan, exploring and observing.

The best part of these nightly walkabouts was the end, when I would visit with the carriage horses that waited for passengers at the southern boundary of Central Park, just across the street from Cleveland's apartment. I always had a little something in my pocket for these stoic animals that I imagined were as out of place and lonely as I. The drivers would put on a moment's worth of charm to ask, in thick Irish brogues, if I wanted a ride. When I declined, they chatted up other potential customers. When I asked if I could pat their horses, or give them a carrot or apple or cube of sugar, they shrugged, which I took to be a yes. In those simpler times, no one wondered if I might poison the horses, or bring a lawsuit if my finger was mistaken for a snack.

The horses possessed a patience I couldn't fathom and stood Zen-like, harnessed, hitched, and forced by blinders to stare straight ahead. Their blinders made it tough to slip them a treat, and sometimes they startled slightly when my outstretched palm appeared out of nowhere. But I thrilled when they gave a gentle snort, or stamped a hoof in appreciation.

Had the drivers been more talkative, I might have connected with them, too—about their horses, or why they came to America. I might even have told them about how, when my Irish ancestors came here (decades before the famine, as my father often reminded me), they set up tents in this very park, just over that low, stone wall. But the men had other things on their minds. Alone, and neither tourist nor resident, I threaded my way through traffic back to Cleveland's apartment.

I took hundreds of calls while Cleveland was out of town, but one was in a category of its own.

"I want to speak to Cleveland, and I want to speak to him now," demanded the no-nonsense voice on the other end of the line.

Many people called asking for Cleveland, and few referred to him as Mr. Amory, but all were, at the very least, civil. It was impossible to know without asking who actually was acquainted with him, and who knew him only by reputation. But I knew one thing about this caller: she was a prickly character. I had no interest in going a round or two, so I played it safe and steered the conversation right down the middle.

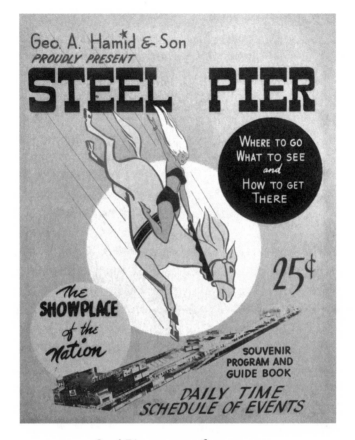

Steel Pier program from 1955

"Cleveland is out of the country, ma'am. If you give me your name and number, I'm sure he'll call you when he returns in a few weeks."

"Didn't you hear me?" she admonished. "I said now. This is an urgent matter. Who the hell is in charge there?"

I paused. "I am."

"Well then, you'd better get on the ball, girl," she commanded.

In the next few minutes she told me of a dire situation involving the Atlantic City Steel Pier Diving Horses. I gasped at the very phrase, diving horses. Had I not been from New Jersey, I might have thought the woman was delusional, or a crank caller making up the most preposterous thing she could conjure. But I knew very well what diving horses were: animals trained to leap, with a woman on their backs, from a forty-foot platform into a ten-foot-deep tank of water. It was an act so unique, and so bizarre, that few visitors to Atlantic City passed up the experience. The horse act was something that seemed always to have been there, and would always be.

I was jolted by the phrase because it took me back to a time and place I hadn't thought of in years, and hadn't wanted to. I saw the act once, in the summer of 1964, when I was eleven. The diving horse was gray, and while I pretended to view the performance the way most people did—as a shocking, even frightening stunt—there was something else about it that left a deep and lasting impression, something I could not put into words yet which moved me deeply.

Now it was a bittersweet memory. Those magical days on the boardwalk were the last time I experienced my life as whole. Only a few months later, my beloved grandfather would die unexpectedly in front of me; my father would sell our house and move my mother and me to an apartment in another state (while losing my cat in the process); and despite my protestations, I would be sent to a harsh boarding school. From that time on, I considered myself an orphan with parents.

The cranky woman brought my attention back to business. The Steel Pier had been sold, she told me, and the diving horses were part of the deal. No one wanted them for diving, no one wanted them for anything. No one, not their former owner and not their present one, had made any provision for them. Despite the fact that they worked for a living and supported dozens of people, no pension or retirement home awaited. No one gave them a second thought.

In the sell-off of fixtures and furnishings, a dapple-gray horse, Powderface, had already disappeared at a bottom-tier horse auction. Horses at these places were, almost invariably, sold by the pound for slaughter and wound up in Canadian abattoirs. It appeared that Powderface's final public performance was in one of those auction rings.

One of the other two horses, the lone mare named Shiloh, was sold to a woman for riding. For now, she was safe. But the remaining horse, a twentysomething bay-colored gelding named Gamal, was in jeopardy: while he had spent a year giving lessons at a summer riding camp, he was soon to be resold at an auction.

Somehow, the cantankerous woman had gotten wind of this information and pressed me for an answer.

"Are you listening? One horse is already in a can of dog food and another is soon to follow. What are you going to do about it?" she snapped.

In a sickening rush, I realized that the gray horse I saw that summer must have been Powderface, the one already killed. The story suddenly became personal. The woman could not have known what the diving horses represented to me; nor how, inadvertently, she had pried open a long-suppressed memory of a lost life. In that moment, I would have sold the family jewels, had there been any, to save Gamal.

Although I was a novice with horses, not to mention lacking the authority to make such a major decision, I realized this was my chance to make a difference.

"We'll take care of him. I promise," I said.

Even I was surprised by my confidence.

"I know you will," she said. "And I'll be watching to make sure." She hung up without saying another word.

I was slightly light-headed as I stood up from the chair behind Cleveland's big desk and looked between the towers of books and piles of papers covering every flat surface of the bay windowsill. I could still hear the Krishnas chanting, but more softly now. Their work in front of our office building was coming to a close and they were moving on to another cathedral of commerce in need of their supplications.

What had I just done? Promise an unknown woman we'd save the last diving horse? Was this the decisive moment I had waited for? Or, in my eagerness to help, had I just gone too far?

The devotees' voices were still ardent, the swirling colors of their robes still shimmering, but fading now as they continued east in the dimming light toward Sixth Avenue, then Fifth. I'm sure they would have been gratified if I took their chanting as a kind of blessing for what had just transpired. And maybe it was.

Chapter Two

That evening, I didn't hang around the office, didn't take my customary walkabout, didn't do any of the things that had become my makeshift routine. Instead, with heart racing, I walked directly to Cleveland's apartment. I told myself I needed to be there in case he checked in, so I could tell him about the momentous phone call, but the truth was something else entirely. The plight of the diving horses unleashed a flood of memories, and all that I had suppressed over the years was now at the surface, demanding attention.

I brewed a pot of tea to keep myself awake and warm, stretched the telephone cord so that it reached outside, and, on that chilly late April evening, planted myself on Cleveland's balcony. The expansive view of Central Park from his apartment inspired equally expansive thoughts, and I often sat there dreaming of my glorious but as-yet-undefined future. But this time my mind drifted squarely to my past.

In late August 1964, my parents and I drove from our suburban Trenton home, through the wild Pine Barrens of southern New Jersey, to Atlantic City. It would be my first time visiting the resort town. My father would be attending the Democratic National Convention, not as a delegate but as part of his job as public relations officer for the state attorney general. My mother and I were along for the ride.

In the days before interstate highways, and even before the Atlantic City Expressway, part of any trip to the southern New Jersey coastline required passing through a vast, sparsely inhabited territory known as the Pine Barrens. It is a gently sloping land of pygmy pines and sugar sand, where lake water, colored by cedar trees, is as cool and clear as iced tea. But I was not lulled into complacency: lurking deep within those impenetrable piney woods and cedar swamps was the Jersey Devil, a sinister legendary character who, since colonial times, had been lying in wait to do God knows what to unsuspecting passersby.

My father never tired of trotting out his old line, "Lock your door—the Jersey Devil is on the loose!"

When I was younger, I would squeal in a combination of horror and delight at the mere mention of the monster. But by 1964, I was too old to fall for it—almost. After all, as I would tell anyone who asked, I was eleven going on twelve, practically an adult and certainly someone who knew the Jersey Devil wasn't real.

I gave my father an exaggerated eye-roll and drew out the words, "Oh, Dad." But when I thought he wasn't looking, I inched my elbow across the inside of the car door and quietly pushed down the lock.

Atlantic City was built on a barrier island, Absecon, just off the mainland and was connected by a long causeway. As we drove across the broad, bright, flat salt marshes, I expected ocean and horizon. Instead, the heavily developed skyline blocked the natural view completely. Like a secular Mont Saint-Michel, Atlantic City rose up and beckoned in the distance, promising a worldly paradise. It shimmered in the late summer heat like a mirage, glimmered in the sunlight as if made of gold. It was accessible, yet just far enough away to be tantalizing. Atlantic City was not shy, and certainly not modest: she was outspread for the entire world to see.

I had been treating my captive parents to a solo version of a new song by the Drifters that alluded to racy goings-on at the beach, "Under the Boardwalk."

As if channeling her youth, my mother countered with an entirely innocent song from her era, "On the Boardwalk (in Atlantic City)."

Something in her stirred as we entered this urban seashore. My mother was a Clothier, a name that held as much sway in Philadelphia as did the Amory name in Boston. Although she was from a lesser branch of the family tree, she bore traces of her pedigree—impeccable manners, an encyclopedic knowledge of the interrelatedness of old-line families, and, above all, a firm belief that it was my father's job to support the household while it was her job to be supported. Fortunately, he shared that belief.

She delighted in telling stories that began, "Now, when I was a young girl . . ." As a youth, she spent part of her summers in Atlantic City with her two older sisters. I was reminded of a photo of the three of them, displayed on the mantel at home. Wearing skirted, industrial-strength bathing suits, they posed in the sand while a many-tiered hotel that resembled a wedding cake loomed in the background.

We drove through the crowded streets, which included conventioneers as well as regular summer tourists, and even I could see that Atlantic City was neither as graceful nor as well tended as "our" genteel seaside resort at the southernmost tip of the New Jersey coast, Cape May. Atlantic City seemed to revel in its lack of order and untidiness and was all about action, a place where people could cut loose and have fun. Bars proliferated and women (not to mention boys and even men) wore revealing bathing suits frowned upon in Cape May. While the hotels here were indeed towering, more like the skyscrapers I'd seen in Manhattan, they seemed less impressive than just plain old-fashioned.

In 1964, Atlantic City was beginning its slow, steady decline from being, as it promoted itself, the World's Playground. Yet like a has-been movie star wearing too much makeup, doused in perfume, and hopelessly out of style, Atlantic City was still treated with deference, not for what she was in that moment, but for what she used to be. Young people like myself knew Atlantic City only in its current state of mild deterioration; but those from just one generation earlier might have experienced the resort in its heyday, or heard stories from their parents, or grandparents.

Atlantic City seemed like an odd choice for a big national event that would be televised. We were, after all, at the beach with half-naked people parading around. Wasn't the town just a little dirty, a trifle run-down? I mentioned this to my father, which led to an inevitable lesson. "This is how the political machine works," he said with a knowing sigh. "A mutual back scratch between Governor Hughes and President Johnson: hold the convention here, in this place that needs a shot in the arm, and we'll deliver the votes for you in November."

Politics aside, Atlantic City in 1964 was still considered a "destination," even if most people beyond the immediate area didn't really know why. Maybe it was because of *Monopoly*, the board game that borrowed the names of the city's streets: Baltic, Park Place, and of course, Boardwalk. It was something that gave everyone a sense of familiarity with the town.

Maybe people felt a kinship because of the Miss America pageant, an event dreamed up by a public relations person in 1921 as a way to extend the summer season into late September. Once they began broadcasting it on TV in the mid-1950s, everyone tuned in— whether to listen to Bert Parks sing "There she is, Miss America!"; to make fun of the various contestants; or to root for the girl from their home state.

Or maybe the country's lingering fascination with Atlantic City stemmed from the incongruous juxtaposition of an actual, year-round city, one with crime and garbage and businesses, mixed with sand and sun and ocean. It gave the impression that life, regular humdrum life, could be more like a full-time vacation, if only you allowed it. Do what you have to do from nine to five, but then hit the beach.

My father was free on our first evening, and the three of us took to the boardwalk for a stroll and in search of dinner. Immediately, we were assaulted by sights and sounds competing for attention. Everything here was oversized, even Mr. Peanut, a somewhat sinister-looking character with one dead, monacled eye, a cane, top hat, spats, and skinny black legs protruding from a giant plastic peanut-shaped body. His job was to wave to tourists and dispense free miniature cellophane packets of Planter's peanuts. Nearby, pigeons, familiar with the ritual and as well trained as any animal act on the piers, hovered eagerly. Once we opened the packets, the birds landed on our heads and shoulders, or sat on our outstretched palms, gorging themselves.

At the Atlantic City boardwalk, age eleven. Gamal and the other two diving horses were performing at the far end of the Steel Pier. August 1964.

Low-flying propeller airplanes buzzed overhead trailing banners that read "Tan, Don't Burn. Get Coppertone" or touting boat rides around Absecon Island. The boardwalk was many times longer, and wider, than Cape May's and I could see why some people chose to be pushed up and down in rolling chairs that resembled adult-size wicker baby carriages. The boardwalk had the feel of a full-time carnival. Although it was not yet dark, lights flashed on every sign. Shopkeepers hawked their wares, cheap souvenirs or beach paraphernalia, while others suggested we try our luck at tossing a ring around a milk bottle or popping a balloon with a dart to win a stuffed toy. Interspersed were high-end specialty stores and even art galleries. Signs as big as those in Times Square advertised everything from Ballantine Beer to Camel Cigarettes. And everywhere, the deafening clang of bells, shrill whistles, or snippets of hurdy-gurdy music.

The three of us were so distracted that we had to jump aside to avoid being run over by the LBJ Bandwagon. It resembled a Conestoga wagon with a giant helium balloon in the shape of a bucktoothed donkey tethered to it. A man dressed as an Indian chief, and for all I know he was the real thing, stood stone-faced against a wall where, for a small fee, people could have a photo taken of themselves with him. A red-faced, bleary-eyed conventioneer attempted to affix a button that said LBJ for the USA to my mother's blouse until my

A diving horse on the Steel Pier while tourists circling
Absecon Island watch the act from the Atlantic Ocean. 1960.

father intervened. The overall atmosphere was one of revelry, excitement, and celebration, not thoughtfulness or contemplation about the momentous decision to be made at the convention.

Even the Republicans got in on the act. A billboard featured a photo of their candidate, Barry Goldwater, with the tag line, "In Your Heart, You Know He's Right." My father explained that this was meant as a slap in the face to the Democrats and would probably not go unchallenged. The next day, Democrats, or at least their sympathizers, erected a small sign directly beneath it that said, "Yes . . . extreme right." Not to be outdone, one of the diving horses was fitted with a red, white, and blue vest bearing the initials LBJ.

Up ahead was Convention Hall, where the Democrats were to gather the next day. In the late 1920s, political boss Enoch "Nucky" Johnson of later *Boardwalk Empire* fame had the gigantic structure built to lure conventioneers and others to the town year-round. It worked: not only were conventions held there, but so were indoor events as diverse as football games, flower shows, and even Greyhound races. It also housed what my father said was the world's largest musical instrument: a pipe organ.

In August 1964, the only thing bigger in Atlantic City than the release of the Beatles' movie *A Hard Day's Night* was the Democratic National Convention being held there. Not to be upstaged, the diving horses grabbed some of the attention by showing support for Lyndon Baines Johnson.

He flashed his press pass to a guard at the door and asked if he could take us inside for a peek. The guard gave us the once-over and with a wordless nod waved us through.

While I had not yet visited the great cathedrals in Europe, I had seen photos. There was something about the hushed, semi-darkened space, this monument to human endeavors, that inspired the same sense of awe.

Giant head shots of LBJ hung above the stage at the front of the room. These were flanked by photos of other luminaries of the party, including JFK and Truman, and the phrase "Let Us Continue . . ." At first, I did not understand what it meant. Then I felt a familiar lump rise in my throat: the assassination, only nine months earlier, cut short Kennedy's term. Now Johnson was promising to carry on his vision. To me, it seemed an almost insulting suggestion, that we should pretend nothing had happened, or that Kennedy could be replaced.

I was still somewhat traumatized by the assassination, we all were in one way or another. Certainly the duck-and-cover air raid drills of my childhood did nothing to foster a sense of security. Still, no one ever dropped "the big one" on us. And while the Cuban missile crisis cast a dark shadow, real trouble had been averted. But when Kennedy was shot, my illusion that evil and terror could never hit close to home was shattered.

Just opposite Convention Hall, a civil rights vigil was in full view. My father explained the reason: black delegates from Mississippi were demanding to be seated alongside the white delegates from their state, not as fraternal delegates. I pretended to understand what that meant, but I knew something was terribly wrong if they weren't being treated just like everyone else. One protester held a sign that read, "Separate but equal is not equal." That, I understood.

My mother lightened the mood by going back to her youth. As she expounded on the relative merits of Fralinger's saltwater taffy (thicker) versus James's saltwater taffy (smoother), she became a girl again, I could see it in her eyes, hear it in her voice. It occurred to me that perhaps her best years, the ones she was most fond of, were behind her.

"See all of these piers," she said, pointing down the length of the boardwalk. "They weren't built for ships or fishing, they were built for entertainment." My father felt compelled to put the piers in context: land on the island was limited, so they expanded the city by building long platforms out into the ocean.

By now it was dark. Up and down the boardwalk, the lights of the piers stretched into the Atlantic like fingers grasping that last bit of undeveloped real estate.

"Oh my goodness," she went on. "There were so many. Let's see, Central Pier, Heinz Pier, Million Dollar Pier, Steeplechase Pier."

At that moment, we happened to be standing in front of another pier, the most well known. My mother looked up and realized where we were.

"Of course," she said, laughing at her omission. "The Steel Pier, where they have the diving horses! It was always our favorite. When you went to the very end, it was just like you were on a ship out in the ocean. We saw Benny Goodman there, and Glenn Miller, too."

"By the way," my father interrupted, "I have something for you."

I thought this third vacation of the year, not to mention summer camp, was gift enough; but I snapped to in anticipation of more.

"You know, I'm going to be working off and on while we're here, but for at least one full day and evening, you and your mother will be on your own."

He reached into the inside pocket of his jacket, and with a flourish, handed me a small white envelope. "This ought to keep you busy for a few hours."

I could not have been more surprised than if he had pulled out a rabbit or a pair of doves: the envelope held two passes for reserved seats to the Beatles' *A Hard Day's Night,* which just opened at one of the Steel Pier's two theaters. Except for a dog and a horse, there was nothing I wanted more in the world than to see that movie. I hugged him, kissed his cheek, and whispered in his ear, "You are the best, best, best daddy in the whole world."

When I pulled back, I thought I saw his eyes begin to water; but had I asked, he would have said it was my imagination, or just from a bit of sand blown in from the beach. But I knew better.

My mother and I were used to being on our own in Cape May, where my father would drop us off for a week or two every summer while he toiled in Trenton; but Atlantic City was something else entirely. Sedate Cape May had only a six-seater Ferris wheel, and a miniature golf course. A jam-packed evening might include watching saltwater taffy stretched on a machine or joining in the Bunny Hop at the small municipal auditorium. Atlantic City offered nonstop entertainment of every kind. I looked forward to packing in as much as possible without my father's well-meaning but dampening constraints. I knew that in my mother's less than capable hands, I would have nearly complete freedom. Our relationship was more like that of sisters (I being the elder); or she as an indulgent nanny and I, her obstreperous charge. She found it easier to let me to do whatever I wanted rather than assert herself.

All day, I ate as much of anything as I wanted. I rented a bicycle (my mother never learned to ride), and while she waited for me on a bench, I tore up and down the boardwalk, well beyond her sight. At one point, I jumped down to the sand to have a quick look under the boardwalk, to see what really went on there. There were no racy goings on, at least not for humans. All I saw were the slightly sinister, glowing eyes of dozens of feral cats.

She and I did a little window-shopping until I decided to turn it into the real thing. A pair of black loafers with whipstitching called to me from the display at I. Miller's shoe store. My mother had a weakness for good quality shoes, so it was not that difficult to convince her to go inside. They had calfskin lining ("As soft as butter," the salesman assured. "No breaking in needed") and cost two or three times what my father would have considered prudent. My mother forked over the cash and arranged to have them delivered to our hotel.

For her sake, we rented an umbrella at the beach. My father always insisted I stay out of the sun, but for the first time in my life I had full exposure: no hat, no sunglasses, no suntan lotion. While she stayed beneath the umbrella (she never learned to swim, either), I hit the waves. I was always the one farthest out, beyond the breakers. The lifeguards called me in so often that one of them grabbed me by the arm as I washed up onshore, returned me to my mother, and demanded she exert some control. I studied her face and saw that just as I had been in over my head in the ocean, she was in over her head with me.

By dinnertime, my head throbbed, my stomach churned, I alternated between fever and chills. I couldn't let on, though, couldn't jeopardize missing out on what I considered the most important event in my life: seeing *A Hard Day's Night.*

As showtime drew near, I began to feel more and more sick. For once, my mother took the lead as I hobbled behind. The brand-new I. Miller loafers dug into my heels and formed deep, painful blisters on my swollen, sunburned feet. My mild case of sunstroke and overindulgence caused the flashing lights and loud noises of the boardwalk to take on a surreal quality. I declined dinner, but my mother insisted I have a Coke, which, to her, was a form of medicine.

We pressed on and stood passively at the end of the movie line that stretched from mid-pier to the boardwalk and curled around the corner. I told her we already had tickets and pleaded that we go up front; but rather than appear pushy, she would accept any second-class treatment. I checked the Timex watch my grandfather had given me for Christmas and realized that at this rate we would never even make it inside.

Just as I was about to give up hope, an officious theater employee strutted past and announced that the show was sold out. I tugged on his sleeve and told him we had reserved seats.

"Well, whattya doin' here?" he scolded. "The show's already started."

He escorted us inside and at random displaced two girls.

And then, after so much anticipation, I fell asleep, dozed right through the nonstop screams of the girls in the audience, not to mention the movie itself. The excesses of the day had taken their toll.

My mother shook my shoulder and told me the movie was over. She suggested we call it a night, skip the rest of the attractions on the pier, and head back to our room at the Ambassador Hotel. I agreed until I remembered the diving horses. Without warning, I reverted from being almost a teenager to being a child: I began to cry.

"I must see the horse," I begged. "I can't miss him."

I was as surprised as she by how much this suddenly meant to me.

The horses performed at the far end of the Steel Pier, far from the boardwalk, far from ordinary reality. Although it was dark outside, the lights on the pier were blinding. Every sight and sound seemed exaggerated, even grotesque: insistent barkers urging people to take a chance on whatever game they were hosting; the deafening noise of the rides; the piercing pop-pop-bing coming from the shooting gallery; and the announcement "All aboard, all aboard to the bottom of the ocean," where a diving bell took people a few feet beneath the surface of the Atlantic to its murky bottom.

We arrived just in time for the diving horse's last performance of the day. A dizzying crisscross of bare light bulbs was strung overhead, but when the act began, they were turned off and spotlights fixed on the horse's ramp and platform. Even with the carnival atmosphere, the scent of French fries mixed with salt air, the crowd jostling for position, despite all of that, the horse had an allure that eclipsed all human activity beneath him. In my altered state of consciousness,

Rider Josephine DeAngelis atop
Deloro, circa 1935–41

it felt like the ocean itself was breathing as waves drew away, then
crashed forward onto the pilings below. A voice boomed from the
loudspeaker, "Ladies and gentlemen, prepare yourselves for the thrill
of a minute. We present Carver's Steel Pier High-Diving Horse!" A
hush came over the crowd.

Out of the darkness, and off to one side, a gray horse appeared
with a handler. The horse was fitted only with a harness. As he and
the handler reached the bottom of the carpeted ramp, the handler set
loose the horse. There was no hesitation, the horse ran forward. The
instant he reached the platform at the top, a helmeted woman in a
bathing suit, who I hadn't noticed before, leapt onto his bare back,
leaned into him, and held on to the harness. They became one.

The horse was now in complete control. He could have sailed forward, but seemed in no rush. He was the star and would do things on
his terms. He lingered and surveyed the audience, as if taking stock,
seeing how many were in the crowd that night, or making sure we
were paying attention. He gazed out at the ocean, then back again
at the crowd.

Without warning, he kicked off from the platform and soared
through the humid night air with precision and dignity. It was a ter-

35

rifying sight, and an unforgettable one. The dive took but a few seconds; but to me, the searing image of the horse's body, pointing like a perfect arrow at his target below, seemed to run in slow motion. I was in awe of his taut muscles, his concentration, his willingness to perform. His plunge into the water was flawless.

Once the horse and his rider emerged from the tank, he trotted to an older woman who fed him carrots, while the same man who turned him loose now rubbed him down with towels. The overhead lights came back on, the audience dispersed, and things went back to the way they were. But I had some trouble returning to ordinary reality.

The wind picked up as we left the pier and carried with it the slightest tinge of autumn. It was still summer, of course, deep summer. Yet the breeze contained a new dimension now, a sad, wistful reminder that things would not be this way much longer, that change was coming whether we wanted it or not. I remembered that we were leaving Atlantic City the next day, and not long after that another school year would begin. Soon, the magic would be over.

I closed my eyes and pictured the diving horse, not as he stood on the platform, nor as he emerged triumphant from the tank; but in midair, leaping into the unknown. I did not want the act to end, did not want the summer to end. I wanted only to keep things as they were on that night when I was still a child, when I could still get away with holding my father's hand, when the Beatles were just hitting their stride and we had not yet chosen Johnson as a candidate. But as much as I wanted this, I knew I could not stop time, could not keep the horse suspended in space.

This realization brought on more tears, and my mother asked what was wrong. I did not have words for the emotion, so I told her I was tired, had too much sun. That much was true; but there was more. Something about how I regarded the world was shaken up that night. Some puzzle, beyond the ken of an eleven-year-old, had been set before me and would take years to solve.

. . .

Just as I intuited, things would not stay as they were on that night on the Steel Pier. Just six months later, on a bleak February morning in 1965, my grandfather, who lived with us, died. Actually, he didn't just die, he died unexpectedly and dramatically, collapsing in front of my mother and me at the breakfast table. She froze, incapacitated by the sight. It was left to me to decide what to do. I ran down the hall to my room and begged God to save him; ran back and phoned a neighbor who was a nurse; phoned our doctor, who made house calls; and phoned my father at work. In the way of a child, I wondered for years afterward if, during those few precious seconds that I wasted lobbying God, my grandfather could actually have been saved by someone more competent than myself.

Afterward, we rarely spoke of him, yet I found myself choking up at inappropriate times—in the middle of class, or in a restaurant. Sometimes, hearing a song he and I used to sing together would bring tears to my eyes; seeing his coffee mug, still in the cupboard, would set off emotions I struggled to contain. At other times, the sadness appeared out of nowhere and engulfed me.

It was no good talking to my parents about it. I tried. When I told my mother how I felt, she launched instead into a discussion of how she felt, about how she thought she saw him sitting in a chair in the living room, or heard his footsteps on the stairs. When she would cry, I was left to comfort her.

Several months later, when I mentioned to my father that I still missed my grandfather as much as ever, he fell back on platitudes that helped him through tough times: "Keep a stiff upper lip" or "Branigans are tough." When that produced no discernible effect on me, he might pull out a photo of his cousin, Tommy Branigan, an amateur boxer. The pale, skinny man, wearing enormous Everlast trunks, raised his gloves as if ready to take on any comers. That, likewise, offered little consolation.

Except for the relief of confiding these things to my big orange tabby cat Cosmo, I was alone in my grief.

.   .   .

Even before my grandfather's death, another change loomed, although I failed to grasp the significance. Not long after our brief visit to Atlantic City, my father decided I would benefit academically and socially from being sent to boarding school. He knew I had a certain intellectual "potential." He had similar potential himself when growing up, but his parents pulled him from school and sent him to work to help support his impoverished family. Undeterred, he studied on his own and passed his high school exams. Afterward, he worked as a cub reporter by day, went to college by night, and eventually attained several degrees. His salary as a state employee was insignificant compared to the returns on his shrewd investments in the stock market. But somewhere along the way he fell prey to the curse of the self-made man: he wanted to give me what he never had. Uppermost in his mind? Not luxury items, but the luxury of a good education.

Catalogues from various all-girls schools began arriving in the mail. In one of the few instances when I did not read something from cover to cover, I thumbed through the pages, looking only at the photographs. They featured fresh-faced girls wearing floor-length gowns and elbow-length white gloves, lining a spiral staircase, and awaiting their fathers, who would whisk them off to the annual father-daughter dinner dance. There were photos, too, of well-muscled, clench-jawed, hawk-eyed girls battling it out in field hockey. There were girls sitting in rapt attention at school desks, taking copious notes; convivial girls chatting in the dining room, leading me to imagine their clever banter. The girls were smiling, revealing perfectly straight, white teeth, and equally straight shoulder-length hair styled invariably in one of two ways, flipped up or curled under. There were innocent girls with wreaths of flowers in their hair, wearing Greek tunics and dancing around an erect May Pole. There were earnest girls documenting chemical reactions by the light of Bunsen burners; and pious girls, illuminated only by the beeswax candles they held, singing in the choir at Christmas vespers. I noticed that all of these girls had well-developed chests, chests that surely required some sort of scaffolding, like the contraption I had yet to need, a brassiere. But above all, I could tell these were pure girls, precocious girls, girls who were perfect in every way. They were as well groomed as purebred Poodles and, like their show dog counterparts, equally at ease in any arena.

Yet although these precious, well-bred girls must have been wanted and were valued by their parents, and were certainly desired and envied by the world at large, they were also girls who did not live with their families. And while thinking about this, I would experience a momentary flicker of unease, as fleeting as a stray cloud dimming the sun, as I attempted to make sense of those two disparate facts: wanted, yet sent away.

Before I was sent away, I was also taken away, from the only house I'd ever known, from my neighborhood, friends, even my state. My father, who loathed homeownership and would complain about constant maintenance if he had to replace a light bulb, decided another change was in order. We moved to an apartment in one of three newly constructed buildings set down in a sea of asphalt. They perched on a crest overlooking the Delaware River with a panoramic view of the Trenton skyline and were five minutes from my father's work.

The apartment was in Pennsylvania, but while only twenty minutes or so from where we used to live, it might as well have been across the country. I could not get back to my former neighborhood to visit old friends, could not even telephone them as it would have been a toll call—something my father would not have allowed. When I pointed this out, he dismissed my concerns. "What does it matter? You'll be away at school."

Was this the same man who took me searching for fossils and Indian arrowheads; included me in his weekly runs to the library; sat me on his lap and sang lullabies as he rocked me to sleep? I no longer knew him, nor, apparently, did he know me.

My sole consolation was that my cat Cosmo, as close to a sibling as I had, would be coming with us. But on moving day, as we arrived at the apartment and got out of our car, the orange tabby cat burst through his cardboard box and streaked across the parking lot. Simultaneously, the moving van arrived. My parents had no time to help me search for Cosmo—they were too busy telling the moving men where to put our belongings.

I wasn't just frustrated or resentful or angry at this turn of events, although I was all of those things. I seethed at the injustice of my recent losses—my grandfather, my home, and now, my cat. But the final indignity lay ahead: the new school with the headmistress who, during my admission interview, listed in humiliating detail my many shortcomings. I assumed, with relief, that my application would be rejected. Instead, she arose from behind her desk, extended her hand, and announced through tightened lips and pitiless eyes, "Welcome to our school."

Now, within a week of moving, it was time to leave for that school. Although we had not found Cosmo, I was given to understand that we had a schedule to keep and that tracking down a truculent feline was not part of it. My parents promised they would continue to search for him, would post "Lost" signs, and put out food every night. Our apartment, they reminded me, was on the ground floor and had a patio. But I suspected all would be in vain. He may have come back to me, his best friend, his ally. But to an adult? To someone taller, and with a deeper voice? Worse, to someone responsible for moving him in the first place? I knew Cosmo as no one else did. He would never come back to them.

My shortcomings were every bit as abundant as the headmistress had observed. Foremost, or so my classmates led me to believe, was my age—the one thing I couldn't change. At twelve, I was younger by a year or more than the other freshmen. The obligatory bullying ensued, name-calling, mostly; but maybe what my father said was true, maybe Branigans are tough. Within a few weeks I learned that showing no outward reaction deflected the feeding frenzy.

The belittling and demoralizing by the staff, however, never subsided, particularly after the mouse incident.

To the extent that you can blame a twelve-year-old for lack of impulse control, no matter how high-minded the motive, I was guilty. I had already committed a series of petty infractions at the school—disorganization, tardiness, inattention; but my precipitous plunge from, as the staff might have characterized it, youthful offender to hardened criminal stemmed from my attempted rescue of a tiny, newborn mouse. After that, and for the rest of my years there, those in charge marked me as someone to be distrusted, and watched.

On a chill, damp November evening I was late, as usual, for an assigned task at the dining hall. But instead of hurrying, I dawdled, trying to delay the inevitable. As I trudged along, I somehow noticed a nearly hairless infant mouse, shivering alongside the walkway. Counting his stringlike tail, he was not much more than an inch long, about the size of a large acorn. His oversized, embryonic eyes were closed, and he was curled inward, probably an instinctual way of keeping warm.

That I saw him was as improbable as his being there. I knew that rodents, like the hamsters I had as a child, constructed nests for their offspring, preferably in a sheltered spot. I could not imagine a female mouse on earth that would willingly, purposely, abandon her newborn. In the wild, reproduction, the continuation of the species, is everything, the whole point of life. Whatever his history, I knew he wouldn't survive without my intervention.

Just as instinct caused the mouse to curl against himself for warmth, so was what I did: I pulled a tissue from my blazer, swaddled the minuscule mouse, put him in my pocket, and hurried back to my dormitory.

I had two roommates who could not have been more different from each other. The unconventional, fun-loving roommate, the one who taught me how to dress, style my hair, and who expanded my musical tastes, was not in the room; but the other, the staid, judgmental one who regarded me and everyone from a distance and with disdain, was hunched over her needlepoint.

She noticed I was more disheveled than usual and asked if everything was okay.

Ordinarily, I would have ignored her or given an abbreviated answer. But on this day, I was so worried about the future of the little mouse that I answered her question with a question.

41

"You like animals, right?"

She didn't hesitate, and assured me that animals topped her list of favorite things.

"I have kind of a situation," I admitted.

"What sort of situation?" All kindness, she leaned forward.

The whole scenario tumbled out, about how I found the mouse, had saved him temporarily, but didn't know what to do next. And as I said this, she looked right at me and nodded her head in sympathy. She understood my predicament, I was certain of it.

"Do you think he can survive until after study hall?" I asked.

She didn't answer, but instead asked if she could take a peek. I slid him out of my pocket and pulled back the tissue. She didn't scream or recoil when she saw him, and I took that to be another good sign. He was dry now and no longer trembled. His breathing had eased, and suddenly everything in the world seemed better.

She said she thought a few hours of rest might do him good, and I resolved to bring back some food for him from the dining hall. With proper care, I would have him on his tiny pink feet in no time and could release him outdoors when he was old enough to take care of himself, perhaps in the spring. I stashed him in the softest place I could think of, my underwear drawer, and hurried to the dining hall.

I was invigorated by my small triumph, and ran the whole way without stopping. For the first time since I arrived at the school, I was more than just someone at the mercy of others, I was someone who could *be* merciful to others. I knew I was unable to save myself from the bleak turn my life had taken, but at least I could save the mouse.

During dinner, I chuckled to myself that, unbeknownst to everyone but my roommate, the little guy was back at the dorm, sleeping peacefully in my underwear and gaining strength. I caught her eye across the room and gave her a broad, conspiratorial smile. She merely nodded in return, but I didn't take it as a lack of enthusiasm, only as a sign of her conservative nature.

After dinner, I noticed that the roommate I now considered an ally was in a huddle by the doorway with my housemother and the assistant headmistress. This was not unusual. Like everyone, she tended to keep company with those with similar interests; but unlike everyone, it was the staff who shared her antiquated hobbies. Yet there was something about the intensity of their posture that alarmed me. It didn't seem like they were having a casual conversation about needlepoint or the upcoming Thanksgiving holiday. Something told me it was more serious than that.

There was only one exit from the room, so there was no way to avoid them.

"Not so fast," my housemother said. "We want a word with you."

All three sets of eyes fixed on me in the most penetrating way.

The assistant headmistress asked if there was anything I wanted to tell them.

"No," I said.

And as I said it, I looked over at my roommate and saw a smug, even savage expression on her face. I realized she had betrayed my confidence.

The housemother came right to the point. "Have you hidden a mouse in your room?"

I smiled the guilty, weak, sniveling smile of someone who had been caught. Yet for the sake of the mouse, for I still had hopes of protecting him, I was desperate to find a way to make a success of the rescue.

I conceded that although I had brought in a mouse, I realized it was a bad idea and put him back outside. In other words, I lied. All three exchanged knowing glances while I waited for what was next.

With unmistakable glee, my housemother pointed an arthritic finger at me.

"No you didn't. You're lying! Your roommate told us the whole story."

In excruciating detail, she relayed how, upon being told about the mouse, she went into my bureau, grabbed the vulnerable creature, and flushed him down the toilet. She warned me that what I had done might have led to an infestation of mice and disease in the dormitory.

But I was no longer listening. I was thinking of the mouse, my little mouse, the one who I thought I had saved but, instead, had delivered into the most treacherous of hands. The whole time I imagined him sleeping or gaining strength, he was already dead. There was nothing I could do to save him now, nothing I could do to save myself, either.

I choked back tears as my attention returned to the housemother. Her attack had reached its peak and she savored each word.

"Yes, you ought to be upset, upset and ashamed. Because the worst thing, the very worst thing you have done, is that you lied." The word "lied" gained a couple of syllables as she expanded it for effect. But she was not finished.

"You have let down the school, let down your parents, and let down yourself. But worst of all, you have let down God."

They didn't expel me, as I had hoped. That would have been too easy, too humane. Instead, a special assembly was convened to expose my perfidy to the student body, and to censure me.

But an unexpected blessing came of the public humiliation: a member of the honor council, a girl I barely knew, took me aside afterward to whisper that she didn't think what I had done was bad. In fact, she said, she thought it was rather nice that I tried to save the mouse. Her remark was nothing short of a lifeline: someone else cared, and not just for the mouse, but for me, too.

Still, I floundered, lost sleep, chewed my nails, developed colitis, and wondered what had become of me and the life I once knew. Anxiety would sneak up on me from behind, like a rogue wave threatening to pull me under. I wondered how the other girls, most of whom did not have my imagination or curiosity, appeared to be not only surviving, but thriving.

Eventually, I found a way to deal with my predicament. When I would lie on my bunk bed and listen to those same girls who seemed so well adjusted by day cry themselves to sleep at night, I realized it was because they didn't know how to turn it off, how to erase the past and focus instead on something else, anything else. I decided the trick was not to go back, not to play home movies in my head of the good old days. Instead, the wondrous time in Atlantic City and the diving horses; my grandfather; my old home; and my cat Cosmo, were relegated to the don't-go-there part of my brain.

Chapter Three

Now that I wanted Cleveland to call to check in, he didn't. After waiting in vain that night on his balcony, I decided that instead of spending any more time staring at the phone and willing it to ring, or, worse yet, taking another maudlin trip down memory lane, it was time for action. I could use his being out of touch to my advantage. Cleveland had a penchant for history. Apart from appealing to his humanitarian nature, I decided another way to bolster my case for acquiring the horse was to rely heavily on details about the origins of the diving act—assuming there was anything worth telling.

I vaguely remembered something my father said in Atlantic City about the diving horses, something about Buffalo Bill. You could hardly get anything more colorful than that. If there was a connection between the diving horses and William Cody, some sort of interesting backstory, then Gamal was as good as rescued. But was there more?

I'd never been a fan of western culture. While growing up, except for marveling briefly at the horses, I avoided the glut of westerns on TV—*Bonanza, The Rifleman, Wagon Train,* and on and on. Even as a child, I was ashamed of our country's overall abuse of native people and animals. And as for settlers, even if they were "just" killing each other, shootouts at the O.K. Corral, or anywhere else, left me cold. I was more Westward No than Westward Ho. And yet, this one clue, Buffalo Bill, led to a curiosity about the post–Civil War American West. I knew there were staged Wild West–type shows. Were diving horses a part of it? What did people consider entertainment back then? And the biggest questions of all: who came up with the idea for the diving horse act, and how were the animals trained?

I began my first tentative moves toward finding out by scouring Cleveland's own extensive library of animal books. It was of considerable help since he had several volumes pertaining to the Old West, leftovers from research for his book *Man Kind?,* where he described the mass slaughter of buffalos for so-called sport, for the fur trade, and various other atrocities. The consensus at the time seems to have been that North America was ours for the plundering, a philosophy known euphemistically as Manifest Destiny.

My first pass at the act's history revealed only the bare bones. The diving horse act was invented, if that's what you can call it, in the late 1800s not by Buffalo Bill, but by a onetime associate, William Frank Carver. "Doc" Carver, as he was known, was a show business impresario who had also been a famed sharpshooter. For a time, Doc Carver traveled with Buffalo Bill's Wild West show alongside another expert exhibition shooter, Annie Oakley.

When I'd gone as far as I could with Cleveland's library, I paid a visit to New York City's flagship library on Fifth Avenue, one of the world's largest. I was confident that if more information was available on anything or anyone related to diving horses, that library would have it.

The two stone lions guarding the entrance of the building, nick-named Patience and Fortitude by Mayor LaGuardia, were, like much of the city in those days, dingy and in need of a good scrubbing. Worse, disheveled men, impaired by some substance or other, slumped on the steps and stabilized themselves against the lions' marble platforms; but despite that, the building was still powerful enough to evoke wonder and awe. I summoned my meager supply of patience and fortitude, reached the top of the stairs, and pulled open the doors.

This next stab at getting basic biographical information revealed that William Frank Carver was born either in 1840 or 1851. The place of his birth: either Saratoga, New York, or Winslow, Illinois, a small town near the Wisconsin border. I decided that could be sorted out later. What I wanted to know about was his connection to diving horses.

The commonly accepted story was that Doc was a dentist. In those days, there were only two dental schools in the country. Most dentists trained as apprentices and required no certification or professional license. Unlike one of his contemporaries, Doc Holliday of O.K. Corral fame, who graduated from dental school, Doc Carver's training was of the less scholarly variety, closer to "have pliers, will travel." He found work at an army installation in western Nebraska. During the post–Civil War years, career soldiers, such as General George Armstrong Custer, switched from fighting the war between the states to fighting the Indian wars out west, in places like Nebraska.

By all evidence, Doc appeared not to have been cut out for the daily grind of dentistry, and early on, he would take time out from his job to work as a scout in the Far West. While at Fort McPherson in Nebraska, Carver fell in with Buffalo Bill Cody, a former soldier and scout who was just then setting up his Wild West show. Cody sensed correctly that Americans who had never been west of the Mississippi hungered for a taste of what was going on in the territories. Cody was ready to capitalize on the public's curiosity by giving them his sensationalized version, a kind of virtual reality for the masses. Mark Twain said the shows offered people "a last glimpse at the fading American frontier."

Carver wanted to join the troupe, and saw it as his ticket out of his dull life; but he needed a specialty. Apparently the steady hand of a dentist served him well because he took up sharpshooting. By 1878, *The New York Times* pronounced him "the best short-range marksman in the world." He was also a larger-than-life character in the flesh. As an imposing, fit man of six feet, four inches, Doc was described by that same *Times* article as being as "fine a specimen of fully developed manhood as ever walked Manhattan Island." In his prime, thrice-married Doc was a bit of a ladies' man. Rumor had it that while appearing in western-inspired plays in Australia, he even had a fling with French actress Sarah Bernhardt. Doc appeared both onstage and off in full western regalia, his presence demanding

Doc Carver, before he conceived of diving horses, rose to prominence as the world's foremost exhibition sharpshooter. 1883.

attention. Yet for all that, he was a teetotaling bad boy who needed unflinching hands for shooting.

For a time, Cody's show was rife with Bills, "Buffalo Bill" Cody, "Wild Bill" Hickok, and "Pawnee Bill" Lillie. Not wanting to be just another Bill on the bill, Carver tried passing himself off as "Evil Spirit" Carver, along with the story that the title was bestowed on him by a Sioux chief. No one bought it. Instead, he was dubbed "Doc" Carver, alluding to his former career as a dentist. For a man who tried his best to live down that staid, respectable profession, it must have stung.

But there was another reason why Doc Carver may have sought to shed his tame life—there was something wilder than dentistry flowing through his veins. Several unsubstantiated but widespread accounts, possibly promoted by Doc himself, reported that while his father was a physician, his grandfather was the well-known eighteenth-century writer, surveyor, and scout Jonathan Carver. If that was true, then young Carver would have heard stories while growing up about how his grandfather, a Massachusetts native, took up the challenge of a royal governor in Minnesota. The British Crown announced a reward

48

of "gold plus expenses" to anyone who found a waterway to the Pacific Ocean, the fabled Northwest Passage. Jonathan Carver never found it, but he discovered lots of other interesting things along the way, many of which he saw fit to name after himself. He asserted that a Native American had given him title to ten thousand square miles of Minnesota land. Jonathan Carver spent all of his savings in legal fees, petitioning Congress to recognize his claim. He was denied, and with his coffers drained, he died penniless in London.

Doc, the alleged grandson with the adventurous heart and dull job, took up the cause. He, too, tried staking his grandfather's claim to lands in Minnesota, but met with a similar result. Nonetheless, living for a time with various Indian tribes, working as a freelance scout and hunting guide, and eventually traveling with Buffalo Bill awakened and satisfied something in him that dentistry never could.

Doc and Buffalo Bill formed a partnership that lasted barely a year. They fell out over the usual culprits: money (with Doc claiming that Cody drank their profits and owed him thousands); and ego (which man should get top billing on posters). Doc sued Cody. The case settled out of court, and Doc started his own competing show, "Wild America." Like Cody's "Wild West," Doc's show featured reenactments of Indian battles and cowboy rope and riding tricks; but Wild America also showcased his impressive shooting skills.

In the late 1870s and '80s, Doc Carver traveled the world both with his Wild America show, and also separately, giving shooting exhibitions. He was so expert that he shattered not only world records, but also five thousand feather-filled glass balls in five hundred minutes straight. The culmination was a command performance before Queen Victoria and the Prince and Princess of Wales. They were so impressed they presented him with a bejeweled pin. Not to be outdone, the last German emperor, Wilhelm II, likewise invited Doc to perform and rewarded him with a large diamond ring.

Once back in the States, middle-aged Doc's career path took a much needed turn. Sharpshooters, after all, don't stay sharp forever. He was approached by a playwright, Alfred Dampier, with an interest in having Doc star in a play he had written for him and based loosely on his exploits before he became a famous marksman. Doc agreed and once again hit the road, now appearing onstage rather than at a fairground. *The Trapper* was such a success that a second play, *The Scout,* was also written for him, this time penned by Dampier and Garnet Walch.

In 1891, and in language as florid as the play itself, an unnamed Australian newspaper critic wrote, "It is as a spectacle, pure and simple, that 'The Scout' must be considered. There is a play, of course, strung together to explain the appearance of Dr. Carver and his cowboys . . . but it is scarcely worthy of attention.

"What dramatic situation could compare with this huge tank, 40ft. long and 12ft. broad by 9ft. deep, which occupies the whole back of the stage and is at the will of the scenic artist, a placid lake in which live ducks paddle about, or a rushing river, in which cowboys, Indians, and horses shout and struggle and splash in admirable confusion? What is left but to fly?"

By the 1890s, Doc's Wild America show had disbanded due to dwindling crowds resulting from overexposure and too many competing shows. *The Scout* and *The Trapper* had run their course. Once again, Doc Carver faced the awful prospect of returning to dentistry. He was desperate for a new angle, a novelty to capture the public's attention.

And then he hit on the idea of something never before seen: horses that dived—not as part of a play, not as a circus act, but as a separate, spotlighted spectacle. As a consummate promoter, Doc recognized the power and poetry in the more refined silhouette of a lone flying horse. From that raucous beginning, the diving horse act was born.

As with other so-called facts about his life, Doc, and others associated with him, gave several versions about how he came up with the idea for the act. In one, it was the proverbial dark and stormy night. While crossing the Platte River, Doc said the bridge collapsed. He and his horse jumped into the water and swam to safety. In another version, he claimed to be fleeing bandits and was forced to dive with his horse into Medicine Creek. Either way, something about the image struck him as marketable and he began training horses—first to leap over jumps, and later into ten-foot-deep tanks of water from increasingly high platforms, occasionally sixty feet, but generally forty.

On August 26, 1894, Doc kicked off his show in Fairmount Park,

Kansas City. The riderless horse was named Black Bess and she leapt from a forty-foot platform into a twelve-foot-deep tank of water. The act was an immediate success.

But despite its early popularity, Doc felt that something was missing, that the act hadn't yet reached its full potential. He soon realized that it would be an even greater attraction with someone on the horse's back, preferably a girl wearing an eye-catching shade of red. And with that, he had an even bigger hit on his hands, so much so that for a time his mini-empire included two troupes of diving horses, one east of the Mississippi, the other, west.

In 1906, headlines on Doc's handbills touted a girl rider as being "The Greatest of All. The Girl in Red. The Bravest Girl in the World." That girl was twenty-year-old Lorena, who initially was billed with the surname Lawrence, then Lorenz, and eventually Carver. At some point, Doc concocted the story that the diving horse act was a family business as a greater draw for his show. Both Lorena and a fellow diver, Sonora Webster, often called Doc "Daddy" or "Daddy Carver."

Lorena Carver, in full Indian regalia, dives into the tank atop Klatawah at the Calgary Stampede, circa 1925.

. . .

By 1929, Sonora and her husband, Al Floyd (who also assumed the surname Carver, but only after Doc's death in 1927), established the act as a permanent seasonal attraction at "the Showplace of the Nation," Atlantic City's Steel Pier.

By then, Atlantic City's previously elegant veneer was beginning to give way to less refined, more affordable attractions. Wealthy visitors, who had been going there for decades and considered it their own, either went elsewhere or were now obliged to rub elbows with blue-collar workers from eastern Pennsylvania and the urban hubs of New Jersey. These new visitors wanted to pack in as much as possible during their one-day vacation, the more sensational and different from their everyday lives as possible.

The original prim-and-proper music on the Steel Pier featured orchestras and opera singers. Eventually it gave way to more popular music, such as that offered by John Philip Sousa and Rudy Vallee, followed by the big band sounds of Benny Goodman and Glenn Miller. Everyone who was anyone played the Steel Pier. Successive generations of vacationers heard crooners like Bing Crosby and Frank Sinatra; the doo-wop groups of the 1950s; the soul music of Motown; and even the Rolling Stones and Herman's Hermits in the 1960s. A regional television show, a forerunner to *American Bandstand,* called *Live from the Steel Pier,* was broadcast every Saturday afternoon from the ballroom and showcased the latest styles of dance, fashion, and music. And as if that wasn't enough, first-run films were shown at the pier's two movie theaters.

There was also a carnival-like side to the Steel Pier. Harry Houdini freed himself from countless forms of bondage, and boxing kangaroos went a few rounds in the ring with heavyweight champ Primo Carnera. Mlle. Alexme, "the Human Projectile," made a career of being shot from a cannon into the ocean, while the claim to fame of a stoic fellow named "Shipwreck Kelly" was flagpole sitting. "Rex the Wonder Dog" balanced himself on something called an Aquaplane as it skimmed across the ocean near the pier, while dancing chickens were secretly induced to perform via a slight electric shock to their

In 1933, four years after establishing a full-time home
on the Steel Pier, the diving horses became, and remained,
the venue's premier draw.

feet through the metal floor of their cage. Children could have their
photo taken with animal celebrities, like Petey from the *Our Gang*
comedies, or Borden Dairy's mascot, Elsie the cow. For those with the
strongest stomachs, there was Dr. Couney's Premature Infant Exhibit.

But of all the acts, the one no one missed, the one that no one
ever forgot, the one that reigned supreme, was Carver's High-Diving
Horses.

Almost a week passed, and I had amassed what I considered a nice
overview of diving horse history. Some of the details needed shor-
ing up. Indeed, some material was downright questionable, but I was
certain it was significant enough to capture Cleveland's attention.

While tracking every lead I could find on the diving horses, I
repeatedly came across mention of New York's Hippodrome. I knew
what a hippodrome was, a place where horses or chariots raced. But
I hadn't known there was one in Manhattan. It was built in 1905 as
a year-round entertainment palace by the same men who built Luna
Park at Coney Island.

New York City's Hippodrome, at one time the city's largest
theater, housed a hydraulically operated water tank that could be
raised onto the stage. It allowed Doc Carver's riderless "Plunging
Horses," and other aquatic performers, to dive. Not long
afterward, Doc came up with the idea for diving horses
with riders as a separate spectacle. 1905.

Theatre Magazine reported that the 5,200-seat Hippodrome
blended "the best acts of pantomime, vaudeville, musical comedy, drama, zoological and aquatic performances." The site, which
stretched a full city block on Sixth Avenue between 43rd and 44th
Streets, was home to what billed itself as "the largest and most famous
playhouse in the world."

While horse racing was never held at New York's Hippodrome,
the phrase "aquatic performances" piqued my interest. Among
other engineering marvels, the Hippodrome had a clear glass, eight-
thousand-gallon tank that could be raised by hydraulic pistons for
swimming and diving shows. My pulse quickened a bit as I scoured
the archives for any sign that diving horses had performed on that
stage. I had just about given up when I studied some photos of the
Hippodrome. The exterior facade of the building was completely
covered with lights, and it was said that the glow of the building

could be seen for miles. But it wasn't the lights that got my attention, it was what those lights spelled out on the marquee: "The Plunging Horses."

The Hippodrome, a place that had once welcomed over fourteen thousand patrons a day, was razed in 1939. High production costs and the Depression were its downfall. Yet although the original building was no longer there, the site where it once stood, where horses had plunged, was only one block west and one block north of where I was now seated. As I left the library that day, I made a point of stopping by. The space was now occupied by a nondescript office building called the Hippodrome, its name being the only vestige of its former vibrant incarnation.

The evening commute was in full swing and pedestrians mobbed the sidewalks. I moved to one side to avoid being trampled, and put my hand against the building as if to make contact with the past. I took secret pleasure in knowing what no one else on the street knew that day—diving horses had been here, and maybe even Doc, too. To me, it was a heart-stopping moment: I was starting to cobble together a bit of Americana and establish a line between Doc Carver, Gamal, and most improbably, myself.

The experience heightened my curiosity, and whether or not Cleveland agreed to buy Gamal, I decided to make it my mission to continue to delve deeper into the life of the illusive Doc Carver and his amazing horses—especially the last one, Gamal.

In the end, I resorted to what I had tried to avoid: staring at the phone and waiting for Cleveland to call. I was eager to deliver my news and close the deal on Gamal's purchase. But when he finally did call, it was he, not I, who directed the conversation.

As was his custom, his first concern was for the welfare of his big white cat Polar Bear. I knew that no matter how much I wanted to lead with the diving horse story, protocol required that we get through Polar Bear's update first. It was not enough that I said that the cat was doing well, I had to relate an incident that would show exactly how well. Only after he was satisfied that Polar Bear was not just alive, but thriving, could we get on to the next order of business: the diving horses.

After holding in the news, after discovering what I could about the history of the horses and the pier, and after rehearsing exactly how I would persuade Cleveland to buy Gamal, it was all windup and no pitch. I had barely outlined the cranky woman's phone call when he interrupted.

"Of course we'll buy Gamal," he said, anticipating my question. "Our ranch will be just the spot for his retirement."

I was elated—except for the part about the horse going to the Fund's new facility in Texas. Gamal and I hadn't even met, and already plans were being made to take him away from me.

Chapter Four

On May 17, 1980, the whole country seemed to be on edge as scientists, with instruments poised at the epicenter of Mount St. Helens, warned it was no longer a question of "if" but "when" the volcano would erupt. I felt the stirrings of a personal tectonic shift, too, as I drove to Harker's horse auction in Indian Mills, New Jersey, where, unknowingly, Gamal awaited his fate. Ironically, I was headed toward the same Pine Barrens of rural southern New Jersey, and on the same highway, that my parents and I traveled on our way to Atlantic City nearly sixteen years earlier. But this time, I would not be seeing a diving horse, I would be buying one.

I sweated and shivered. I wasn't sick, nor was the weather excessively hot or cold. What was running hot and cold was my confidence.

In theory, it was a simple enough task: buy a horse that was for sale. Yet this was the first time since I began working for the Fund that I was carrying out a major project, one that I initiated. I had to make a success of it.

I vacillated between picturing Gamal shaking in the corner of a dimly lit stall and feeling the full weight of my assignment. Entrusting me with this task, not to mention giving me a blank check, was no small gesture on Cleveland's part—it meant he was confident I could get the job done. Now I had to convince myself.

As I neared the auction, I worried how little of substance I knew about horses and how ironic it was that this first big project should involve one. As a Fund employee, I had educated myself about the perils facing many creatures, but I had not spent much time in the company of horses. My few personal interactions amounted to tedious trudges around a dusty riding ring at summer camp; watching girls at boarding school, born to the saddle, put their horses through paces; and most memorably, surviving a hair-raising trail ride at a mountain resort atop Old Joe, an enormous horse who decided he'd had enough and galloped from the group while I hung on for dear life. I was distinctly not a horse person.

Of course as a child I always wanted a horse. What young girl doesn't? I may not have plastered my walls with photos of horses, or collected plastic models of them as did some of my friends; but on those weekly trips to the library with my father, I read the requisite horse books such as *Black Beauty, National Velvet,* and *Misty of Chincoteague,* and saw every film adaptation of those works. But when it came to acquiring an actual living, breathing horse, I knew my parents would give me the same answer as when I asked for a dog.

Yet although my direct experience with horses was scant, I had done my homework. And as my car made its way down the dark two-lane road leading to the auction, I thought about the many dangers facing these most docile of creatures.

Despite their size, horses were pretty much defenseless, and relied on speed to escape predators. For millennia, the measure of their worth had been their value to humans—carrying loads, pulling plows, and submitting to saddle and bridle. But those jobs had long since been eclipsed by the internal combustion engine. Now, for the most part, they owed their existence to their entertainment value: riding, racing, or in Gamal's rare case, diving. Modern-day horses were in a precarious position because when times get tough and budgets are trimmed, luxuries are the first to go.

Horses that had lost their entertainment value still possessed one last bit of usefulness: their bodies. Their flesh for meat, hooves for glue. Weren't great musical performances made possible by their manes stretched on a violin's bow? Didn't their tails carry paint on brushes to create masterpieces on canvas? It all sounded like the ultimate in recycling except for one fact: horses were not machines that could be stripped for parts. Horses had a sense of self, they related to us and to each other. They felt pain.

George Orwell's words in *Animal Farm* rang in my head: "All animals are equal but some are more equal than others." Was I guilty of species bias? To me, it wasn't that horses were better than other livestock, but they were different; and it was we humans who made them different. Domesticated horses were conditioned from birth to trust people, to relate to people, to depend on people. We fed them. We named them. And we were capable of betraying them in the cruelest way.

There was also the manner in which these horses were sacrificed. I read that if a horse was destined for the dog food can, it was slaughtered in the United States. But for those whose fate was a human's dinner plate in Canada or France or even Japan, a long, arduous journey lay ahead, since butchering a horse for human consumption was illegal here. Any horses purchased for slaughter that night at Harker's would be loaded into one of the idling double-decker horse trailers parked behind the main building. From there, they would make a grueling all-night journey north up Interstate 81 to Canada. From auctions in southern parts of the country, horses would be shipped alive to Mexico. Either way, the living cargo would neither be fed, nor watered, nor afforded any pain relief. After all, it was a one-way trip.

I hoped with everything in me that this auction would be different, that I could somehow avoid seeing evidence of those widespread horrors.

A day earlier I had been in New York, picking up a check from Cleveland. Now, at the auction in Indian Mills, New Jersey, the contrast to the city was striking: here the landscape was green and rural, and people looked like they had just ridden in from the back forty. And maybe they had: small road signs proclaimed that America's oldest weekly rodeo, Cowtown, was just a few dozen miles south.

Clearly, these were horse people, but not the sort I was accustomed to—the sort who wore black knee-high boots, khaki-colored jodhpurs, velvet-covered, beanie-shaped riding hats, slim-fitting tweed jackets, and who carried the ever-present (and slightly threatening) riding crop.

Surrounding me here was a sea of brightly colored plaid shirts, blue jeans, and disturbingly pointy-toed cowboy boots. There were a few cowboy hats here and there, and even a smattering of bolo neckties adorned with a chunk of turquoise and pulled up tight against the throat. Some horses among the forty or so that would be sold that evening were saddled up just outside the main building to strut their stuff to prospective buyers. Even the saddles were different from the minimalist English-style ones with which I was most familiar. Western saddles were twice as big, featured a prominent horn, fat wooden stirrups, and a leather seat as cushy as a La-Z-Boy recliner.

As I made my way across the room to register at the auction office, a gravel-voiced Conway Twitty crooned "Oh Lord, I love the lady wearin' tight-fittin' jeans" over the loudspeakers. I showed the manager the blank certified check, and took a number and program. I'd only been to one other auction, accompanying my father to Sotheby's in New York for a sale of Roman coins and artifacts. I was unsure if the routine was the same here, and risked showing my inexperience by asking how to bid. The man behind the desk gave a condescending smile. "Raise your number." Chastened, I managed one more question: confirming the information I'd been given earlier on the phone—that if I bought a horse, it could stay in their barn overnight until I returned the next day with transportation. He nodded, and I felt his eyes follow me as I went off in search of Gamal.

Like the layout of a cathedral, where, by design, you are drawn down the aisle to the nave and then the altar, Gamal's stall was also at the end of an aisle. As shrewd horse traders, they knew that putting him at the end also meant you had to pass the stalls of other horses being sold and might be inspired to do a little impulse shopping along the way.

My initial instinct was to sprint toward Gamal, but, just as they planned, I stopped at the first horse I saw. I peeked over the stall door and saw he shared the space with a donkey. Neither animal looked up, something I found disturbing. I had a feeling there was a story there, but not one I wanted to hear.

I didn't have to wonder at the next stall. A young teenaged girl was crying as her father explained for what surely was not the first time that he took no pleasure in selling her horse but that they no longer could afford the upkeep. "It's more than just water and hay," he said, his own eyes glistening. I regarded the plump, honey-colored mare, who hovered by the stall door as if at any moment it would open and she would be reunited with her special girl. The horse had a pink bow in her forelock, a parting gift, no doubt.

The card affixed to the next stall said its occupant was a Thorough-bred, a former racehorse. Even to my untrained eye, he looked pained. He put no weight on his right hind leg and it appeared swollen. That story spoke for itself.

Next to him, a Methuselah of a horse with a concave back that seemed as if it had bowed under the weight of concrete sacks. He was going at the hay like there was no tomorrow, and perhaps for him there wouldn't be.

I'd seen enough, too much, and made my way straight to Gamal, more intent than ever to spirit us both away from all of this.

Gamal's brightly lit stall was bedecked with red, white, and blue crepe paper, along with a hand-lettered sign that read, "The Last Atlantic City Steel Pier Diving Horse." Of course, Shiloh was still out there somewhere, but they weren't going to let a little detail like that spoil the sales pitch. Propped on an easel were newspaper clippings glued to poster boards and I strained to read them over people's shoulders. There was something about the history of the diving act, an interview with a former diver, and the latest news that Gamal was headed for the auction.

For his part, Gamal seemed unfazed by the burgeoning crowds, the popping of flashes, the blaring country music. I wondered if, for him, this was business as usual. He was, after all, used to being the center of attention. It was impossible to get close to his stall door for the throng, so I caught only a few tantalizing glimpses of his dark shape as he ate a little, drank a little, dropped a few piles of manure.

Once or twice, he stopped, raised his head, and surveyed the crowd in what to my amateur eye seemed to be a judgmental manner. At no point did he hang his head or quiver, as I had feared. Gamal, I began to realize, was a horse that had been around the ring a few times.

What must it have taken for Gamal, for any of the horses, to have performed? To have leapt from such a tremendous height then land in such a small tank? Courage, of course. And athleticism. But was there more? Was Gamal a proud horse? I could already tell that he had a certain indefinable something that other horses did not. What was it? Since our lives were about to become entwined, I had a feeling I would soon find out.

At show time, I took a seat on the bleachers directly opposite the auctioneer's stand. To my dismay, the family selling the honey-colored mare sat right in front of me. It was no longer theoretical: I was now experiencing firsthand the danger she and the other horses faced—sale to a slaughterhouse. I looked around the auction and wondered who in the audience might be capable of such treachery? My eyes lit on a small cadre of men lingering in the back of the room. They looked like regulars—relaxed and well familiar with the proceedings. I suspected that these denim-clad businessmen were the ones who traded in horse flesh.

As I waited for the first horse to enter the ring, I felt my body tremble with rage, with fear, and with grief that beings as magnificent, as sentient, and as helpful to humans as horses would ever be treated with anything but the utmost respect and reverence. Most of these horses weren't sick or lame. They were simply between owners, or had the misfortune of being owned by people who did not necessarily care where, or how, the horse wound up. And if one of these horses was incurably ill, if it could no longer perform its function, then it had the bad luck of being owned by people unwilling, or unable financially, to have it euthanized humanely.

After the first three or four horses, I could tell which potential buyers wanted a horse to ride, and which had more sinister plans. Horse people checked the horse's gait, the way it moved around the ring, and its conformation, how close to perfect was its anatomy. Horse meat people, or "killers," as they were known, eyed the animals differently. You could almost see their brains calculating how much flesh was on the bone. Some of the horses, like the ones I saw when I first arrived, were past their prime and clearly had but one bleak future. I fingered the blank check in my pocket and had the fleeting thought that I could save them all: the donkey and horse pair, the lame Thoroughbred racehorse, the ancient horse, and even the honey-colored mare. But just as quickly, I knew I couldn't. Where would I put them? What would Cleveland say? And where would it end?

I held my breath as the honey-colored mare entered the spotlight. Most horses wore only a halter and were led around the ring. The mare was saddled and ridden by a teenaged boy. She was calm, well trained. The family in front of me held each other in suspense. After a few descriptive words, the bidding began. The men in the back bid once or twice, but once they saw their competition was a family that bore a striking resemblance to the one selling the mare, they dropped out. There was, apparently, an unspoken code of honor that stopped them from buying serviceable horses if they were wanted elsewhere. The mare was sold to the new family and, on that night at least, her life was spared. The other horses I was concerned about were not so lucky.

An hour or so later, it was time for the grand finale: Gamal.

The auctioneer began, "And now ladies and gentlemen, the moment you've all been waiting for. We've saved the best for last."

He gave a brief history of the diving horses (somewhat at odds with what little I had uncovered), but made no mention of Powderface's fate. I knew that if the same hoopla had surrounded his sale, he, too, would have survived.

A young, athletic girl who couldn't have been more than ten or eleven led a saddle-less Gamal into the ring. The auctioneer barked at her, "Go on, now. Git up on him." Like an ancient Minoan bull leaper, the girl sprang from a standing position, landed astride the horse's back, and began circling the ring—all in one fluid movement.

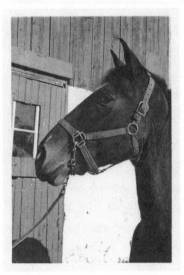

Gamal, a confident, self-assured horse. 1981.

"Yes, ladies and gentlemen, now you can own a piece of Atlantic City history. This world-famous act, in operation since the 1920s, has come to a close. It's the end of an era."

The auctioneer may have said more, perhaps even important things. But I was so struck by Gamal's entrance that I could no longer hear the background music, could not see the people around me, and for the first time that night did not even think of the horses headed for slaughter. The moment was not in slow motion, it was motionless, encompassing only my awareness of this glorious horse, who, even then, I suspected would come to mean everything to me.

Gamal's dark brown coat gleamed beneath the harsh overhead lights. Everything about him indicated composure, professionalism. He was perfectly obedient, yet simultaneously in control as each step, every movement, was precise and deliberate. As much as it surprised me to think such a thing, he seemed to take a certain pride in his performance. Far from being a beaten-down, trembling old man, charismatic Gamal owned the room.

Dimly, I became aware that the auctioneer's introductory pitch had concluded. He shifted gears and was now all business.

"Do I hear five hundred dollars?"

Several of us raised our numbers, including, to my horror, the meat buyers.

"Do I hear six hundred?" he asked a millisecond later. The meat buyers dropped out.

I had trouble keeping up with the auctioneer's breakneck speed, and could not really understand his staccato, speaking-in-tongues routine. My heart was racing, my palms sweating. Whenever I heard a dollar amount, I raised my number and probably bid against myself a few times.

At about sixteen hundred dollars, the bidding stalled and I thought we were done, that I had sealed the deal. But the auctioneer earned whatever commission the seller paid him as he renewed his pitch by reminding us, "One of a kind, ladies and gentlemen. One of a kind."

Although the meat buyers were no longer interested in Gamal, he was not home free. The bidding was down to three of us. One, I learned later, "felt sorry" for Gamal and would have taken him home, wherever that was. The other said he wanted to put Gamal "on display" at local carnivals. As I neared what Cleveland strongly suggested should be a $3,000 limit, I dueled with the carnival man. My winning bid was $2,600—$2,600 for a horse that, had his past been unknown, might have fetched $500.

I'm sure some of those at the auction that night thought I had been suckered, that the man from the summer riding camp had put one over on me; or that I didn't realize the horse I just bought was vastly overpriced. But all I could think was that perhaps for the first time in his life, Gamal's value had nothing to do with money and everything to do with his welfare.

Once the auctioneer slammed down the gavel and pronounced Gamal sold, the little acrobatic girl slid from his back and handed me the reins, assuming, wrongly, that I was as experienced as she in handling a horse. Reporters from newspapers, television stations, and even wire services besieged me. I was aware that Gamal was somewhat well known, but I hadn't expected that much interest.

Someone instructed me to smile for the cameras, while others peppered me with questions about who I was and what my plans were for the veteran performer. I explained about The Fund for Animals, and about how Gamal would soon be heading to their new facility in Texas, the Black Beauty Ranch. The whole time, all I really wanted to do was get a good look at the horse. But getting that look would have to wait: I had hired a stable owner near me to pick him up and board him for a short time until the fencing at the ranch was finished, and she was not available until the next day. I knew as little about her as I did about horses. But she came with a recommendation: she was the daughter-in-law of a friend of a friend. With her farm being only a few miles from my house, it would be easy to visit Gamal often.

In one last bit of business, I settled up with the auction staff, and they handed over the clippings that had been on display. Although they assured me, repeatedly, that Gamal would be well cared for overnight, I worried anyway. What if he was stolen? Or broke loose? What if someone made a mistake and loaded him onto a truck headed for Canada? Still, I had no choice. With more than a little trepidation, I left Gamal at the auction and anticipated a sleepless night.

Chapter Five

I thought I hadn't slept at all, that night after buying Gamal. I thought my body had hummed and buzzed like an overloaded electrical outlet; or that I had thrashed and twitched, and punched my pillow, trying to find the single position that would simultaneously cradle my head and calm my mind. I was as overstimulated as if on a caffeine drip, as visions of the auction and the animals replayed in my head. I assumed it had happened, that there had been that overlit, noisy barn on the edge of the Pine Barrens. But because I had no time to get to know the object of my efforts, Gamal, I had every reason to wonder if the whole thing had just been my imagination.

Yet although I thought I hadn't slept, I awoke with a start the next morning. As reality set in, I dressed and rushed to a corner store to get a newspaper. If there was any mention of Gamal, it would be proof that the previous night was real. Besides, I was longing to see him again, and if there was an article, I hoped it would include a photo.

There he was, on the front page of most papers. In fact, the only bigger story was that Mount St. Helens had finally erupted.

I read the various accounts of Gamal's purchase with a mixture of amusement and concern. It was my first experience of being misquoted, and I hoped Cleveland would believe me when I explained the situation. Several stories reported that I had bought a ranch in Texas, or that I intended "to fill the ranch with as many abused horses as possible." Most said Gamal was twenty-six, but one said he was twenty-three. One reporter described Cleveland only as a "humorist," and I wondered if Cleveland would find much humor in the term. I knew he preferred "social critic," "author," "animal advocate," or all three. I was beginning to understand how false stories and rumors develop. After all, if Cleveland, with all of his connections, couldn't control the press, who could?

Just a few hours later I found Gamal, the picture of contentment, alone in a large green pasture and up to his knees in clover. As I watched him graze, I was surprised by his size. Even at a distance he seemed huge, with a thick neck and powerful hindquarters. Quite an impressive sight, I was sure, even to as experienced a horse person as Wendy McCook, the woman who would be boarding him until he went to Texas. I was about to point out his imposing size to her, but before I had a chance, she commented first.

"Oh, he's just a little bit of a thing," she said.

I studied her face to see if she was kidding. She wasn't.

"He can't be more than 15.2 hands," she added, as if that would make things clearer. Horse talk was beyond me, and I realized I needed a crash course in this foreign language.

I had just met Wendy and didn't want to get off on the wrong foot by correcting her, so I let it go. Besides, more important than his size was his temperament, and based on my experience with him the night before, I knew he was an agreeable animal. He had been calm, gentle, and stood patiently as photographers snapped flashbulbs in our faces. As Wendy and I climbed over the fence and walked toward him, I thought about how lucky I was that my first horse should be so tame.

Once again I was about to share my insight with her when she spoke up first.

"He's got a real mulish look in his eye."

From her tone, I took this to mean that any similarity to a mule was not a good thing. I began to question whether Wendy really knew horses as well as I thought she did. Clearly, he was big. As for the mulish look, well, how could she tell from that distance? Perhaps the sun casting shadows across his face gave her the wrong impression.

Privately, I stuck to my opinion that he was a tractable horse, and we walked in silence toward Gamal.

The plan was to approach him in the pasture, attach the lead line to his halter, and bring him in. Simple enough, I reckoned. It would be just like walking my Border Collie, Stockbridge. I offered to do the honors. I thought I noticed an indulgent smile on her face as, without argument, she handed me her rope.

"Gamal," I called out, much the way I would have called a dog.

The horse didn't lift his head and continued to munch on the fresh green grass. Poor old thing, I thought. His hearing is probably shot, maybe from the diving tank's water.

"Gamal," I called again.

This time he shifted his eyes in my direction, but kept right on tearing at the grass. He must really have been starved, I reasoned.

I could feel Wendy's eyes on the back of my head and it heightened my sense of insecurity. I had told her of my extremely limited experience with horses, but led her to believe I was a competent person in general. I was hoping Gamal would not prove me wrong.

"Gamal," I called, and this time it worked. He lifted his head and acknowledged my presence. I stopped walking forward and regarded him, and he, me. Now that I was closer I realized I had seen bigger horses, but there was no denying his muscles. Even though he was somewhat thin, I saw the outline of some very strong curves.

It occurred to me that Gamal was not a show type, or a race type, or any fancy type of horse. In fact, if he was a type at all, you would have to say sturdy and hearty, of no specific breed. I was beginning to like his type better and better. Gamal, I decided, was not a sissy horse, not a high-strung, overbred, rearing up and whinnying type of man-made horse. Almost certainly, he came into this world the old-fashioned way. Somewhere in a pasture, not unlike the one in which we were standing, his father and mother did what came naturally, and, from that brief union, Gamal was created.

But if there was one thing I was certain of on that warm day in May, it was that Gamal knew who he was. There was no question in my mind that he had a strong sense of self, of purpose, and of dignity.

The look I saw in his eyes was not mulishness, whatever that was, but perceptiveness, a kind of shrewdness, and perhaps taking it to an extreme, I would say he looked like he was a pretty good judge of character.

Emboldened by his acknowledgment of me, I closed in on him.

Gamal lowered his head, threw back his ears, and pawed the ground. More horse talk, this time from the horse himself.

I edged closer and, just when I was within a few feet of him, he snorted, let out a squeal, and took off in the opposite direction. Although I could have, and even should have, turned to Wendy for advice or asked her to fetch him, I did not. This was my first one-on-one interaction with Gamal and I wanted to do it on my own.

I assumed I had frightened the old guy, but persisted—slower this time. After all, I reminded myself, he had been through a lot recently.

"Gamal," I said in a bright, encouraging tone. "I've come to take you home."

While it was beginning to occur to me that calling him was fruitless, even ridiculous, I never thought it might also be dangerous.

Gamal responded in an even more animated manner. Again he lowered his head, again he pawed the ground, but this time he charged in my direction. Even though I didn't understand horse talk, I knew what it meant to have a half ton of horse coming my way. While I was trying to decide whether to dart to the left or the right, he made a deliberate sharp turn and barely avoided running me down. Had I not been so stunned, I might have been impressed by his fancy footwork. He had come so close I could almost feel the heat of his sunbaked coat on my skin. He stopped short a few feet away, and through fiery eyes, glared at me over his shoulder.

I had just been rejected by a horse, and was as crushed as if Gamal had actually trampled me. To make matters worse, Wendy sauntered out into the field and, without so much as a word, attached a rope to his halter and led him away. He was the very picture of obedience. I know my face was reddened by what had happened, but I was able to force back tears. Was this dismissal by a horse, the one I was already so fond of, an example of my incompetence? Was it proof that just

With Gamal. He was not in great shape in the beginning, as evidenced by his thin neck and prominent hipbones. He grew into a healthy horse from eating plenty of fresh hay, grain, and the many carrots I gave him. 1980.

as I had not been the right fit for picket lines, penning the Fund's publications, or lobbying legislators, even the pasture was a bust?

As Gamal approached the trailer's ramp, he stopped and looked at me again. This time, though, there was something different in his gaze. This time, it was not mean or cruel or judgmental. His relaxed eyes had a mischievous twinkle as if to say, "Gotcha!" He looked at me in a jolly way, a merry way, and, above all, a kind way. In fact, his look was so benevolent that despite what had just happened, I made the decision not to despair, not to give up.

And so our courtship began.

That night, after making sure Gamal was safely tucked away in his temporary home, I decided to read up on horses from my library. Over the years I had amassed a large collection of books about all kinds of animals, including equines. My idea was to familiarize myself with some of the more common horse terms so I would at least understand what people, if not animals, were talking about.

I was still annoyed that Wendy thought Gamal was small, so my first stop was at the word "hands" as applied to measuring the size of a horse. I discovered that a hand represented four inches, and that the number of inches from ground to withers determined the height of a horse. The origin of the term "hand" was not discussed, although I assumed it had to do with the width of an average hand. Withers? In the book I was consulting, no definition was given for "withers," but by cross-referencing I found out that the withers are the top part of the shoulder. Therefore, Wendy's estimate that Gamal was about 15.2 hands meant that he was 62 inches at the shoulder. Most Thoroughbreds, like those Wendy typically dealt with, are more than 16 hands. To my chagrin, it meant that, having seen him only from a distance, she was right about his size.

Next I looked up horse colors, and was amazed by the variety. I knew Gamal was a dark mahogany brown with a black mane and tail, and that the combination was known as bay. I realized I had heard the word "bay" before, in the Stephen Foster song "Camptown Races" ("I bet my money on the bob-tailed nag, somebody bet on the bay"). But my certainty about Gamal's color was somewhat shaken when the author warned in a reproachful tone that bay horses were not to be confused with chestnuts, which are similar, but do not have the requisite black mane, tail, and lower legs. Worse, it was noted that in some parts of the country, chestnuts are known as sorrels; but for now, I put aside that tidbit. I was all but certain I had a bay horse until I read the final part: a dark brown horse is sometimes called a seal brown and a lighter brown is called a dark bay. Was there someone out there to whom this made sense?

I remembered that Gamal had a distinctive white patch on his forehead and that, too, had a name: a star. At least I thought it was a star. Again, the author issued a warning: a star was not to be confused with a snip, a stripe, a blaze, or, God forbid, a bald face. I settled on a star.

I recalled that he had one white foot, but after doing more research, I realized I was badly mistaken. There was no such thing as a white foot. He may have had a white coronet, a white pastern, or a white ankle; and it was even possible for him to have had a white sock, a white stocking, or white spots on his coronet or heel. But I was dead wrong about the white foot.

After plowing through all of this, I thought it might be easier to determine exactly what type of horse he was. But I was wrong about that, too. If the varieties of color were bewildering, it was nothing compared to varieties of breed. Early on it occurred to me that Gamal may have been a mixed breed and that, of course, muddied the waters considerably.

First, I had to decide if he was what was known as a hot-blood or a cold-blood. Lest I thought a thermometer might be needed, the book made it clear that the terms had nothing to do with a horse's body temperature. Hot-bloods descended from the Arab and Barb horses of northern Africa. They are lithe and light-boned and contributed to the stock of such breeds as the Thoroughbred, the Quarter Horse, and the Standardbred. Cold-bloods are from northern Europe and helped create such big-boned bruisers as the Clydesdale, the Percheron, and the Shire. Although Gamal was sturdy, I couldn't really see him as a relative of one of those giants. I went with the hot-bloods.

I eliminated Thoroughbreds (which, it was noted, is the name of a breed and not another name for purebreds), as well as the so-called gaited horses, ones that move their front and hind legs in a particular pattern, such as Tennessee Walkers or Missouri Fox Trotters. When I realized that Standardbreds (also a breed) were also gaited and, what's more, were divided into either trotters or pacers (according to their specific gait), they, too, went out the window. Happily, there was no need to pursue any of the parti-colored breeds such as Appaloosas, Paints, or Pintos.

I had narrowed Gamal's ancestry to Quarter Horse or Morgan Horse when I realized the absurdity of my pursuit. If I had learned anything from my brief encounters with Gamal, it was that these endless delineations of size, of breed, of color, of attempts to narrow him were beside the point. There was nothing narrow about Gamal. Nothing.

It had been a long day, and that, combined with the dizzying array of facts about horses, brought on a strong wave of fatigue that pulled me under. But before I was fully submerged, I had one half-delirious thought: Gamal is safe and is mine.

· · ·

Of course, Gamal was not mine. Legally, he belonged to The Fund for Animals: they bought him, they paid his considerable bills. Yet, when I showed up at the barn early the next morning, eager to spend my first full day with him, it was Gamal himself who reinforced this idea of, if not ownership, then at least special friendship.

Until Gamal arrived, I had never before been inside Wendy's barn, although I had driven past it hundreds of times. As I surveyed Gamal's new lodgings, I realized I had made an unconventional choice.

Wendy's barn was neither of two types that predominated in Bucks County, an area where real, working farms were fast disappearing, and where gentlemen's farms and housing developments were taking their place. Some barns were prefabricated, soulless but practical metal structures, better suited for storing machinery than livestock; others were grand showplaces rivaling many houses in amenities and seemingly staffed with workers assigned to catch manure before it even hit the ground.

Wendy's humble red barn had seen several hundred years of constant use, with traces of previous occupants clinging to its walls and windows by way of nicks and dings, cobwebs and stains. The entire structure listed slightly to one side, and seemed to grow organically from the ground. A grass-covered earthen ramp led to the second story, where hay, carriages, and farm equipment was stored. The first floor, where a dozen and a half horses were boarded, had an old stone foundation slathered with flaking whitewash. It was a modest barn that, arguably, would have benefited from a cash infusion of a few hundred thousand dollars—an amount that, as with anything concerning horses, wouldn't have gone far. But no amount of money could have bought its character or charm.

Equally charming were the enthusiastic, horse-crazy girls who took lessons at the farm and competed in shows at larger venues. On show days, when both they and their horses were done up in snazzy equestrian attire, you might leap to the conclusion that they were mean, elitist girls. They were not. I was about twice the age of these young teenagers, yet they took the time to show me the ropes, sometimes literally. When I wasn't trailing behind Wendy, trying to stay out of her way while gleaning as much as I could from her several decades of experience, the girls tutored me and were patient with my ignorance. They taught me everything they knew with a cheerful readiness, and were eager to spruce up the former diving horse. One time, they thought it would be amusing to braid Gamal's mane. As I watched their nimble fingers execute a string of tiny braids along his neck, it wasn't hard to read the mortification on the old performer's face. He was, as I came to understand, something of a tough guy, a man's man, who took little pleasure in frivolity. Mercifully, he took the indignity in stride.

These girls, and their horses, were part of what is known as the hunter-jumper set. I was to learn that it is a type of English riding activity that highlights the horse's and rider's athleticism and grace as, together, they jump over fences or stone walls or hedges of varying heights and widths. It is a form of virtual foxhunting, originally developed as practice for the real thing, or to compensate for areas where foxes had been decimated by actual hunting and land development. Over time, the sport also became an art form, with horse and rider merging, and knowing each other's pacing, strengths, and weaknesses. Horses that compete in this sport tend to the long, leggy Thoroughbreds and Thoroughbred blends. Except for the farm's free-ranging resident goat, Dinner Bell, Gamal was an entirely different sort from all the others in the barn.

On that first sultry day in late May, it was ten or fifteen degrees cooler inside the barn, thanks both to those thick stone walls and to the building being tucked into the hillside. The air hung heavy with the robust fragrance of horse: sweat, urine, sawdust, manure, compacted dirt, tanned leather. It was the scent of ancient memory, although I was breathing it for the first time.

Inside the doorway was a bulletin board, and between show ribbons and notices about upcoming competitions, someone had posted a few newspaper articles about Gamal. Immediately, the girls, who I hadn't yet met, mobbed me and wanted to know his history, how long he would be staying, and where he would be going. One told me she had fashioned a star from cardboard, covered it with aluminum foil, and attached it to Gamal's stall door. After ten minutes, I had gotten no farther than the entryway.

Dimly, I was aware of a loud, insistent whinnying coming from deep inside the barn. I didn't know one whinny from the next, nor that there could even be a difference. The sound grew louder, and over it boomed Wendy's voice, one I definitely recognized.

"Aren't you going to visit Gamal?"

I looked down the aisle, and saw Gamal craning his neck over the half door of his stall, bobbing his head up and down.

I had come bearing gifts, a five-pound bag of carrots, and hot-footed it down the aisle to deliver the coveted goods.

"He recognized the sound of your voice, you know," Wendy said.

I was still unable to tell when she was kidding and gave her a quizzical look.

"He didn't start that racket when anyone else was here," she said.

He recognized the sound of my voice? From only our two brief encounters? While that concept sank in, I realized to my embarrassment that I hadn't recognized his. Once again, the horse had outdone me.

Wendy gave me her first deliberate lesson: how to feed carrots to a horse without losing fingers. Gamal needed no tutelage, and before long, polished off the bag.

By now, the barn had cleared out, and I decided to go into Gamal's stall to get to know him at closer range. After all, I reasoned, since he recognized my voice, he must have wanted more of me.

It never occurred to me that entering his stall, which was not only a confined space, but also his space, was a bad idea. I opened the stall door and stepped inside. Immediately, Gamal pressed his body against the back wall. Still, I saw no cause for alarm and figured he was just making room for me. A second later, he swung around and turned his rump in my direction. His tail switched impatiently from side to side. From the deep recesses, I remembered the warning issued at a summer camp years earlier: never stand directly behind a horse. Now here I was in exactly that vulnerable position. I made a fast exit, and as soon as I did, Gamal turned around and ambled back to the stall door.

"Gamal," I said. "It's time for us to have a little talk."

I explained to him the only way I knew, with words, who I was and how I happened to be involved in his life. I began by telling him about his guardian angel, the cranky old woman who alerted us to his plight. Then I told him that Cleveland and the Fund had come to his rescue. This act of compassion had little effect on his composure. There was no discernible gratitude, or thankfulness in his demeanor. But he stood quietly and was patient, and that was enough to encourage me to continue.

To assure him that I was qualified to take care of him, I explained that he was not my first brush with a diving horse, that I had seen the act on the Steel Pier in 1964. I did not mention Powderface, and instead told him that he might have been lazing in one of the stalls on the pier that very evening, having already performed earlier in the day. When I felt I had pretty much covered the situation, I made him a promise. I pledged that from that point on, we would take things at his pace. I would not force myself on him, nor would I allow anyone else to do so. This was his retirement, I said, and my goal was that it would be the best part of his life. I didn't want to overload him with too many details and made no mention of going to Texas.

I was so engrossed in what I was telling him, I didn't realize that in his way he was trying to tell me something. He had placed his head and neck outside the stall and was resting on my shoulder. The most obvious interpretation of his body language was that he was leaning on me, as in depending on me; but there seemed to be more to it. Somehow, the realization that in many ways this large creature's life was in my hands gave me confidence, rather than the reverse. It was almost as if Gamal was telling me that he knew I could do it; and so, I could.

I stopped talking, and for the first time had a closer look at this animal in my care.

I stood on tiptoe so I could see over the stall door and considered his body. Gamal was thin, but well built and compact. I had been right about one thing: he was a powerful-looking horse. His color, whatever it was called, was like dark, rich chocolate. His thick wavy mane and tail were blue-black, and on top of one of his hips was a dark patch the size of my palm which looked like a berry stain. Three of his four hooves were a deep charcoal gray, but one, the one attached to what I still thought of as a white foot, was lighter, the color of a ram's horn.

I stroked his throat and felt his warmth. Under the mane he was warmer yet. His dusty coat was smooth, yet the hairs of his mane, which were tangled with bits of hay and sawdust and grass, were very coarse indeed. But beyond all of that, Gamal had an inner glow, something that neither grooming nor better nutrition could have improved.

I inhaled his scent: sweet, salty, pungent, and distinctly his own. The soft area around his nose felt as if it was covered in velvet. As his delicate nostrils flared slightly with each breath, they tickled my cheek. His warm exhale, a perfume of carrots and sweet feed. Without trying, I found myself getting into the same rhythm of respiration. I put my ear to his neck and listened to his heartbeat.

For a long time, and I don't know how long, Gamal and I held that position. I was listening to him, breathing with him, and he with me. This moment with Gamal marked the first time in years, perhaps since my ambles in the White Mountains, that the constant chatter of my mind began to recede. Soon, I became conscious only of breathing: in and out; in and out. My awareness of the barn slipped away, my awareness of the stall slipped away, and there was nothing separating Gamal and me. We were simply breathing, in and out, in and out.

I was shocked by this mystical intimacy with a horse. I had expected to learn a lot through my contact with him, but I was thinking more along the lines of bits and bridles, saddles and stirrups. Suddenly I was faced with the possibility of something else entirely. I didn't feel I could speak to anyone about it. What would I say? That Gamal and I had a heavy-breathing session in the barn? I could only imagine Wendy's reaction. She was a decade or so older than I, with the look and bearing of Julia Child. My few experiences with her told me she was a practical, no-nonsense sort of person. This is not to say she didn't have a sense of humor, but she tended toward dry wit and sarcasm, and I didn't want to be on the receiving end of one of her pointed observations. Besides, for all I knew, this was something all horses did, and I was not keen on exposing yet another example of my ignorance.

It was possible, I thought, that Gamal had some kind of asthma, or breathing disorder. But since the veterinarian was coming to examine him within the week, and since the horse didn't seem to be in distress, I decided that for the time being I'd keep his condition to myself.

A few days later, I showed up early at the barn for the veterinarian's visit. I didn't want to miss a minute, as I knew this would be a good opportunity to take notes on Gamal's overall condition, learn more about horses, and, assuming doctor-patient confidentiality extended to vets and horses, broach the subject of his breathing. No sense revealing my ignorance to everyone in the barn.

I had dealt with many veterinarians in my life, but never one who specialized in horses. My only frame of reference was veterinarian James Herriot's *All Creatures Great and Small* series of books. I assumed this vet would be similar: that he'd dispense folksy wisdom along with medication, and establish a warm rapport with both patient and client.

This clinician came highly recommended by Wendy. He had cured horses when others had given up. He was much sought after at the most exclusive farms and, during the winter, traveled to Florida to tend the U.S. Olympic Equestrian Team's horses. I was pleased that my old pensioner was at last going to get what he deserved: the best.

Sensing I might be overwhelmed by the task, Wendy's husband, Jon, took Gamal from his stall and placed him in the cross-ties. Gamal greeted me with widened eyes and looked for evidence of carrots. I did not disappoint. As we waited, he crunched his vegetables with contentment while I patted his shoulder and kept an eye out for the veterinarian.

At the appointed hour, a diesel Mercedes sedan pulled into the driveway. A small, fit man in his late thirties, with a tidy waxed handlebar mustache, emerged from the car wearing spotless khakis and a short-sleeved golf shirt bearing a prominent designer's logo. I assumed he was either a friend of Wendy's, or someone looking for directions. I also thought he might be a reporter, although one seemingly more well paid than I ever was.

He entered the barn as if he had been there before, and as he whisked past, he said to no one in particular that he was looking for the diving horse. I wasn't certain, but it almost sounded as if there was disdain in his voice.

I pointed to Gamal and explained who we were. "Good," the vet said. "I wanted to be sure he was ready. I'm here to examine him." As he said this, he glanced at the thick gold bracelet on his wrist that doubled as a wristwatch. He went back to his car, opened the specially outfitted trunk, pulled out a few tools of his trade, then returned with a black bag and clipboard.

I was prepared to tell him a little about Gamal's history, after which I expected he, like Herriot, would give the horse a reassuring pat, along with some encouraging words for me. Instead, he asked who would be responsible for Gamal's bill. He added that the standard procedure was payment when services were rendered. I stammered that technically, I did not own Gamal, that I had only just met him; but I assured the vet that the Fund would pay promptly. He took the news with a downward twist of his mouth, but at least he accepted the arrangement. I had a suspicion that the paltry amount in my checking account was unlikely to cover even the cost of his car entering the property.

He wrote down Gamal's vital statistics: age, color, and sex, then asked about the horse's health. I explained, again, that I had known Gamal for only a few days and, in what must have been obvious, admitted that I knew very little about horses. I added, though, that I was hoping to learn more by watching the exam. "I figure this will be a little like watching a mechanic check out a used car that I already bought," I said, trying to lighten the mood. I meant no offense, but offense was taken. I'm not sure if it was by comparing him to a mechanic, or the very idea of a used car that annoyed him, but he looked at me in a most disapproving way.

It probably would have been part of any physical examination, but this man seemed to carry out his task with a particular flourish, as if drawing attention to his competency and skill. He whipped the stethoscope from around his neck, and blocked first one of Gamal's nostrils, then the other, as he listened intently to the horse's lungs, then heart.

"For a horse his age," he said, "he sounds good."

I could have done without the age reference, for Gamal and I were just beginning our relationship and any hint that it might not be a lengthy one was anathema to me; but at least his airways were clear.

If ever there was an appropriate time to ask about Gamal's breathing, this was it.

"Gamal's breathing," I ventured, "can be rather . . ." I took a second to choose the right word.

"Can be what," he jumped in. "Has he been breathing hard after running?"

"No."

"Has he been huffing?"

"No."

"Panting?"

"No."

"Wheezing?" This last question contained more than a touch of impatience.

"No," I said, eloquence failing me. "None of those. But the other day, he hung his head over my shoulder and just stood there breathing in a kind of deliberate, almost dreamy way. He's done it a couple of times since. What do you think he means by it?"

The minute those last words escaped my mouth I realized how stupid I must have sounded to this dour man who had devoted his life to what can be proved and what can be measured, not what can be imagined or sensed.

He made a noise resembling "Hrumph" and repeated my question, "What did he *mean* by it?"

An uncomfortable pause hung between us.

"He's a horse," he said. "He feels fear, pain, hunger, thirst, and sexual arousal."

Intuition told me that there was more to horses than just that. And although my experience with Gamal was limited, I already suspected he was unusual, even among the general horse population. I wanted to suggest to the vet that perhaps Gamal did mean something by what he did, something else entirely from basic animal instincts, that maybe he was expressing something wonderful, possibly magical. But I didn't say any of those things. I dropped the subject in favor of getting on with the exam and allowing the vet to do what he did best.

By now, Wendy had joined us, and judging from the vet's half smile, his first of the appointment, he seemed relieved to have someone more experienced at hand who spoke his language. As she took my spot at Gamal's head, the vet told her to thread the chain at the end of the lead rope through Gamal's halter and stretch it across the bridge of his nose. From the look on my face, Wendy realized I had a question. She explained that the chain gives a person better control over a horse. I found this puzzling, since so far Gamal had been a model patient; but I allowed for the fact that he was a large animal whose temperament was unknown to the vet.

The vet examined the horse as any careful, highly trained doctor might. He scratched lightly at Gamal's coat so he could see his skin; parted the hair in his ears and with a scope, peered deep inside; and shined a flashlight in each of his eyes. He lifted Gamal's lips and examined his teeth, pulled on his tongue, and glanced at the lining of his mouth.

After kicking a fresh sample of Gamal's manure, he told Wendy he needed to tube the horse. I didn't know what he meant, but as he went back to his car to get what he needed, Wendy explained that what the vet was about to do would look worse than it really was, but was a necessary evil in order to rid Gamal of internal parasites.

It was hard to imagine how it could have looked worse. The vet fed at least five or six feet of a white plastic tube down Gamal's nose and into his stomach. From a gallon jug, he poured a milky white liquid, the dewormer, into a funnel he held over Gamal's head while gravity transported the concoction. The horse flinched only a little, and I had to take Wendy's word for it that it wasn't so bad.

Next, the vet lifted all four of Gamal's hooves. When he finished cleaning their undersides with a specially designed pick, I could see they did not have the smooth surface that his hoof prints had showed, but instead a somewhat rippled one. He pointed out one particular hoof to Wendy and said, "See that?" She nodded in well-experienced agreement. I looked over her shoulder but saw nothing unusual. Wendy reached out and touched the hoof. "It's warm, too," she said.

The vet cut away at the warm hoof and within seconds, a stream of thick, yellow-green pus broke loose. Gamal had been suffering from an abscess, something that not only had been painful, but would have led to a more serious condition if left untreated. He packed the hoof with some sort of medication, and gave Wendy instructions on how to care for the wound. He said the hooves also showed evidence of something called "thrush," but I didn't dare ask for an explanation.

I had been startled by the tube worming and the pus-letting, but that was nothing compared to what was next: the vet scooted beneath Gamal to check the horse's penis. As he touched Gamal's underbelly, the horse startled and stepped sideways. He didn't rear up on his hind legs, or kick, or flail his front hooves in the air, but apparently his sudden movement was unacceptable. In an instant, the vet jumped up and told Wendy to get the twitch, a two-foot-long wooden rod with a noose-shaped chain at one end. She complied, and as she was about to speak I interrupted her.

"I know," I said. "It's going to look worse than it is."

"Actually," she corrected, "it's not only going to look awful—it's going to be awful."

The vet took the twitch, inserted Gamal's upper lip in the opening, then twisted the chain until the lip was pinched tightly to one side. He handed it over to Wendy, and without another word, scooted back beneath the horse. He grabbed Gamal's crotch in what I thought was an unnecessarily aggressive manner, and pulled the massive member from the foreskin. After looking up one side, down the other, and at the top, he released it, stood up, and made another notation on his paperwork. The rest of the exam was conducted in near silence.

The final assessment of Gamal's health was that, overall, the horse was in good shape but in need of a few things to prevent existing problems from getting worse and to make his life more comfortable. He advised Wendy that she, or the girls in the barn, could take care of most items on the list. He never mentioned how, or if, I might participate, never even looked in my direction.

. . .

I took a look at the vet's list: hoof trimming (farrier required); tooth filing with further examination (veterinary dentist required); and the rest, which could be done by Wendy: treatment for thrush, bath, and sheath cleaning. I was desperate to find something, anything, that I could do, and thought I might be able to handle the bath. As it turned out, even with that I needed help.

For a horse that spent so much time in water, he jumped and reared at the sight of the spraying hose and I feared he was going to break loose from where I had tied him. Yet, as in the pasture at the auction house, as soon as Wendy came outside to assist, he was the perfect gentleman. She said a few calming words to him, let him sniff the hose, and let him see the water spray against the barn. Once he knew what was happening, he was fine and I took over. As warm, sudsy water steamed from his broad back, he leaned into the massaging nubs of the rubber brush. He lifted his upper lip in pleasure, for there was no question that he was enjoying it. I held the hose sideways to his mouth, and he seemed to delight in lapping the running water. Later, Wendy showed me how to dry him with what was called a sweat scraper, a foot-long, specially made U-shaped piece of aluminum. As I dragged it across his skin, the metal worked like a gutter on a house: the water collected and rolled off. I had seen something similar in the *Masterpiece Theatre* series *I, Claudius,* as Roman slaves scraped the skin of the nobility luxuriating in hot baths. This would not be the only time I sensed a master-slave parallel with horses.

I asked to be taught how to clean Gamal's hooves—a backbreaking job that required me to bend in half, lean into his body (presumably to get him off balance), and then lift his several-hundred-pound leg between my knees to expose the underside of the hoof. With the pick, I was to dig out the accumulated dirt in his hooves, especially in the frog, a V-shaped indentation that took up the middle section. It was here that acrid-smelling bacteria created the condition known as thrush, the result of damp conditions and lack of care. The cure was an old-time remedy, one that Doc Carver himself might even have used. Kopertox was a green liquid that had to be applied daily until the condition cleared up and which, I discovered the hard way, stained both hands and fabric if not handled carefully. Later, the visiting farrier paid even more attention to Gamal's feet. I was amazed to learn from him that just by slanting the hooves at a slightly different angle, there would be less stress on the horse's muscles and skeleton, making him more comfortable.

Likewise, the itinerant equine dentist, not a veterinarian but someone who specialized in this often neglected part of a horse's body, was able to correct several problems. I wondered briefly if Doc Carver used his dental skills to take care of his horses' teeth.

In yet another quaint but unfamiliar horse term, the horse dentist told me he needed to "float" the horse's teeth. To prove his point, he encouraged me to feel the sharp hooks of enamel on the surfaces. If the teeth were more level, he said, the horse could grind his food better and get more nutrients out of what he was eating. As a bonus, the hooks would no longer scrape Gamal's cheeks and tongue. Before I knew it, he pulled out a long metal rasp with an equally long wooden handle and filed down the rough edges as one might plane a board.

The veterinarian was right to order further examination of Gamal's teeth: the dentist found one tooth was abscessed. He whipped out a giant pair of pliers, and with someone holding the twitch, extracted the tooth with one hard pull. Like a fisherman with a prize catch, he held up his trophy: a white, bloodied square the size of a half marshmallow. Blood and pus and saliva streamed down Gamal's chin and just as quickly was absorbed by the sawdust on the barn floor. I steadied myself against the wall at the sight. The dentist handed me the tooth, and suggested I drill a hole across the top, put it on a chain, and wear it as a necklace. "It's a real conversation starter at a party," he advised without a hint of irony. Apparently he and I attended different parties.

But there was one item left on the to-do list, the thing that made no sense to me whatsoever: cleaning Gamal's sheath. I knew what a sheath was, a covering. It was also a kind of slim-fitting, unadorned dress best worn on someone with a flawless figure. When I was a child, my mother had a few in her closet. But in this case, what was the sheath covering? Then I remembered the veterinarian's intimate, invasive examination of Gamal, and it came to me in a revolting rush: somehow, Gamal's penis had to be scrubbed, flushed, or for all I knew, power washed.

Wendy explained that male horses, geldings in particular, accumulate dirt and secretions called smegma in the sheath covering the penis. Smegma! Now there was a word I hadn't heard since my boarding school days. It was routine, in some circles, to hear an unfortunate girl being told she smelled like smegma. While I didn't know what it meant, I was careful, always, to err on the side of overbathing.

If there was anything worse for a horse than ordinary smegma, it was a related condition where a hard, pea-shaped lump of smegma, known as a bean, formed in a pouch at the tip of the penis. Untreated, it could cause anything from discomfort, to severe pain, to urinary blockage. I could see that this was a serious business indeed, but for once I was glad to be too inexperienced to even try to carry out this necessary task.

Like taking out the trash, sheath cleaning was a vital job no one wanted (and I'd be suspicious of anyone who did). But Wendy was made of strong stuff. She rolled up her sleeves and went at it barehanded. I half watched, half shielded my eyes from the awful sight, which involved lubricating jelly, and warm, sudsy water. Her long arm disappeared beneath Gamal's belly as she felt around like a blind person. Soon, she was peeling off ribbons of the dreaded smegma. I asked what horses did in the wild, horses without human slaves to assist in their grooming.

"There are no geldings in the wild," she told me. "Stallions get cleaned by breeding."

I was about to ask about those females on whom the stallions cleaned themselves. How did they get clean? But before I had a chance, Wendy exclaimed, "Aha!" and interrupted my thoughts. You'd have assumed she discovered a nugget of gold, but in fact, it was a bean. She offered to show me the prize, but I declined. The stench alone was enough, and had I fainted, there would be no living it down.

Chapter Six

I would not have been my father's daughter if I hadn't continued to be curious about diving horse history. Although there were fewer bonds between my father and me than there had once been, one connection remained unbroken: viewing the world as what is, overlaid on what was. Gamal's appearance reawakened the childlike sense of wonder I experienced when I saw a horse dive at the Steel Pier. Now, my life and Gamal's life had intersected, and I felt that if I knew more about his past, our connection would only deepen.

But there was more at play than just my own interest. After I acquired Gamal for the Fund, reporters would show up at the barn from time to time and question me not only about Gamal's personal history, but also the act's history—as if I was an expert. In fact, they may have known more than I did. Soon, my curiosity mingled with theirs and it became imperative to delve more deeply into this horse with a history.

Gamal had already enchanted and challenged me beyond anything I thought possible. I wanted, even needed, to know everything about him—where he performed, how he was trained, where he was stabled. Anything that could bring his background into sharper focus was vital to my understanding of this magnificent but somewhat inscrutable horse.

I had uncovered some general diving horse history while preparing my case for buying Gamal, but I knew it yielded some dubious information. The biggest mystery: Doc Carver, the enigmatic man who invented the diving horse act. Gamal was incapable of telling me about all he had seen and done during the course of his life. But Doc Carver purposely left behind a scramble of stories, one more incredible than the next. Was it even possible to discover the truth?

The newspaper clippings I was given at the auction were my only tangible link to Gamal's history, the history of the diving horse show, and Doc Carver's life and times. I dove into them, assuming I would get my answers. I did get a few leads on people who were still in Atlantic City and who might give me some firsthand information. But, just as when I began compiling information to help persuade Cleveland to buy Gamal, I realized these clippings also contained contradictory information. In one article, Doc was referred to as a country doctor, while in another, a dentist. And here, again, the dates of his birth were at odds—1840 or 1851?

If the date of Doc's birth was untrue, it cast doubt on every other statement. If he was born in 1840, the Civil War would have been a greater influence on his life. He might even have participated. Yet I saw no evidence of that. And if it was Doc himself who had floated various versions of his life story, then what was he trying to promote—or hide?

Gamal was a living link between Doc and me. While Doc never knew Gamal, Doc owned, and trained, the first diving horse. Lorena, who had been with the act since the beginning, worked with Gamal at the end. And now he, the last diving horse in the Carver line, was in my care. Despite my misgivings about what may been involved in training the horses, the safety of the act, or even the questionable ethics of using animals for entertainment, I would not have known this remarkable horse were it not for Doc. If only for that reason, I had to know more.

The frightening yet compelling image of a horse in midair had gripped the imagination of hundreds of thousands of people for nearly a hundred years. A traditional interpretation might say the act was popular because Doc tapped into two age-old fascinations: sex (the slightly risqué sight of a woman in a bathing suit) and violence (or at least its potential). But neither explained fully its fascination to me.

After all, as a child, neither sex nor violence was of particular interest. I was simply in awe of the horse. I needed to know why.

Despite my intense concern for animal welfare, it was too easy to dismiss the whole thing as just another example of animal abuse. Yes, Gamal narrowly escaped Powderface's tragic fate. But to define him solely as a victim somehow diminished his accomplishments. Certainly he had been used and discarded; but he also excelled in the diving act. He did something that not many horses could do. I was reminded of something one of the early diving girls, Sonora Webster Carver, said in a newspaper interview: "And as I often tell people when they marvel at the act, horses are like people: some of them have nerve, some of them don't."

Gradually, my mind began to be flexible enough to hold two opposing thoughts: that the act held the potential to be dangerous

When the staff found a name they liked, they stuck with it. Over the years, there were several horses named Red Lips, and several named Powderface. Sonora Webster Carver was riding this Red Lips when she hit the water off balance, causing retinal detachment and eventual blindness. She never held it against the horse, though, and continued to ride him, and others, sightless. Here with her husband, Al Floyd (Carver), Major the dog, and Happy the goat, circa 1932.

to both horse and rider; and that the horses and riders were courageous and talented.

Part of that mental flexibility was the result of a book I had just
read that put a human face on those involved with the act. *A Girl
and Five Brave Horses* was an "as-told-to" story by that same Sonora
Webster Carver. From my earlier research on diving horse history, I
realized that her book contained as much fiction as fact; but it was a
jumping-off point for more about Doc and the horses.

In Sonora's telling, she began her diving career in 1924; married
Al in 1928; took the diving horse act to the Steel Pier in 1929; and
retired with Al in 1942. More than half the book centered on an
accident she suffered in 1931 while diving. She neglected to turn her
head quickly enough as she and a horse named Red Lips entered the
water tank. The impact detached her retinas. Although she became
blind, she continued to dive, sightless. Diving, she said, was the thing
she loved to do more than anything else.

How she overcame adversity was a powerful theme. It was not,
however, what I found most interesting. She was someone who knew,
and worked closely with, Doc. I scoured the pages, looking for firsthand anecdotes about the man's character and more about the horses.

Sonora described the elderly man she met at her job interview as
tall and "seemingly indestructible," with a "ruddy face and penetrating eyes." Almost every anecdote she relayed about him revealed a
tough taskmaster. She cited numerous instances of Doc's imperious
and demanding ways: requiring her to wear modest clothes, both
onstage and off; forbidding her to mingle with the crowds so as to
maintain an air of mystery; and berating her for the slightest mistake
during her performances, such as forgetting to bow to the audience.
Somehow, though, she stayed on and cared for Doc until his death.

Yet, there was one conversation between them, about his early
buffalo-killing prowess, where he revealed a more introspective side.
He confided to her that he regretted killing as many animals as he
had in his early life. As he explained it, he had been "too young to
feel any sense of shame."

. . .

After becoming blind, Sonora not only continued her performances, but learned Braille and taught it to others. Later, her cowritten memoir was made into a 1991 Disney film, *Wild Hearts Can't Be Broken.* Clearly, the woman's bravery was not limited to diving on horseback.

But there was one way in which she chose to be blind: glossing over the real dangers associated with horse diving.

Sonora repeatedly painted a sanguine picture of the act. She stated that in many towns, local humane societies would protest the show, and in one case got as far as having a California court issue an injunction to stop it. But, she proclaimed, once the judge examined the horses, he found them fit and healthy and threw out the case.

She implied that the act was, if not risk-free, then at least only mildly risky. The most obvious refutation of that was her own blindness. Elsewhere, I read of a tragic incident involving a diver that, although it took place before Sonora's time, is something she would have known about: eighteen-year-old Oscar Smith, who plunged to his death while diving on a horse. She did not mention it in her book.

Smith was something of a child prodigy, an up-and-comer in what passed for entertainment at the turn of the twentieth century, bronco riding. Doc promoted him as the Champion Boy Rider of the World. Young Smith had also been a scout for Theodore Roosevelt and, as if that wasn't enough, he occasionally filled in by riding the diving horses when the girl in red, a Miss Lawrence, was "indisposed." It was while taking her place in San Antonio, Texas, on February 17, 1907, that young Oscar Smith met his demise.

According to eyewitness accounts, "the horse made a beautiful dive. The horse hit the water nose first with Smith sitting gracefully on his back. The crowd broke into cheers as the horse and rider went under water. The horse came up but no rider. Men jumped into the tank and retrieved the boy's lifeless body. When taken out of the water, it was found he had a large bruise over his left eye, evidently caused by a kick from the horse." The horse, one of the first named Powderface, was unharmed and continued to dive for several more decades.

Most of the stories that Sonora did relay in her book were upbeat, but there was one heartbreaker: Lightning, the only diving horse to die on the job. Lightning was a 1,500-pound mare and one of Doc's original diving horses. Sonora speaks fondly of the horse, who spoke in "little whinnies and nickers," and was possessed of a "gentle friendliness." Despite her name, Lightning had an extreme terror of electrical storms. The mare had a few names in her day: "Babe," when Doc bought her; "Lightning," as he thought it was more dramatic for the show; and finally "Duchess of Lightning" in honor of a duchess who saw the act in Canada and wanted to buy the horse. Would that she had.

In 1927, toward the end of Doc's life, two horses, John the Baptist and Lightning, were contracted to dive at what Sonora called Lick's Pier in Ocean City, California. It was a kind of Steel Pier of the West, both in popularity and attractions. A twist in the usual way the act was performed is that the horses were to dive without a rider into the Pacific Ocean, rather than into a tank on the pier. Whether it was Al or Doc who signed the agreement is unclear, but the outcome was disastrous.

As Sonora tells it, John went first, and despite choppy seas made his way back to shore. Lightning was next, and executed a perfect dive. But when she became aware of the crashing waves, she panicked and swam not to shore, but beyond the breakers and out to sea. Lifeguards went after her in a boat, but that frightened her even more and she swam farther. Although they were able to lasso her and bring her in, she had already drowned and was dead upon arrival on the beach.

Doc was in Nebraska at the time, attending a convention of old-timers associated with western reenactment shows. In order to shield Doc from the horrible news, Al sent a telegram, saying only that Lightning was hurt and that he should return to California immediately. That alone was enough to cause Doc extreme anguish. According to Sonora, he kept repeating, "Oh my horse! My pretty horse. I should have known something like this was going to happen. I had a dream about a month ago in which Lightning was hurt. Oh, my pretty horse!" This, from a man who, despite his gruff exterior, always referred to himself as his horses' "Daddy."

When Doc got back to California, they told him the rest of the story: Lightning was dead. Doc canceled the contract immediately.

Sonora said, "From that moment on, the life seemed to go out of him, as if it were visibly ebbing." He died only weeks later.

To get closer to the diving horses than just historical research, I decided to take a trip to Atlantic City, the place where they had once performed, and from where their fame spread nationwide. I sensed that visiting what I was told was now a ramshackle town with a shuttered Steel Pier might resurrect the memory of my personal experience with the flying horses, something that still affected me these many years later. I knew I wouldn't get all of my answers in one day in Atlantic City, and that it was entirely possible that my visit might raise more questions. But it made sense to begin at the beginning.

As I drove down the streets of this city by the sea for only the second time in my life, it looked like the morning after a party, a big, messy affair that hadn't yet been cleaned up. The party could easily have been named "The Wrecking Ball," as, in its aftermath, almost all of the gorgeous, rickety, hopelessly outdated but supremely interesting old hotels had been blown up, flattened, then bulldozed and hauled away to make room for brand-new gambling casinos. Those few left standing gave shelter only to pigeons who huddled on windowless windowsills.

I passed block after block of rubble, with some now vacant lots being used to park front-loaders and backhoes that awaited their next assignment. No wonder that in 1979, French film director Louis Malle was able to use real locations, rather than sets, while shooting his movie *Atlantic City*. The town provided a ready-made backdrop for a film about broken dreams. I had a dream there once, too, a dream about how my life was going to unfold, about what was permanent and unchanging. Somehow, in a way I still did not understand, the image of the diving horse kicking off from the platform played a part in that narrative.

The demise of the grand hotels was one thing, and sad enough; but tragic was the fate of the diving horses. The once iconic living symbols of the city were, also in a moment, sold to the highest bidder. Their dead-end destiny was part of the "out with the old, in with the new" maxim that was being promoted as a cure-all for the town's ills. I needed to know how the horses' final owner could have discarded the three remaining performers—Gamal, Powderface, and Shiloh—with such indifference. He knew the animals, had known them for years. And they had made money for him, also for years. Had he no conscience?

My first stop was at a place that seemingly had no connection to casinos, the Steel Pier, or diving horses—but thanks to one of those newspaper clippings that accompanied Gamal, I knew it did.

I felt a little shell-shocked as I got out of my car at the Marine Mammal Stranding Center. The small, nondescript building was located on an inlet at the less populated northern end of town and had been founded just a few years earlier, in 1978. Yet despite its unassuming exterior, it had the distinction of being the world's first nonprofit, twenty-four-hour facility dedicated to rehabbing and rescuing marine life—mainly seals and dolphins but also a few sea turtles. I was there to interview the center's founder, Bob Schoelkopf, to satisfy my curiosity about the diving horses—animals with which he had a slender connection.

Bob's journey to establishing the center did not follow a straight line. He did not, as I might have imagined, graduate from college with a degree in marine biology. He did not even grow up at the shore. In fact, his career path almost seemed like chance.

Around the time I had last been in Atlantic City, innocently watching the diving horses, and while the Democrats were nominating Lyndon Johnson for president (in part to reduce our involvement in the Vietnam War), Bob Schoelkopf was in Reading, Pennsylvania, enlisting in the Navy. He was, of course, sent to Vietnam. As a corpsman, he went on to receive scuba diving training as part of a special operations unit.

Near the end of his service, he was medically evacuated to the naval hospital in Philadelphia. After his recovery, he was assigned to the naval shipyard nearby to finish out the remainder of his stint.

While there, he became aware of a place called Aquarama, a combination aquarium and aquatic performance center in South Philadelphia. It was owned by George Hamid Sr., the same man who owned the Steel Pier.

After the Navy, Bob needed a job and Aquarama was hiring. With his underwater experience in the military, Bob was certainly overqualified, but a job was a job. And so he began, in full scuba gear, cleaning the inside of the animals' tanks. His first glimpse of the diving horses was when, from time to time, they and their collapsible tank and ramp would be hauled the sixty miles from Atlantic City to Aquarama. The idea was to give Philadelphians a taste of what they were missing at the seashore.

Aquarama existed for only seven years, from 1962 to 1969, but Bob was too valuable an employee to let go. Hamid offered him a job at the Steel Pier, and soon he developed his own show, Captain Bob and His Dolphins. The animals did similar stunts to those at Aquarama—leaping through hoops, clapping their flippers at the appropriate time, and even gyrating on their tails to "The Twist."

Soon, Bob was promoted to manager of the pier, and in addition to his show he had one more duty: interacting with the diving horses. Despite many published reports that the act was all good times, fun and games, Bob didn't see it exactly that way. He claimed that upon surfacing after a dive, it was not unusual for a horse to vomit whatever food was in its stomach—half-digested grain or hay—from the force of hitting the water. Bob admitted that while technically the horses were not forced to jump—no whips or prods were involved—they had little recourse but to jump once they reached the top of the ramp. The platform was too narrow for them to turn around, and backing down forty feet was not part of their skill set. He also divulged that once his wife, Claire, leapt into what was then a fifteen-foot-deep tank atop a horse, just for the experience.

And what was it like?

"She told me it hurt, hurt her chest," he said. "And if it hurt her, it must have hurt the horses, too."

Bob had exhausted his diving horse stories. When I pressed further he said I really needed to speak to a man who had long since left town, a man known as the diving horses' master trainer, Bill Ditty. The name rang a bell: he was mentioned in one of the articles given to me after the auction. Bob didn't know where Bill lived, but felt sure that if I wanted to locate him badly enough, I'd find a way to track him down. I made a mental note to do just that.

My next stop that day was at a tumbledown establishment, and I knew immediately that I would be seeing and hearing things I would rather avoid. After all, I was about to meet the man I held responsible for selling the last three horses—caring not one bit for what became of them. I considered driving away, but it was too late— Walter, whom I also read about in newspaper clippings given to me at the auction, was expecting me and was heading toward my car. The old man's dilapidated farm in nearby Absecon was crisscrossed with broken-down fencing delineating pastures of mud. I knew that during the Steel Pier's off-season, the horses were boarded at his farm and I shivered at the thought of my precious Gamal ever having lived there.

I did my best to be courteous, and strained to come up with excuses for why the place was in such a state of disrepair. But one thing I could not overlook was that he was the very person who had put the horses in harm's way.

Before I could even begin to question him, he insisted on showing me two horses in his care.

"This here's Goliath, the world's largest horse," he said. The grossly oversized creature lumbered through the muck and sniffed me all over, probably hoping for another meal.

"And this one's the world's smallest horse."

I didn't really know the difference between a small horse, a pony, or a miniature of either. But I knew an animal with dwarfism when I saw one. The animal had a large forehead, wide-set eyes, and a small jaw. As he nibbled my sleeve, I could see crooked, overlapping teeth, too many teeth for such a small mouth. How on earth did the animal manage to eat?

Walter was oblivious, slapped each animal on the rump with a chuckle, and sent them back into the muck.

I started off with what I considered a neutral question, if he knew how the diving horses were trained.

"Trained?" he asked, incredulous. "They weren't trained. You kicked them in the ass and they jumped."

He must have noticed the shock on my face because he backtracked a bit.

"It was gradual, see. First they'd jump a few feet, then a few more, until they got to the top of the ramp. It wasn't nothin' special."

I asked how it came about that he owned the diving horses. Walter had a ready answer, and a prideful one. "When those guys sold the pier to Resorts, it included all of the fixtures."

I knew what that meant. In legal terms, the diving horses were chattel, personal property.

"Then Resorts sold everything not nailed down," Walter said. "What would a casino want with three broken-down nags? Anybody could have bought those horses from Resorts. But I was the one with the sense to do it. I knew I'd make something back on my investment."

Earlier, in 1973, George Hamid Jr. sold the pier to a group of well-heeled Atlantic City businessmen. At that point, even though overall revenues were declining, the diving horses were still a fairly big draw. Those last owners of the pier were hometown boys who had known one another since high school. They grew up seeing the horses dive, and they, like Hamid, knew the emotional attachment people had to the scene of their summer memories. From a business standpoint, they also knew the pier's value was directly connected to the horses and the tourism dollars they represented.

These men may have been pillars of the community, devoted family men, generous philanthropists. They may have even loved the family dog. But when they sold the pier to Resorts International in 1978, not one of the trio considered the welfare of the horses. Not one considered excluding the horses from the sale and giving them a proper retirement. Likewise, none of the accountants or executives at

Resorts, when looking over the pier's inventory, ever considered the fact that the horses were living beings. Not one saw this as an opportunity to repay the horses for their labors. None of these supposedly astute businessmen even had the sense to recognize that, if nothing else, finding homes for the horses would have been good publicity.

In a shameful chapter in Atlantic City's history, there was one final display of insensitivity and greed: not only did Resorts not give away the horses, they sold them to old Walter for a few hundred dollars, as if that paltry sum made any difference to the casino's bottom line.

In newspaper reports, Walter claimed Resorts told him to "get rid of the horses as quickly as possible." The company denied it and said that since he had been boarding the horses, it only made sense to sell him the animals—not that that was much better. What Resorts couldn't deny, of course, is that, one way or another, they did not take care of the horses; they disposed of them.

Shortly after I acquired Gamal, I approached the publicity director at Resorts to see if the casino might like to reimburse the Fund for saving Gamal. I pitched it as good publicity, and a way for them to make amends for overlooking the horses the first time around. Initially, my idea was well received and he went as far as setting a date for a ceremony, one that Gamal would attend. I bought a suit for the occasion, a not-insignificant expense given my salary. And then, the deal was off, with the only explanation that "the powers that be" had decided against it. In retrospect, I figured out why: to acknowledge Gamal now would also mean acknowledging the casino's terrible oversight in selling the horses in the first place. Worse, it would mean admitting that Powderface was missing and presumably slaughtered. Better, they reckoned, just to keep quiet and wait for interest in the horses to wane.

Walter told me he resold the horses immediately for the highest price he could get. A New Jersey horse dealer bought Powderface. Without thinking to disclose to anyone the horse's colorful career, the dealer took the horse to a low-end auction in Iselin, New Jersey, where the majority of animals were sold for meat. He didn't keep track of who bought the horse. Another New Jersey man bought Shiloh from Walter, but owned her only briefly. He then resold her to a woman in Pennsylvania for riding. And Gamal, after his stint at a summer camp in Maryland, was also sold again, this time at the auction where he was miraculously delivered into my care.

There was one last stop I needed to make, and it was the one about which I had the least enthusiasm: the Steel Pier. It was still owned by Resorts International, and still closed. Many plans had been proposed in the years since its purchase about a renovation, a reopening, and about making it, once again, into a world-class tourist destination. Even Donald Trump had similar plans when he acquired the Steel Pier just a few years later in 1988.

As the fog rolled in, a chill, damp wind blew off the Atlantic. On the streets, on the boardwalk, and on the beach, it was deserted. It was late afternoon, but already the lights of Resorts, and the few run-down shops surrounding it, glowed with a forced cheeriness.

Just opposite, on the ocean side, was the Steel Pier, now a mere stub compared to its one-mile length in its heyday. Over the years, it had been wracked by waves, hammered by hurricanes. Now, totally neglected, it had fallen into decrepitude.

Cyclone fencing across the entrance prevented access from the boardwalk, but the post-apocalyptic landscape could still be seen through the diamond-shaped chain links. The floorboards of the structure were either buckled or missing, and much of every surface was coated with pigeon droppings. A few small buildings were boarded up, their former brightly colored paint jobs now faded and peeling. In the far distance was the one thing I came to see, but also wanted not to see: the two-tiered diving horse ramp.

Facing the ramp, some of the bleachers, the very ones on which I sat with my mother, still remained, as if awaiting an audience for the next show. Even from far away, the horses' platform seemed incredibly high, and incredibly fragile. I imagined Gamal, and Powderface, and all the others, that, over the years, had galloped up that ramp as the announcer promised "the thrill of a minute." Now, the only sounds were the wind whistling through the slats, and waves slapping the shore.

During the hurricane of 1962, the pier was in danger of collapse. A barge broke loose and smashed into it, splitting it in half. The horses were at the far end of the pier, with no way to escape. As the story went, their trainer and handler, Bill Ditty, lashed together the four horses—Dimah, Phantom, Lorgah, and Gamal—and jumped with them into the ocean. Ditty, who couldn't swim, reportedly held on to their manes and guided them to shore.

There were other stories that made headlines over the years, too, like the time Kenny Rogers had a few drinks after his last show, ran up the horse's ramp, and announced he was going to dive—that is, until he looked down forty feet into the tank. He decided to come back down the same way he went up. Band leader Buddy Rich complained that every time it was announced that the horse was about to dive, visitors would rush to witness the spectacle, leaving Rich with a half-empty ballroom. And there was the Timex wristwatch ad with the famous tagline "It takes a licking and keeps on ticking." Among the many durability tests was one that featured a watch strapped to the foreleg of Lorgah before a dive. Although the timepiece fell off in the tank, damned if it wasn't still ticking upon retrieval.

It had been a troubling day, and I was chilled as much by the temperature as the scene. As the shadows of dusk settled, I became more than a little spooked by ghosts that seemed to surround me. Against my normal driving habits, I took Bob Schoelkopf's advice not to stop at red lights due to the area's high crime rate and frequent car-jackings. As I sped past gambling's ancillary businesses—pawn shops, dive bars, and bail bondsmen—I realized that while my visit didn't yield exactly the sort of information I was seeking, the trip was well worth its discomforting aspects.

Chapter Seven

It was predictable, inevitable, perhaps even fated—the more time Gamal and I spent together, the more attached I became to him. Initially, I did not realize this was a problem. In the beginning, I was keen only on saving the horse, and, while he was in my care, I wanted him to be comfortable and secure. I had every intention of sending Gamal to Texas when the fencing at the Fund's ranch was complete. But life conspired against that plan: completing the fencing took longer than expected, by several months. The result was that as days, then weeks, passed, and I got to know Gamal better, the thought of

Gamal after a dive on the Steel Pier, ridden by Patty Dolan, late 1960s

sending him to Texas cast a long, dark shadow over our otherwise sunny relationship.

There was a selfish reason for my wanting to keep Gamal: I loved him. Although grooming was included in his boarding fee at Wendy's barn, I would add to it whenever possible by brushing, bathing, and even cleaning the underside of his hooves—anything just to spend time with him. The increasingly close bond we were developing had many benefits. Gamal didn't exactly give away his affection, but when he exhibited any trace of it, like giving my cheek a gentle push with his nose even when no carrots were in play, I would be thrilled. The thrill was doubled if whatever he did, such as whinnying when he heard my voice, was done exclusively for me.

I never blamed him for not doting on me, or not responding in kind when I would hug and kiss him. After all, how many people had he known during the course of his life? Some were kind, I'm sure; but I'm equally sure that some were not. Eventually, he must have decided that it was in his best interest to play it cool with new people, to take his time to see how someone was going to treat him. I did my best to build his confidence in my benign intentions, while asking nothing in return. Well, almost nothing. After a few close shaves in the beginning, I told him firmly that any attempt to kick, or bite, was completely out of the question. Gamal understood the tone, if not the words, and complied.

But I can't say I was getting nothing from Gamal. The affection coming my way may have been a bit scarce, but his unique means of boosting my self-confidence was not. Sometimes, I would confide to him those things I told no one else. Other times, I would tell him about some little triumph I'd had on the job, or would complain about someone's real or imagined slights. But no matter the content, he did not abandon me, did not correct me, did not judge me. To me, that was worth a hundred nuzzles.

But other times when we were together, speaking was unnecessary. In near silence, we would connect via what I came to think of as meditative breathing. I had no formal instruction on that front, but it didn't matter. The only instruction I needed was from the horse himself. Time spent breathing consciously with Gamal, his head draped over his stall door and onto my shoulder, or his body pressed against mine alongside the pasture fence, was time well spent. It afforded me the simple luxury of experiencing a kind of serenity I had rarely known. Somehow, just slowing down with Gamal, watching him get into the "zone" and then doing my best to copy him, produced simultaneously a kind of euphoria and a calm that gradually began to change the way I viewed the world. I was beginning to see things in a broader context, one fueled less by personal drama and more accepting of the vicissitudes of life. When a session was over, for inevitably one of us had other business to attend to, I would come to as from a dream. There stood the inscrutable old horse—eyes at half-staff, head lowered slightly. Not asleep, yet not entirely in this world, either.

Softly, so as not to startle him, I would murmur his name.

"Gamal," I said.

His eyes would open fully as he turned to me.

"Thank you," I would whisper.

He would swish his tail, bob his head a few times, and once again lower his eyelids.

But there was also an unselfish reason for wanting to hold on to Gamal: I wanted him to have a home, a real home, a home with me. As far as I could tell, he had always been the new horse in the barn, going from one herd to another. I didn't know where Gamal was born, how long he had been allowed to stay with his mother, or even his exact age (most estimates put him at twenty-six, and my veterinarian agreed). I knew he had experienced a lot during his life, and must have formed meaningful relationships along the way. But all of those bonds had been severed—not because he wanted to sever them, but because someone decided to do the severing for him.

I had no reason to think that Gamal would be treated by any but the kindest hands at the ranch in Texas; but they would not be my hands. To my knowledge, no one before had noticed his otherworldly, meditative side; but I was open to whatever teachings he had to impart. Would that be the case if he went elsewhere?

At the ranch, he would not be one person's horse, he would be one of many. I wanted Gamal to be one of one. I wanted to be his home, the person in his life who would never abandon him; someone he could trust to have his best interest at heart. I wanted to be the voice he heard and came galloping to across a green meadow; the one he knew, and who knew him like no other.

If by some miracle I was able to keep Gamal, I was certain of one thing: I would be getting the better part of the deal.

Cleveland did not buy the ranch as a diving horse sanctuary. In fact, before the purchase of the original acreage in northeastern Texas, the Fund had been strictly an animal advocacy and humane education organization. The Fund's mission was to inform the public of the various perils facing animals, and suggest, sometimes forcefully, what steps could be taken to prevent them. Over the years, its mission expanded slightly by supporting a modest but exemplary rabbit sanctuary in South Carolina; a one-man wildlife rehab center on Sanibel Island in Florida; and a somewhat larger wildlife rehab center in Ramona, California. But those were the exceptions to the Fund's primary work: humane education. Animal husbandry was not part of the plan.

Before buying the ranch, one hands-on project that nearly came to fruition for the Fund was accepting ownership of a privately funded animal shelter in New Jersey and turning it into a model facility for the rest of the country. For over a year, Cleveland sent me on weekly trips to the place. I was to observe how it was being run and report back to him on what worked and what didn't.

Few things were more heartening than seeing animals that otherwise would have had no chance get adopted into loving homes. It changed the lives of the animals, and the people's lives, too. The motto inscribed over the front door, "There is hope for those who enter here," was a spin on a line from Dante's *Divine Comedy* ("Abandon hope all ye who enter here"). Often, the shelter lived up to the optimistic proclamation.

But there was the other side of the story: learning firsthand about the often unrealistic expectations people had when they adopted, and the endless excuses adopters gave when they returned an animal. My elation at watching a trusting cat or dog get into a car with its new family was sometimes overshadowed by watching another family show up with an animal that had, in some way, become a burden. Some people expressed regret, even angst, as they signed the surrender papers; but most did not, and never looked back as they drove away. After witnessing many adoptions, both good and bad, I realized that assessing a potential adopter's ability and desire to stick with an animal for the long haul was a critical part of the process. Making sure the animal was a good fit with the people to begin with was another. It was always better to reject an applicant, rather than adopt an animal into incompetent hands.

In addition to learning the adoption ropes, I was also charged with making suggestions on how the shelter could promote its available animals and educate the public about humane care. But there were problems—not with the animals, but with the employees. Lack of leadership, and differing opinions about who should do what and how it should be done, threatened the facility's future. Adding to the tension was that the shelter's founder, a kindhearted dowager who could always be counted on to make up any financial deficits, died unexpectedly. Not long thereafter, the idea of an acquisition was abandoned. Overall, Cleveland and I felt that was a good thing.

But as the years leading up to the ranch purchase passed, it became obvious that letter writing and boycotting, lobbying and demonstrating, even filing lawsuits, only went so far. An emerging, younger group of activists, ones who increasingly used the term "animal rights" instead of "animal protection" or "animal welfare," agitated for more direct involvement. If Cleveland was to remain relevant, not to mention true to his mission of "putting cleats on the little old ladies in tennis shoes," then he had to change with the times or risk becoming obsolete. Not only did his reputation demand it, so did his principles.

The direct action door began to open with the appearance of Dexter Cate, a fearless young man from Hawaii who, with the Fund's help, flew to Iki Island in Japan. By dark of night, he kayaked alone to a pod of captive dolphins slated for slaughter, and freed them by cutting the net that fishermen had used to ensnare them.

Next was Canadian Paul Watson, who sought and received help from Cleveland to purchase and renovate a trawler he would name *Sea Shepherd*. Middle-aged Cleveland, more accustomed to transatlantic crossings on the *QE2,* accompanied the crew to Canada and helped spray-paint baby seal pups on the ice, rendering their pelts worthless to pick-axe-wielding hunters. Later, Watson formed his own group, the Sea Shepherd Conservation Society, and went on to disrupt whaling ships across the globe.

Dovetailing with the Fund's activism expansion was a plan announced by the National Park Service (NPS) to exterminate burros living at the base of the Grand Canyon. These animals existed in that nether world of being neither fully wild nor fully domesticated: feral. They were descendants of those domesticated creatures abandoned by luckless gold prospectors in the mid-1800s. Stoic, pack-

Cleveland Amory was not an armchair activist.
His travels to protect animals led him to Canadian
ice floes to stop a seal hunt; to the Grand Canyon
to oversee the rescue of feral burros; and here, to
Chincoteague, Virginia, to ensure the safety of feral
pony foals being sold to the highest bidders as an annual
fundraiser for the local fire department. 1985.

bearing burros (or donkeys as they are generally known east of the Mississippi) became the very symbol of the rugged, crusty men who were lured west by the promise, or hope, of getting something for nothing. Some stopped in Arizona on their way to the California gold rush and never left. Others already in California headed back when word of gold in Arizona reheated their fevered imaginations. Riches were to be had for the taking. All they needed to realize their dreams was a shovel, a panning screen, and a string of long-suffering pack animals to carry their scant belongings on the way in and haul treasure on the way out.

For a select few prospectors, the dream "panned" out. For most, it did not. When the possibility of a gold strike faded, men who were barely able to keep themselves alive regarded their animals as just more mouths to feed. Burros were abandoned by the thousands all over the West and left to fend for themselves in inhospitable lands not suited for grazing.

But burros are a canny lot, and almost to their disadvantage, they did not succumb to heat and thirst and hunger. While Thoroughbred horses would have faced almost certain death under similar circumstances, and even Gamal might have had a tough time of it, the burros not only survived, but multiplied. And it was in the multiplying that they got into trouble.

For years, the NPS conducted intermittent extermination campaigns against them, popping off a few dozen here or there. But by 1980, the government decided that enough was enough: all of the burros were to be cleared from the Grand Canyon, as they were competing with native animals for the area's limited food supply. Worse, they said, some of the few edible plants were endangered. The burros were pests, the NPS warned, the equivalent of rodents, or cockroaches. To support these claims, trigger-happy wildlife biologists, paid by the NPS, recited the well-worn mantra of game commissions across the country: you have to kill them to save them. In reverential tones, they assured the public that killing was good science and sound land management. Compassion, apparently, was beside the point.

Some of these wildlife biologists were so adamant on this point they offered to help with the slaughter.

No one could argue that living some six thousand feet down at the bottom of the Grand Canyon, with freezing winters and scorching summers, with little food and few sources of water, was an easy life. But there had to be another way to help the animals, Cleveland reasoned. He found it suspicious that the only solution the NPS recommended was shooting, that they did not suggest removing the offending animals. In fact, it had. Over the years, the NPS tried to remove the animals but had failed. It was a feat, they claimed, that could not be accomplished.

If there was anything in this world that set Cleveland's teeth on edge, it was being told that he couldn't do something. He believed that the burros could be removed, and he felt so strongly about it that he hired a lawyer. A court case ensued, culminating with a judge issuing an injunction against the NPS. "Thirty days," the judge told Cleveland. "You have thirty days to prove there is another way."

It was, of course, an absurdly short amount of time to plan or assemble a crew. I can imagine the NPS employees snickering over what appeared to be a victory for the Fund. Based on their halfhearted efforts over the years, they were convinced such a campaign was infeasible. But, of course, they didn't know Cleveland.

Despite the constraints, the Fund accomplished in one day what the NPS claimed was impossible: three burros were brought out, alive and kicking. By the end of the trial period, more had been herded, hauled, and hoisted to the canyon's rim than in all the decades of the NPS's feeble attempts combined. The Fund was given permission to continue until all the burros were removed, a number that eventually reached 577.

Cleveland spent months off and on at the Grand Canyon, overseeing the project. The Boston-bred city slicker was entirely hands-on, and worked out tactics in a temporary corral with former rodeo cowboys and cattle ranchers, men whose occupations he might otherwise have criticized. But their very specific set of skills—roping, hog tying, and herding—were exactly those needed, either to airlift by helicopter the captured animals in slings; or raft them down the Colorado River on a pontoon boat to flat land. On some nights, beneath the wide dark western sky, Cleveland must have marveled at the unexpected turn his life had taken, from his days as a rookie reporter in Arizona when he witnessed a bloody bullfight in nearby Nogales, Mexico, to directing a massive animal rescue project.

Removing the burros from the Grand Canyon was a success, and every last animal had literally dodged a bullet. But once they were out, another problem immediately asserted itself: what to do with them. Adding to the original 577 came word of more burros and wild horses, known as mustangs, in jeopardy. Since the Fund had done such a good job at the Grand Canyon, one would have assumed the NPS would have copied their methods and adopted a similarly humane method for animal removal elsewhere in the West. But they did not, and the same shooting scenario was proposed for Bandelier National Monument in New Mexico, and in California at the China Lake Naval Weapons Center and Death Valley. Again, the Fund stepped in to save the animals. In the end, the group rescued over six thousand burros and four thousand mustangs over a three-year period.

Clearly, not all of those animals could find homes in the vicinity of the evacuation areas. As a solution, the Fund purchased land in Texas that came to be known as Black Beauty Ranch, named after the title of the Anna Sewell book that had affected Cleveland as a child. He was adamant that the ranch was not to become a zoo. Instead, it would be a staging area for animals that would later be sent to adoption centers across the country, and a retirement home for those too old or sick to travel.

It was an expensive proposition, both the rescue itself and the purchase and outfitting of the ranch. In addition to needing money, the Fund also needed homes for the animals. Just as the photo of Cleveland hugging a baby harp seal on an ice floe was effective in swaying public opinion against Canada's inhumanity, so, too, did another photo have an equally profound effect. In a staging area at the Grand Canyon, *People* magazine featured a shot of Cleveland in a black cowboy hat cradling an animal not much larger than a lamb—a fuzzy, long-eared, big-eyed, newborn burro. Money poured in, as did offers of help.

When this image of Cleveland and a baby burro rescued from the Grand Canyon appeared in *People,* animal lovers from across the country responded by offering to adopt, or by making their farms available as satellite adoption centers. 1981.

Television took a keen interest as well, resulting in a barnyard casting call for a young, tractable, photogenic burro to appear with Cleveland on *Good Morning America* at the show's studio in Manhattan. The truck hauling that burro from the ranch would have one lone occupant traveling north from Texas, and another on its way back—Gamal.

Whatever plan I hatched to keep the horse with me had to be carried out in a hurry. Once Gamal was sent away, ours would be just another of his severed relationships—and of mine.

Gamal and I were outside the barn as I contemplated the plan for his imminent move to Texas. We had progressed to where he now allowed me to walk him around on a lead rope as if he were a very large dog. He was even more tractable when he realized our destination was the deep green grass of the overgrown lawn that surrounded Wendy's house. I knew that while he may not have become as attached to me as I was to him, I was at least a part of his world. For now, that would be enough.

I heard the throaty rumble of a motor in the driveway and, without even turning around, recognized it as the diesel Mercedes of the veterinarian. On this day, however, something about his uptight, pompous manner gave me an idea: Since he was so well known in his profession, meticulous and expert in every way, why not use that to my advantage? Why not get him to certify in his less-than-humble opinion that Gamal was unfit to make an 1,800-mile road trip? As much as it galled me to ask anything of this man, I did what I had to do.

Before he even got out of his car, Gamal and I approached him. I asked if, while he was there, he would have time to examine Gamal. My request gave him the opportunity to display his gold wristwatch again as he checked the time. Without answering, he asked if the horse had been having a problem. I explained that he seemed to be doing well, but that I had concerns about how an animal his age would fare on the long haul to Texas.

After informing me that even though he was already on the premises there would still be a travel charge for his visit, he said he could manage to squeeze us in. Gamal had had enough with standing around—the lush lawn was calling to him, as was Wendy's grape arbor, which he seemed just to have noticed. As he dragged me for the first time in a long time, I hoped the vet didn't notice my lack of control.

I watched Gamal going at the grass with unmistakable vigor and became concerned that, with the help of professionals, I had initiated an almost too good rehabilitation job. Between the deworming, the additional food, the dental work, and the bath and grooming, he was the very picture of an animal in his prime. His coat gleamed; his mane, now unknotted, waved freely in the breeze; and he stood on his trimmed and healed hooves with complete confidence. Gone were any signs of prominent ribs or hips. Gone, too, or nearly so, was the cantankerous streak he displayed in the beginning: Gamal was beginning to trust me.

Wendy's lawn was well nibbled by the time the vet indicated that he was ready for us. I brought in the horse, his lips green and his breath fresh from the chlorophyll, and unlike during his first exam, I was able to put him between the cross-ties by myself. The vet seemed not to notice and conducted a routine exam. This time, there was less, if anything, wrong with Gamal so the inspection was brief.

"He looks just fine," the vet proclaimed. "His previous conditions have cleared up." And here he paused, as if deciding if he wanted to say more.

"You seem to have done a good job of it." I was surprised by the grudging credit.

Then he was back to business with the accompanying irritable air. "What is it that you want from me?"

Ah, the million-dollar question. And if I'd had a million dollars, I had the feeling he would have done anything I'd wanted. But in fact, I did not. All I wanted was to hold on to an old horse who, to my knowledge, never experienced the comfort or security of having one person be his advocate and his friend, forever. On the spot, I came up with a plan, one that, admittedly, played fast and loose with the facts.

"I expect Mr. Amory is going to want you to certify that Gamal is capable of making the trip to Texas. Can you do that?" I asked. "The truck to transport him should be here in a month or so."

"Certify?" The vet frowned. He knew "certify" was a loaded word, one with legal implications. I knew it, too.

Drawing on nerve I didn't know I had, I continued. "I understand this will put you in a tough spot. If Gamal does make the trip and something awful happens, won't someone, somewhere, wonder why his veterinarian didn't discourage the trip? I don't know about you, but I think it would be safer to certify against the trip than for it. After all, he's twenty-six, a senior citizen of a horse."

I had the fanciful impression that Gamal understood if not the words that people spoke, then at least the gist of their conversations. Upon hearing the phrase "senior citizen," the horse shot me a proud look that indicated he was fully capable of making the trip to Texas, even if he had to walk the whole way; but it was followed by something else, a softness in his eyes which had not been there when we first met and which told me that although he could do it, he'd rather not. That look gave me the guts to press the subject in a way I wouldn't have otherwise.

I noticed the vet was staring at the floor. He knew what I wanted of him and was not comfortable with it. I, too, looked at the floor as I continued my appeal.

"What if," I said as I traced a small circle in the sawdust on the floor with the toe of my shoe, "Gamal was a twenty-six-year-old retired show horse."

He pursed his lips as if he was having trouble imagining it.

"What if he was being sent, let's say, to a breeding farm, or even just to live out his years on his rider's farm, somewhere far away. What if Gamal was more like one of your regular clients?"

He jerked up his head at that last supposition and, for the first time, looked me in the eye. I had managed to get him to make the leap and think of Gamal as something personal, something valuable, a some*one* instead of a some*thing*. I pushed harder.

"Would you let one of those horses go to Texas? And if you would, would you let him go now? Or would you say he needed more time to recover from his recent illnesses?"

I offered this last suggestion to give him an out. He didn't have to say "never," but instead could say "just not yet." I figured that if Gamal stayed with me a few more months, he would surely be too old to travel by anyone's standards. Besides, who knew when the next truck might be coming up from the ranch? It could be years. All I needed was time.

I could tell from the anxious look on the vet's face that I had him right where I wanted him.

Without saying a word, he pulled out his stethoscope and proceeded to give Gamal another going-over. While his first exam seemed adequate, this one was even more so. He prodded and trotted Gamal, and after some time put away his instruments and revealed his findings to me.

"If one was to err on the side of safety," he said, "then midsummer is probably not the ideal time for Gamal to make a long trip to somewhere even hotter."

He felt compelled to add that barring a catastrophe (my mind raced—suddenly elevated temperatures? engine trouble with the truck? flat tires? stuck in traffic?), Gamal would probably survive the journey.

"But, of course," he added, "there can be no guarantees."

He began to explain how his usual clients, the more refined, more delicate Thoroughbreds, might have difficulties that Gamal would not; but by then I had stopped listening. Gamal was as precious as any million-dollar horse and I refused to entertain any suggestion that his hearty, mixed breed heritage would somehow work against him, or my plan.

I asked the vet to put his conclusions in writing, especially the part about how he could not guarantee Gamal's safety on such a long journey. He agreed. Once he was out of earshot, I whispered to Gamal that we had just bought ourselves a little time.

A s it happened, there wasn't that much more figuring to do: the solution was practically in plain sight. I remembered that technically Gamal was not the absolute last Atlantic City Steel Pier diving horse, he was the last in the long line of the original Carver horses. Apparently there was one other former diving horse out there, a chestnut mare named Shiloh. She came on the scene after both trainer Bill Ditty and rider Lorena Carver had left the pier, had been trained by a newcomer, and had performed only briefly, just before the whole enterprise was shuttered. During the second round of sales, a woman bought Shiloh as a riding horse. Through old newspaper clippings, I tracked down the woman, also named Wendy, and gave her a call. If I was able to acquire Shiloh, then she could go to Texas on the return trip, and Gamal could stay with me.

When I reached her by phone, it almost seemed as if she had been waiting to hear from me. She had kept up with the news, and knew that the Fund had purchased Gamal a few months earlier. I was to discover that she also knew how much we paid for him.

My plan was to determine if she might sell Shiloh for some reasonable price. Knowing how attached I was to Gamal after such a short period of time, I considered it unlikely that she would part with Shiloh after having her for over a year. Still, it couldn't hurt to ask.

After some small talk, I broached the subject. I had barely finished asking the question when she answered not with words, but with a number, "Twenty-six hundred."

Had I been Cleveland, I would have known what she meant. Had I been Cleveland, I would have been prepared to bargain. But I was not Cleveland.

I repeated the number to her, twenty-six hundred, but phrased it as a question.

"I want twenty-six hundred for Shiloh, the same as you paid for that other horse," she said.

That other horse was my Gamal, and it rankled to hear him referred to in such an impersonal way.

There was an awkward pause, but soon she filled in the silence.

"Look, Shiloh's only eight, less than a third the age of that other one. You'll have her that much longer."

I considered reminding the woman that the Fund was a nonprofit group; or that we were dedicated to helping animals; or that we would give her horse a wonderful home. But from her tone, I knew it would be to no avail: anyone who could sell her own horse that easily was unlikely to be swayed by sentiment.

I explained I'd have to clear it with the main office first, but that I felt certain we could strike a deal.

"Don't wait too long," she teased. "They aren't making diving horses anymore."

The next day I was at the Fund's office in New York to make my pitch. In my purse was the letter from the veterinarian attesting to what I hoped would be interpreted as Gamal's precarious health. That, and the story of how I had contacted Shiloh's owner and that she was willing to sell the horse to me, a complete stranger, would form the basis of my argument. I decided not to mention my growing attachment to Gamal. It would be too easy for Cleveland to see that as a sign of weakness, or selfishness. Best to stick to the facts, I thought.

We went through what had become our usual routine: Cleveland delivered a stream-of-consciousness account of the Fund's various activities, called his stockbroker, made another call to his club to see if a chess match was still on for the next day, and took several incoming calls. After each interruption, he would take up his narrative exactly where he had left off.

I bit my lip and waited for the right time. But there was no right time, and on some level I knew it. Still, I hesitated, and squirmed, and nearly brought up the subject any number of times. Cleveland had already told me we would not be having dinner that night as we usually did—he had other plans—so it was now or never.

"I need to speak to you about Gamal," I said.

Cleveland gave me his trademark skeptical look, with one eyebrow arched theatrically.

I handed him the letter from the vet and, as he read it, I explained that Gamal was only just beginning to recover, physically and emotionally, from the many changes in his life.

Cleveland said nothing and waited for me to say more.

"It's just that, well, as the vet says in the letter, it might not be in Gamal's best interest to go to Texas."

"Really," he drawled.

Since he didn't disagree immediately, I saw it as an opening.

"He's an old horse, you know, very old. Why, if he was human he'd be about . . ." And here I struggled, because I had no idea of the horse-human age conversion rate.

"Would you say he was like a person in his early sixties?" Cleveland deadpanned.

"Oh, definitely," I said before remembering that Cleveland was in his early sixties.

"What's it going to cost me?" he said, stifling a laugh.

I took my cue from Shiloh's owner.

"Twenty-six hundred."

Cleveland knew I was talking money, but he didn't yet know what it was for.

I explained about my conversation with Shiloh's owner, and, exaggerating a bit, said I was afraid that if she didn't sell the horse to the Fund, God only knew what the woman might do with her. Before he asked, I told Cleveland she was firm on the price.

"Look at it this way," I added, again taking a page from the woman's book. "Since Shiloh's only eight, she's a lot younger than Gamal and you'll have her that much longer." Even as I said it, I thought it was my only false note. It just wasn't in me to make that kind of a sales pitch.

"Marian," Cleveland bellowed to his assistant in the adjoining room. "Tell Alice to make out a check for twenty-six hundred dollars."

As I made my way to the door, clutching the precious check in my hand, Cleveland called out to me.

"We've known all along that Gamal wasn't going anywhere. Not since we heard you gushing about him."

I waved over my shoulder, but didn't turn around. I couldn't risk letting him see the tears in my eyes.

Chapter Eight

Whatever qualms I may have had about Shiloh's owner—how she could let go of the horse so easily, or what condition the horse might be in—disappeared when the woman brought the lovely mare out of a spotlessly clean barn. Shiloh was the color of a newly minted penny, and her copper-colored coat gleamed in the sun. She was plump, shiny, and her pale hooves were well trimmed. I didn't foresee any veterinary bills in her near future, nor would she be a rehabilitation project, as was Gamal. The former diving horse sported a new red and blue halter adorned with tiny white stars, befitting her celebrity status. The woman was equally lovely, and I realized I had misjudged. She knew Shiloh would be well cared for by an animal protection organization, and she displayed real affection for the horse when saying her goodbyes. As Shiloh was led without protest up the ramp and into the trailer, I noticed a certain sway to her step, almost a sashay.

One thing that troubled me was the question of whether Shiloh was in foal, or if she had given birth while the woman had her. I remembered reading an old newspaper clipping that quoted her as saying that the mare might be expecting. I wondered if she had been? Or if the woman had bred her again and she had delivered more recently. The thought that there was even a chance that I was taking Shiloh away from her foal didn't sit well. Then again, even if that was the case, what could I do about it? Then I remembered something

Shiloh, 1980

Wendy often advised: Don't ask a question if you aren't prepared for the answer. I wasn't prepared, and so didn't ask.

As soon as we unloaded Shiloh at Wendy's farm, I began comparing her to the other two horses in my care, Gamal and AmFran, a young Thoroughbred gelding I purchased from a slaughterhouse buyer at an auction. Wendy named the colt after the AmFran (America to France) Meat Packing Company, from which I bought him for $50 above what the company representative had paid moments earlier. My idea was to have Wendy give him some basic training, and then place him in a caring home. Eventually, we did.

Shiloh, a chestnut, was the lightest in color of the three horses, with a striking white blaze that ran the length of her face. Long eyelashes framed her large, dark eyes and lent a coquettish quality to her appearance. Like Gamal's body, but unlike AmFran's rangy frame, Shiloh had a thick and compact build. Despite her considerable girth, Shiloh was a dainty horse who was unmistakably female.

I wasn't the only one who noticed her feminine qualities. I imposed on Wendy's good nature by having her, and one of her girls, introduce the two former divers on lead while I observed. I was eager to watch Gamal and Shiloh revel in their reunion. But the revelry took an un-

Stable owner Wendy McCook, right, with Shiloh, aided my equine education. Here, Gamal and Shiloh on her farm. 1981.

anticipated turn. After just one sniff beneath Shiloh's tail, Gamal whinnied, flared his nostrils, and seemed ready for action. Although he was a gelding, some basic instinct had been awakened, and he was willing, although unable, to get to know her in the biblical sense. Shiloh took considerable umbrage at his impudence. She squealed, she bucked, she performed an amusing sidestepping trot to avoid him. Based on what I saw, I had to conclude that either Shiloh did

While Gamal, right, was initially enthusiastic upon being reacquainted with Shiloh after several years apart, she was less keen. Eventually, the two former performers treated each other like another member of the herd. 1981.

not remember Gamal and was annoyed by the liberties being taken by a stranger; or that she did remember Gamal but never cared for him to begin with. Soon, the novelty of her presence wore off and things were back to normal.

Normalcy lasted two days. I had been expecting a burro to arrive by truck from Texas in about a month, but Cleveland called with a change in plans. It seemed that the rescue effort out west was going so well that some burros had to get off the ranch and into homes immediately. To do so, they needed publicity: the *Good Morning America* segment was going to take place sooner, rather than later.

"We have too much of a good thing," Cleveland said. "Your burro will be arriving by the end of the week."

He dropped this news as if he was talking about something ordinary, or of little consequence. I suppose if I, like he, had seen hundreds upon hundreds of burros floated, herded, and airlifted to safety, then I might not consider the arrival of one man with one burro a big deal. But since I hadn't, it was a huge deal.

To say that my previous exposure to burros was brief is an understatement. There were random photos in *National Geographic* and fleeting images on TV westerns. And a decade or so earlier, I had met one—two if you count its mother. But just because our encounter was brief didn't mean its effect wasn't long-lasting.

The summer after I graduated from high school, my parents insisted I accompany them on a tour of Spain, Portugal, and Morocco.

Morocco was the final country on our itinerary and daily temperatures reached 120 degrees or more. Despite what tour guides said ("It's dry heat, you won't even feel it"), it was at least as hot as one of the outer circles of hell. During a visit to the medina in Fez, it seemed as if we had crossed into one of the inner ones.

At the entrance to the ancient, walled part of the city, snake charmers set a nightmarish tone, as cobras writhed like drunken belly dancers to the sounds of high-pitched, tuneless flutes.

Narrow, labyrinthine lanes brought on claustrophobia as we picked our way past endless rug shops, spice shops, brass ornament shops.

Indolent men smoking hookahs or sipping mint tea looked me up and down in a combination of lust and disgust. Women were nowhere in sight. An alarming number of people with watery, clouded eyes begged for alms. We had been warned not to give them anything as it would cause a frenzy. Still, the temptation to press a coin or two into their outstretched palms was great. I wanted to bolt. But how? And to where?

From a distance I heard "Balak! Balak!" which I soon realized meant "make way" or "look out!" Careening around a corner was one of the hundreds of overloaded donkeys that crowded the city. Many of the thin, flea-bitten animals had open sores from wearing unpadded harnesses. This one was different, though: she had a small, fuzzy foal by her side. The untethered, knock-kneed donkey was trying to keep up with his mother, who was being whipped to keep her moving beneath an enormous weight. Briefly, he became separated from her by a cart that had become wedged at the turn.

As shouting men attempted to free the cart, the solitary foal let out pitiful, panicked cries. Instinct took over, and I leaned down to stroke his neck. From the way he ducked his head, it appeared he did not expect to be petted. He looked up at me, his large eyes wide and frightened. What followed, though, was another look, which I experienced as a kind of merging between our two terrified souls. On some level, we understood each other. Judging from how he stopped crying, he was comforted. For just a moment, the background cacophony receded and a calm descended over both of us.

Of course I wanted to scoop him up, find his mother, and abscond with the pair. Instead, the cart was freed, the foal ran down the alley to reunite with his mother, and the momentary peace between us was shattered. But the look in the little donkey's eyes—terror replaced by hopefulness—would stay with me forever.

After hearing Cleveland's announcement that a burro was headed my way I leapt to the good-news/bad-news scenario. The good news was that Shiloh and I would have limited time to bond before she was loaded onto the truck for its return trip to Texas. Contrary to my usual way of thinking, this was an advantage since I now knew that I was very good at taking in animals, but not very good at letting them go.

The bad news was that while I had been doing my best to educate myself about horses, burros were something else entirely. I was not the equine novice I had been when I met Gamal, but I had not yet shimmied up to the burro branch of the family tree.

Wendy had aided my horse education immeasurably, but there was no similar burro mentor on the scene. As had been the case so many times in my life, I turned to books. I knew I would have to cram for this course like someone who had slept through a semester and then pulled an all-nighter before the final exam. But my motivation was stronger now than it had ever been in school: a knowledge of burros in general would help me take better care of the specific one heading my way. And secretly, I had one other aspiration in mind—I hoped to know more about this type of animal than anyone else in the barn.

There was not a plethora of books on burros in the library system, and none in my local branch. At least there were encyclopedias, and they confirmed what Cleveland had told me: there was no difference between a donkey, a burro, or an ass. What they were called depended on where in the world they were located. Mules, which many people confused with burros, were actually hybrids and usually sterile. A mule has a horse for a mother and a burro for a father. The more rare hinny is the reverse: a horse for a father and a burro for a mother.

Invariably, burros were described as "sure-footed" or "slow" or that intriguing word, "stubborn," but I felt sure there was more to them than that. All of their descriptions led me to suspect that there was something intelligent going on behind those long ears and that doleful expression. In the scant references to burros in books on horses, you could almost see authors rolling their eyes, as if burros were the embarrassing, eccentric uncles of the equine family.

Through the interlibrary loan program, I was about to place a request for Frank Brookshier's seminal work *The Burro* when the librarian advised me that it might take a week or more to arrive. I explained that I didn't have that kind of time. Her book-loving eyes widened in horror at someone desperate for information. Apparently she lived to satisfy this sort of thirst for knowledge, no matter the subject. She sprang into action. She pounced on the telephone, as if getting me that book pronto was a life-or-death matter. Her hard work paid off: a copy was waiting for me at a library some fifty miles away. Since I needed the book immediately, all I had to do was go there and get it.

I was on the road just outside town when I passed the local saddle shop and remembered that among bits of equipment, they sold a few books, too. It was worth a try. Besides, I always enjoyed going there and experiencing the creaky wooden floors and the scent of fine leather and polish, salt blocks and sweet feed. All the way at the back of the store, on a bottom bookshelf, was the dusty tome I was looking for. I thought I detected a sneer on the face of the clerk as she rang up my order, as if, finally, they found a chump to buy at full price a book that had probably languished there for decades. But I wasn't put off by what I was to discover was widespread condescension about burros. To me, the book was as priceless as I anticipated would be the burros themselves.

Within a few pages, I became drawn in by the habits and history of these ancient, underrated animals. To the extent that I had ever before thought of burros, it was of the resigned beasts I witnessed in Morocco—trudging glumly beneath too heavy a burden. I was, of course, familiar with their otherworldly braying and, if pressed, I would have said they were mostly gray in color. I could not have been more wrong in this limited view.

I was struck by burros' incredible varieties: Mammoths, Miniatures, and Standard Donkeys. There were those known variously as Maltese, Majorcan, and Mallorcan Asses. There were those miniatures known as Sardinians or Sicilians. There was a variety called the Poitou that had a long, shaggy coat that hung in dreadlocks, but they originated in France, not Jamaica. And there were others called either Wild Asses or Wild Burros, depending on where in the world they lived. They ranged in color from black to white to spotted. But, apart from the fact that some were a little larger or a little smaller, or had more or less hair, all shared the same characteristics that set them apart from their equine cousins, horses: long ears, upright short mane, a tufted tail, different hoof shape, different pelvic shape, different numbers of chromosomes. Their distinctive hee-haw sound spurred satirist Jonathan Swift to refer to burros as "the nightingale of beasts." Elsewhere, they were called everything from the "Rocky Mountain canary" to the "desert contralto."

Reading about burros was a guided tour through history. Burros, I learned, are native to the Middle East, where their history goes back over five thousand years. Yet in their native countries, where these original beasts of burden transport both people and products, they are more reviled than revered. In both Judaism and Islam, they are considered "unclean," and unfit for human consumption—something that may be the only advantage to their lowly status. Christianity, however, holds them in a somewhat more favorable light: it was a burro that carried the pregnant Mary to the manger, and later witnessed the birth of Jesus. Coming full circle, Jesus made his final journey into Jerusalem atop a burro on Palm Sunday. The distinctive dark stripe on a burro's back, along the spine and across the shoulders, resembles the sign of the cross. Folklore has it that the mark was given in recognition of the animal's sacred role.

In the New World, burros were brought on Columbus's second voyage to Hispaniola in 1493 to help carry the expedition's supplies. Other animals on board were brought for grim purposes: Greyhounds, to chase down native people and wildlife; Mastiffs, to control or kill the same; and pigs, to feed the explorers. Later, Spanish conquistadors brought burros to Mexico and then to what is now the American Southwest.

While burros are often portrayed as the horse's ugly cousin, their physical characteristics are a perfect example of form following function. Long ears are ideal for hearing things far away, such as across a desert. Those ears may also help cool a burro, something important in hot climates. Their bray, which can last up to twenty seconds, can also be heard over a distance of nine miles—handy if you are calling out to others of your kind who may be somewhere out there in the wide-open spaces. Those little boxlike hooves make burros more sure-footed than horses and better able to navigate rugged terrain. And as for their reputation of being stubborn or stupid, I was delighted to read that this was largely a matter of interpretation. Because their prey instincts are highly developed, they are equally highly cautious. If a burro doesn't want to do something, there is a good reason for it. Far fewer burros than horses are bitten by rattlesnakes or swept away in raging rivers.

Yet despite all of the burros' marvelous attributes, writers from Homer to Aesop, and from Shakespeare to Cervantes, chose to portray them as objects of derision. While horses are regarded universally as noble, dignified, and brave, burros are considered servile, surly, and sullen. The ultimate put-down is to call someone an ass, or say that their behavior is asinine. And, as if to indoctrinate children in burro derision at an early age, pin the tail on the donkey is a favorite birthday party game.

But, as I came to realize through personal experience, burros belong to a select club of creatures—one that includes such disparate members as Afghan Hounds and parrots, otters and goats—that have highly developed personalities, something I associate with intelligence. Foremost among their qualities are mischievousness and a sense of humor. They enjoy taunting, teasing, playing for the sake of play, and above all, getting up to no good in the most fun-loving way.

The more I read, the more it seemed to me that civilization had much for which to thank burros. Returning the favor by saving them from slaughter in the Grand Canyon and elsewhere was the honorable thing to do. I was ashamed that, throughout history, we humans rarely gave them the respect or credit they deserve. I even began to harbor a heretical thought (although not one I shared with Gamal): in some ways, burros are superior to horses.

Just as I'd only met a burro once before (and briefly, at that), I'd never met a Texan, ever. But that didn't stop me from thinking that I knew what one, or all of them, would be like. My impressions were formed by a mishmash of television images: Davy Crockett dying at the Alamo; LBJ lifting his Beagles by the ears; J.R. plotting revenge on the nighttime soap opera *Dallas;* and the real-life drama in Dallas, Kennedy's assassination. From that, I decided that Texans were consumed with that tiresome, trite trio of sex, money, and power. By all rights, the man hauling the burro from Texas to Pennsylvania should have had a knife in his teeth, a sexy swagger, and the cool cunning of a cutthroat businessman. At the very least, he should have been someone who knew where he was going.

Yet somehow this man who managed to get himself and the burro the roughly 1,800 miles from the Fund's ranch in East Texas became lost, or at least disoriented, in tame Bucks County, Pennsylvania, where street signs are clearly marked and the roads are paved. Worse, he reached his personal Alamo at, of all places, the Rendezvous, a popular gay bar painted a brilliant, beckoning shade of lavender.

It was high noon when he called me from a pay phone in the parking lot of the place. "Miz Branigan," he drawled. "Ahm in New Hope, I think, but, well . . ." And I could hear that while he was lost, he did not want to admit it. I offered to drive over (not that he needed my help, I assured him) and lead him to Wendy's farm, a distance of not more than two miles. I think he said something like, "Much obliged, ma'am."

As I pulled up, he was leaning against his truck, legs crossed at the ankles, and gnawing on a toothpick. He was a little too short, too paunchy, and too middle-aged to be a long, tall Texan; but he did look like an extra from a honky-tonk bar scene—scuffed cowboy boots; the requisite bold, silver belt buckle on a hand-tooled leather belt; high-waisted utilitarian jeans; a short-sleeved, polyester western shirt; and, a white cowboy hat. Oddly, he wasn't the only one in the parking lot wearing similar attire. Not only had country music and style gripped the nation in general, but it also influenced a subculture, the gay community. Like the Village People disco band, some favored uniforms of hyper-manly working men, but presented with an ironic, flamboyant twist: construction workers, firemen, lumberjacks, and, yes, cowboys. That last set sported the real Texan's pointy-toed boots, but which were more likely to have silver-tipped toes; and western style shirts and jeans, albeit body-hugging. Many even had the real Texan's mustache, but meticulously trimmed. But the real Texan's cowboy hat added a unique, authentic touch that drew admiring glances from some of the patrons heading inside.

We shook hands briefly, but I was in a rush to see the burro that I was told was called Jose. As I rounded the trailer, I decided the animal's name would be the first thing to go. I was disappointed with my first peek at the trailer's lone occupant: the burro's hind end, and farther forward, a pair of long ears that flicked occasionally on an otherwise motionless animal.

Wendy had swapped stories and shared beers with people from all walks of life. But when the Texan pulled into her drive, it was a toss-up as to what she found more exotic—the Texan, or the burro. My eyes met Wendy's for just a second as the Texan began unloading the animal, and I could see the look of amusement on her face. He led the six-month-old burro, not even half the size of Gamal, into the paddock and showed him the water and hay.

The burro's coat had an unusual rusty rose hue that I had not read about, and resembled a blend of cinnamon and nutmeg and salt. He looked as if he still had to grow into his more than foot-long ears, and his large dark eyes had an all-knowing quality tinged with a slight sadness. Of course, given his many experiences in his short life, I suppose that shouldn't have been surprising.

There was something else that should have come as no surprise: since he was the one chosen to appear on television, he was an exceptionally well-put-together animal. From my reading, I knew that, as with horses, people, and all creatures, not all burros were created equal. Good conformation was not a beauty contest: a well-constructed animal is better able to perform his tasks, and, ultimately, better able to survive.

As I looked him over, I remembered reading about some of the words used to describe burros in shows. Perfection, which surely this little burro had achieved, received only the weak appellation of "good." But judges of burros were far more elaborate in describing faults. An animal could be "buck-kneed," "calf-kneed," "tied-in at the knee," or "knock-kneed." The pasterns of a burro were to be neither "short and straight," nor "stumpy or sloping." But the worst invectives were reserved for burros described as "coon-footed or splay-

Sparkplug arrived in the summer of 1980 and was about six months old. He had already shed his fuzzy baby coat. Initially, his chest seemed narrow, giving the impression, lower down, of knock knees. That winter, his coat grew to several inches in length and was impenetrably thick. By spring, his chest had expanded, partly from confidence, partly from better nutrition. He became the picture of perfection.

footed," "bow-legged or pigeon-toed." This young burro, straight from the Grand Canyon and the result of natural selection, possessed none of those bad attributes. As inexpert as I was, he seemed to be flawless.

As Wendy, the Texan, and I stood by the fence and regarded the spirited newcomer, he regarded us right back. The barn's occupants were not to be denied an opinion, and they erupted into a cacophony of whinnies and thumps. It wasn't long before the burro matched them with his own unique voice. He threw back his head and, with his ears draped down his neck, let loose the first real-life bray I had ever heard. It was so loud, and so long, and so unexpected coming from the small creature, that it quieted even the horses. The burro stood in the center of the paddock and brayed again. The horses did not respond or join in, but just listened, or perhaps asked each other, in their own way, what the hell kind of creature had just invaded their domain.

For a third time, and somewhat plaintively now, the burro let out a final bray—but again, no response. While the sound might have been amusing for a first-time listener, for me, it wasn't entirely so.

For one thing, it was a reminder of the little burro in the medina in Morocco. But for another, I remembered from my research that this was how burros called out to others of their kind. He must have been waiting for a response, for the comforting hee-haw of another burro somewhere in this foreign land. But his efforts were in vain: there were no others in these parts and his calls were met with silence. He had become an orphan, far from his mother, his herd, and his home.

As Wendy and the Texan went into her house, I stayed behind to do what I could to comfort the burro. Carrots helped. After I was sure he was acclimating, and saw him take a long drink of water, I, too, went inside and pulled up a chair to the kitchen table. The Texan was all too happy to treat us to stories about the Grand Canyon, about Cleveland's interactions with the cowboys, and about the Fund's ranch, where the Texan now lived with his family. But no matter the tale, the stories always seemed to end with the suggestion that it was he, not Cleveland, who was instrumental in the success of the burro rescue, and even in the founding of the ranch itself. Again, my eyes met Wendy's and we shared a moment of skepticism.

The Texan recounted the time he jumped into one of the ponds on the ranch to rescue a half-drowned burro and then swam back to shore with the animal on his back; and how it was he, not Cleveland, who insisted that mothers and nursing foals had to be rescued together. And how it was he, and not former rodeo roper Dave Ericsson, who devised the sling system at the canyon that made the tandem hoisting possible (something Cleveland and everyone else involved with the effort attributed to Ericsson). But the man was a good storyteller, or perhaps more accurately a good BS artist, and I decided to accept his anecdotes for what they were: tall tales.

The sun was beginning to set, and it was nearly time for the dinner reservations I'd made for all of us. I led the Texan to where he would be staying, a place I realized too late was even more a case of "when worlds collide" than Wendy's farm: the Hotel du Village. The two stately, ivy-covered stone buildings had once been dormitories for a girls' boarding school and were now transformed into a quaint country inn with adjoining French restaurant. As the Texan and I got out of our respective vehicles I saw a look of deep concern on his face. I assumed even he recognized the accommodations were a poor choice on my part.

"Do they have a safe here?" he asked in a low tone.

"You mean in your room? A safe for your valuables, like jewelry or something?"

What, I wondered, could he have brought that needed safekeeping? A special plug of tobacco?

"Yes'm," he said. "I'm carryin'."

I struggled to translate from Texish to English what "carrying" might mean. Was it the same as "holding," as some of us used to say back in the 1960s if they had a stash of marijuana or hashish tucked away somewhere on their person. Had the Texan brought drugs? I was trying to wrap my brain around the awful thought when he indicated I should come over and take a look in his duffel bag. Just beneath some freshly pressed jeans and starched western shirts (because he was, after all, going into New York) was a leather holster. And nestled in that holster was a handgun, a very large handgun. Just as I'd never before seen a Texan, I'd also never seen a handgun.

"What kind is it?" I whispered, as if speaking louder might cause the gun to discharge.

"Three fifty-seven Magnum," he said with a fair amount of pride.

I remembered hearing that back in Texas he was also a part-time deputy sheriff. Like many Fund employees, myself included, he moonlighted to make ends meet. Perhaps that's why he carried a gun. But then those TV images reappeared in my head and I thought it equally possible that this was just another Texan trait: they all carried guns. Why the Texan thought he'd need one on this particular trip eluded me, unless it was just another of his little weaknesses, like exaggerating, or calling me ma'am.

I was in a tough spot. I was a semi-regular at the restaurant, on a first-name basis with the owner. I wasn't eager to sully my reputation by bringing up the unsavory subject of handguns. I doubted that the restaurant owner's usual guests asked if she would hold their weapons for safekeeping while they tucked into their steak au poivre.

Should we ask her if they had a safe? Or should he hide the gun under the mattress? What if the maid found it and set it off accidentally? Mostly I wondered why in God's name I hadn't booked him a room at the Holiday Inn. In the end, I suggested he keep the gun with him at all times, hidden of course.

Early the next morning, the toll collector at the Lincoln Tunnel, who had surely seen just about everything, did a double take as he surveyed first the Texan, in full Lone Star State regalia; then me, in my best equestrian-inspired attire; and finally, the tips of the burro's oversized ears through the windows of the trailer. The weary-looking man, probably nearing the end of the eleven-to-seven shift, shook his head, made change, and gave the Texan a receipt.

But as foreign a sight as we were to the toll collector, it was nothing compared to what Manhattan must have looked like to the burro. He'd gotten his first glimpse of the world from the hard stone floor of the Grand Canyon. The rush of the mighty Colorado River was the first sound he ever heard. Apart from the underside of his mother, the first sights he ever saw were five hundred million years of geologic history in layer upon layer of multicolored rock walls—sage green, russet brown, coral pink—until it opened to the unattainable blue sky. The young burro's mother, perhaps not much older than he, was undoubtedly as thin and malnourished as were the others in the herd; but she was fit enough to bear him, nurse him, and present to this planet yet another traveler on an uncertain journey. The unusual turn his life was to take, national television, was beyond anyone's imagination.

When we emerged from the tunnel, I experienced the city as never before—through the eyes of a burro. I realized that he was seeing canyons again, but this time the man-made variety. As the Texan unloaded him at the ABC studio, I noticed the burro looking up at the skyscrapers. The Texan walked him up and down the sidewalk and the little fellow followed at a trot. Perhaps this would be one of those counterintuitive moments; perhaps the burro was somehow comfortable here.

That idea was put to rest as soon as we entered the building. The television crew had the forethought to roll out a carpet (although not red) so the burro would not slip on the smooth floor or trip on the crisscross of electrical wires. But there was no way they could have anticipated his aversion to bright lights. He blinked and balked and even trembled slightly. As much as the Texan and I tried to push and pull the burro onto the set, he would not budge. The creature's final comment on the proceedings was to sit down.

"Five minutes to air," a stagehand called out.

David Hartman, host of *Good Morning America,* rubbed his nervous hands together as he watched the burro's obstinate performance. I imagined he was doing a quick mental calculation of how many tens of thousands of dollars each minute of airtime cost the network. Cleveland glared at me as if, somehow, this was my fault. I consoled myself with the fact that at least he didn't blame the burro. But the pressure was on. Cleveland knew that the success of the entire rescue effort was at stake. Just one glimpse on television of the young homeless burro, a creature that would otherwise have been shot to death by the government, would be worth a thousand written appeals.

"Three minutes," the stagehand warned. The Texan tried wrapping the lead rope around the burro's hind end and pushing, but it was fruitless. All of us began to sweat—all, that is, except the burro.

I regarded the little character sitting on the floor of the studio. There had to have been something that I came across during my research that would be helpful in this odd circumstance. I remembered reading that poking, prodding, or, God forbid, striking, would be of no use. But something positive, something enticing, might do the trick. What, I wondered, would it take to motivate him? What did he like?

Just beyond the burro, I noticed a service table set up for the crew. It was laden with doughnuts and coffee, sugar and cream. I rushed across the room, tore open some sugar packets, and poured them into my hand. I ran back to the feisty fellow, sat down next to him, and gave him one free lick. After that, if he wanted more he had to work for it. Seconds later, as well trained as a trick pony, he followed me onto the set.

"Open your hand," I commanded Cleveland. To my surprise, he obeyed. Once I filled his palm with sugar, he had the burro eating right out of his hand.

"By the way," I told him as I darted out of camera range. "His new name is Sparkplug."

The director called out, "Quiet on the set."

A few minutes later, a sticky Cleveland, with Sparkplug sporting a sugar-frosted mustache, ambled off the set like an old prospector and his burro. Cleveland had struck the kind of gold he was seeking. He instructed me to stay behind to hold the burro while he led the Texan across the room to meet David Hartman. But before he did, he mentioned that I should keep Sparkplug indefinitely, just in case other publicity opportunities arose. And with that, I had struck gold, too.

The Texan didn't return to his home state immediately. Who can blame him? When he told me temperatures on the ranch reached well over a hellish 100 degrees during the day, the low 90s here must have seemed cool. Even the gruesome local tour I took him on—a visit to an infamous horse auction; another to a forsaken city zoo; and a stop at a high kill rate animal shelter (that at least resulted in his adoption of a doomed dog)—was preferable to him than returning to the Texas oven. Yet although his respite was short, it was long enough for all other plans to fall apart.

Shiloh had only been with me a few days longer than Sparkplug, and I was still getting to know her. She continued to be demonstrably more affectionate than Gamal. Far from copying his hard-to-get routine, she was ready to nuzzle or whinny at anyone passing her stall. While it would have been easy to get sucked in by her indiscriminate advances (and in fact, I did slip her more than her share of carrots), her attention was almost too easy, too unselective. Gamal made me work for his affection, but when he gave it, I knew it was for me and me alone. But Shiloh was a friendly, outgoing girl, and seemed robust and contented in her new digs. I had no reason to think she would have any trouble on the trip to Texas, nor that she would fit in there equally well.

Then, she coughed.

When I first heard it, I wasn't quite sure it even was a cough. Horse coughs were something else new to me. It was a hollow, rumbling sound, something that seemed to come from a deep, cavernous place and almost sounded like the woof of a big, hoarse dog. I reasoned that Shiloh could have been trying to clear a piece of carrot from her throat. Or that maybe she was speaking in another kind of horse language I hadn't heard before. Since I heard the sound only once, I said nothing. I was tired of being the dumb novice with yet another inaccurate observation. Besides, both Wendy and the Texan heard the sound and neither expressed alarm, so I took my cue from them.

The following day, Shiloh coughed again, twice. This time, I spoke to Wendy. She reminded me that Shiloh had come to us with papers stating that a vet had examined her recently. Still, she went into Shiloh's stall and checked her out. The mare's eyes were clear, her nose was clear, and she was eating and drinking normally.

"We'll keep an eye on her," Wendy said. "But I don't think there's anything to worry about."

Not worrying was never my strong suit. By the third day, Shiloh was still coughing, but still without any accompanying symptoms. I thought about her trip to Texas, only a few days distant. What if she was sick and something happened to her along the way? As much as I hated to call the vet, for surely I would hear about the expense from Cleveland, I felt I had no choice. Shiloh was going to Texas in Gamal's place, and just as I wanted to protect him, I had no desire to endanger her.

When I called the horse vet's office, I was pleased by how fast an appointment was made. The vet was in the area, the receptionist said, and could be there within the hour.

I had the gleaming Shiloh between the cross-ties when he arrived. No need for the nose twitch with her, nor the chain across the bridge of her nose. Shiloh was a personable girl who welcomed attention, even from a vet. I explained about her intermittent coughs, but that otherwise she seemed fine. And I told him that it would be Shiloh, and not Gamal, who would be making the trip to Texas.

He placed the stethoscope to her ribs, closed his eyes, and listened to her heart and lungs for what seemed like an interminable amount of time. He looked into her eyes, up her nose, and into her mouth. He took her temperature. For good measure, he even looked into her ears. He pressed on her throat in a way that elicited a cough. He did it again, and as if on cue she coughed again. He pursed his lips in deep thought, but said nothing. I had no idea if Shiloh was perfectly fit, or ready for intensive care.

Without saying a word to me, he went out to his car, put away his instruments, locked them in his trunk, and presented me with a bill. I could wait no longer to ask the obvious question.

"Well? How is she?"

"Overall, fine. I suspect she has a slight allergy to something either in the barn, or the pasture." I was reminded of the ultra-clean environment of her previous barn and thought his diagnosis made sense.

"So, she can go to Texas in a few days?"

"I didn't say that," he corrected. "In fact, I don't think she should go."

"Why not?" The pitch of my voice rose a bit at this unexpected news. The usual thought ran through my mind: What will Cleveland say?

"As you know," he said with a touch of sarcasm, "it is safer to advise against travel, than for. Besides, if she stays here, I'll know soon enough if it was allergies and will treat her accordingly."

The thought of the empty truck rumbling back to Texas without either diving horse was horrible to contemplate. Would Cleveland believe me when I told him what the vet advised? Or would he think I had become an equine hoarder at his expense?

"Could you put that in writing?" I asked the vet.

"I already have," he said. With a slight flourish, he presented me with a handwritten note, jumped into his Mercedes, and sped away.

A few days later, after Cleveland complained about my animal management skills and how I was going to bankrupt the Fund, the truck did indeed return empty to Texas.

And I never heard Shiloh cough again.

Chapter Nine

My mini equine empire continued to expand as if someone had added yeast and water to flour and placed it in a warm spot. Only one member of the growing herd, AmFran, was of my doing. Cleveland, either in a moment of weakness or a moment of compassion, was responsible for the others—and one wasn't even a horse.

In the sort of call that could only come from Cleveland, he informed me early one morning that I needed to drop everything and pick up a llama named Hot Britches. Much like the llama himself, the hows and whys were fuzzy, but it was not my place to question, only to act. Hot Britches was the only non-human boarder at a boarding school in Vermont.

Wendy agreed to accept the unusual hauling job, and she and I set off in the teeth of a blizzard that worsened at we drove up Interstate 91. It was midafternoon when we arrived at the school where we were directed to the stables. There stood the magnificent but haughty creature whose visage let us know that it was we, not he, who would be in service. We were told that he had been the project of one of the students, and apparently once the project was done, the student was done with the llama. Britches was predominantly white, except for a black patch over one eye. He sported what looked like a pair of rust-colored Bermuda shorts from his waist to his knees—hence the name, Hot Britches. The staff told us to be careful, that if someone displeased him he would spit in their direction. Displeasing a llama was unknown territory to me, but I knew that food goes a long way toward pleasing most creatures. As he whittled down a carrot with incredible speed, I saw that we were off to a good start. The only other thing we were told was that he had been trained to do one thing—lie down upon hearing the command "Kush." I never asked why, but perhaps teaching the animal that trick had been the boy's school project.

Like a king sent into exile, Britches maintained his regal composure at a stately, measured pace, as he glided silently up the ramp into Wendy's trailer. We drove south, then west to skirt the worst of the storm and make the most of the dwindling daylight. We got as far as the Red Lion Inn in Stockbridge, Massachusetts, when weather and fatigue ended our journey. It was a place with a no pets policy, which, after some debate, we decided included llamas. Wendy assured me that Britches would be fine in the trailer overnight. After all, she said, llamas are native to the Andes. Unbeknownst to the innkeepers, a well-fed Britches spent the night in their parking lot buried in straw in the trailer. When we opened the trailer door the next morning, it was so warm inside that the escaping steam crystallized as it met the icy mountain air. To the astonishment of the locals, we trotted Britches up and down Main Street to stretch his legs, re-trailered him, and made it back to Wendy's farm by noon. Within a few hours he had buddied up with the animal that would become his best friend, Sparkplug the burro.

Sparkplug, the burro, and Hot Britches, the llama,
were of a similar size, were the only nonhorse boarders
at the farm, and shared a paddock. It didn't take long
for them to develop a deep friendship. 1981.

. . .

Cleveland's other contribution to the animals in my care was a twelve-year-old former Standardbred racehorse from Long Island named Prince Nelson. Despite Cleveland's grouchy exterior, he was no match for a desperate plea on an animal's behalf. When a sobbing woman he hadn't known previously called one day to say she had a horse and needed his help, he caved. She had nowhere for the horse to go, she said, and the one-month board bill she paid in advance was about to expire. She hinted that the horse, too, might expire without Cleveland's assistance. The next thing I knew, Wendy and I were crossing the Verrazzano Bridge with a horse trailer, then trying to dodge aggressive drivers on the Long Island Expressway.

At journey's end we met the horse, and the woman who saved him. We were in a fashionable part of Long Island's North Shore, a district known as Muttontown (named for the vast herd of sheep that once grazed in its meadows). Although it was relatively undeveloped for that part of the world, gamboling spring lambs were long gone. Some massive old estates remained, though, as well as a few horse farms, including this one, the aptly named Gamboling Farm. It resembled neither Wendy's picturesque but modest farm, nor the spotlessly clean but characterless abode where Shiloh had been housed. This place was the stuff of cinematic fantasies about how horses live. Sixty horses were boarded in high style on its sixty acres. As soon as we passed through its gates, rolled silently across the Belgian block courtyard, and saw the perfectly groomed, placid boarders cast disinterested eyes in our direction, I could see how Prince Nelson's savior could afford only one month's board.

Prince's owner was an incongruous figure in the barnyard— sobbing and wearing a skirt, heels, and plenty of costume jewelry. She told me she had followed Prince for his entire career, and was so enamored of him that she borrowed $4,000 to buy a one-sixth share of the animal. Over the years, she had watched him transform from a young, inexperienced Pacer with energy to spare to a middle-aged veteran, beaten down by too many races, too many drugs, too many losses. Inevitably, an injury ended his racing days, and he was sold in a claiming race without her knowledge for a mere $600. She spent the next several years searching for him until she found him in Canada, headed for a slaughterhouse. She borrowed another $1,200 to get the horse, as she put it, "outta they-uh."

A claiming race was a new term to me, and to Wendy's dismay I revealed my ignorance and asked what it meant. The woman put her well-manicured hand on my forearm and explained with great patience that horses that can't quite keep up in the top tier can increase their worth if they can be sold afterward. It makes them more desirable if they can be picked up for a reasonable price. I asked what was considered reasonable, a few hundred dollars? "Oh Gawd," she said as she threw back her head. "It's such a range, dear, from hundreds to a hundred thousand." Earlier, the woman mentioned that she was a secretary who lived alone. I did the math, and realized that buying back the over-the-hill racer may have dented, if not decimated, her savings.

"I committed the number one crime in horse racing," she admitted. "I fell in love with that big beautiful animal."

Prince Nelson was a stallion, my first. Wendy had one comment as the perfectly proportioned blue-black horse with a long, wavy mane was led from his stall: "Not bad for a Standardbred." With her Thoroughbred bias, I knew that was high praise. To me, he seemed like the equine equivalent of Michelangelo's *David*. As much as I may have extolled Gamal's beauty, objectively speaking he finished a distant second to Prince Nelson. There were the rippling muscles, thickly arched neck, and those gorgeous, rounded cheeks. There was also a fire in his eyes that reflected a barely contained, explosive energy. He frightened me a little, but was awe-inspiring, too. I could see how he mesmerized the woman as, year after year, he trotted his magnificence around the racetrack.

The woman was still sobbing, even more so, as we readied to leave. She told me that the only thing he liked better than carrots was when she sang "You Light Up My Life" to him.

"You'll sing to him once in a while, won't you?" she pleaded.

I promised I would (and did, in private). As I hopped into the

Standardbred stallion Prince Nelson was one of the rare racehorses to be reclaimed by his owner when his track career ended. But when the cost of his upkeep became prohibitive, Cleveland Amory agreed to take him. Prince, along with several other Fund animals, was eventually transported to the Fund's Black Beauty Ranch in Texas. 1981.

truck, she pressed a twenty-dollar bill into my hand, but I pressed it right back.

"You've done enough," I told her. "You saved the horse's life."

On the way back to the farm, Wendy explained that Prince would have to be kept in the stallion stall, the one with metal bars on the door so that, unlike the other horses, he could not stretch his neck into the aisle of the barn and cause trouble. I learned later that the word "stallion" comes from the Old English for "stalled one," a reference to this centuries-old practice of segregating intact males from both the mares and the geldings for everyone's safety. As it happened, Prince Nelson was the gentlest of stallions, surprising even Wendy. He did, of course, have eyes for Shiloh—all the boys did; but he seemed more in love than in lust, and appeared content to admire her from afar.

Gamal was not one to be denied attention during the comings and goings of the other animals in my life. He and I continued our special relationship, both on and off the farm.

Apart from our private time together, we had a few public appearances. In the fall of 1980, we were invited as guests of honor at an enormous street fair in Philadelphia called Super Sunday. A broad boulevard was blocked off from City Hall to the Museum of Art, the steep steps of which had become famous from the first *Rocky* movie. Gamal and Sparkplug, Wendy and I, were assigned a prime spot in front of the Rodin Museum, right by the sculpture called *The Thinker*. It wasn't long before I was thinking, too: why were we here?

Everyone in Philadelphia was familiar with the diving horse act, and initially I thought that was a good thing. But after a couple of hours of people asking sarcastically when Gamal was going to dive, or saying how sorry they felt for him, or making every ass joke in the book about Sparkplug, we packed up, left the spot cleaner than we found it, and forced our way through the crowd by beeping the horn and flashing the lights of the horse trailer. I was dismayed when, the next day, a reporter who I thought was sympathetic when we spoke, seemed only to have been looking to make a name for himself when he wrote, erroneously, that we left behind piles of manure.

A few months later, another public outing involved an appearance on *Those Amazing Animals,* a national network TV show that was a spin-off of *That's Incredible!* Given its provenance, I should have realized it would bear little resemblance to a thoughtful PBS production, but I was flattered by their interest in my charges and agreed to participate. After all, this was not something I initiated: both Gamal and Sparkplug had been sought out, invited for what we were told would be an on-air interview.

As it happened, Sparkplug never even made it out of the trailer— not enough time for him, the producers mentioned in passing as we arrived. Gamal was made to wait outside the studio in frigid weather, making me glad I packed his winter coat. Finally, he was called onstage only to be portrayed as something of a freak, a sideshow performer. Unlike most people, who at least felt sorry for Gamal, the host of the show made fun of him by asking if he wore nose clips and goggles when he dived.

In fact, neither view of Gamal, pathetic abused animal or mindless performer, was accurate. Portraying him that way diminished his skill, his artistry, and his courage, and didn't come close to representing what I considered to be his special mystical gifts.

.   .   .

For a time, I acquired other horses on my own—horses who would otherwise have wound up in the knacker's yard. This was because I had acquired something else—the bad habit of attending horse auctions to see how widespread was horse slaughter. But in the process, I found it impossible to leave without making at least one purchase. In addition to the first, AmFran, there were others I bought along the way, horses that I named Luck of the Irish and Beautiful Boy, and a pitiful, half-starved mother-and-daughter pair. The rescues were rewarding, but the eyes of those not so fortunate haunted me.

One visit, to the infamous New Holland auction located in the Amish country of Pennsylvania, was especially tough. The juxtaposition of the area's well-manicured farms and barns, many adorned with hex signs—places you might actually want to visit for a scenic, old-fashioned holiday—was offset by unchecked cruelty at this, the largest horse auction east of the Mississippi. It was impossible for me

An emaciated Amazing Grace, left, and her mother, Royal Virginia, two of several horses I purchased at auctions to save from slaughter. Here, the day after the sale, they already looked better from having been given water. The foal and mare were in deplorable condition, but over time, and with nutritious food and veterinary care, they transformed into healthy horses. 1981.

to shake the images of the condemned animals, and those people who sent them to their deaths without so much as a moment's hesitation.

That evening, when we returned to Wendy's farm, I wasn't quite ready to go home—I needed to unburden myself to someone who understood, someone with a sympathetic, nonjudgmental ear. While Wendy and I were friendly, we weren't exactly friends, did not confide in each other or socialize. But Gamal was just the man for the job of listening.

I led him outside to the lawn and began sharing what was on my mind. I told him about the suffering I had witnessed that day—about the cruel Amish farmers who felt the need to give their former equine slaves one last whip lash on the back to show them who was boss before they sent them into the auction ring; the terrified foals penned with stallions; the fighting horses; and the horses too weak even to stand. I nearly broke down while revealing to Gamal the fate of the majority, the ones I was unable to save. I told him how the horses' suffering had now become my suffering, and indeed how suffering seemed to be the endless undercurrent of the world. I knew that he heard me, that he realized my words were directed at him, but what he gleaned beyond that would have been conjecture. I know what the horse vet would have said: Gamal understood nothing.

I disagreed.

Once I told Gamal my story, we stood together in silence. A few times, he lifted his head and looked at me hard in the eyes; but mostly he grazed. I watched Wendy go into her house, the stained glass lampshade over the kitchen table glowing softly. I could see her talking to her family: her husband, Jon, and her two children, a teenager and a toddler. Jon handed her a tumbler of wine from a gallon jug, and I imagined she told him she needed it after the kind of day she had. I experienced a momentary pang that there was no similar scene waiting for me at home—no husband, no children, no one who really cared about what I had to say or how I felt.

I was in danger of slipping into a morass of melancholy until I glanced over at Gamal, my Gamal. If I'd had a regular domestic life, it might have diluted, or prevented, my close relationship with him, might even have prevented me from going into the kind of work I

The bond between Gamal and me took time to develop. When it did, it was life-changing for both of us. 1980.

had chosen. Besides, I reminded myself, if I'd wanted a traditional life, I could have had one. After all, most people do.

Gamal seemed to sense that my mood had lightened. The lead rope by which I held him felt as if it was conducting the energy between us. He lifted his head from the grass and nestled his big face next to mine. His warm breath caressed my cheek, and with that, I was reminded I was not alone.

Chapter Ten

As much as I loved all the animals in my care, some were destined
to move on. There was an ever-changing roster of auction horses;
and Prince Nelson, Shiloh, and Hot Britches were slated to go to
Texas. All of this separation was potentially troubling. Over the years,
I had trained myself never to get too close to anyone unlikely to
stick around—which, to my way of thinking, was almost everyone.
I'd had enough of the revolving door of people and places during
my adolescence and was not keen on continuing the process. I told
myself that keeping a slight distance from the temporary herd was
in my best interest.

I might have put Gamal in that temporary category, too, since, according to his paperwork, he was an old horse. By common measure-
ments, a twenty-six-year-old horse is nearing the end. Yet Gamal
possessed such a strong combination of youthful vigor and natural
wisdom that I never gave his age a thought.

I couldn't say the same for Sparkplug. He seemed defined by his
youth. My research revealed that burros could live thirty or forty
years, sometimes longer. Since he was barely a year old, I fantasized
that we could grow old together.

I was impressed by the many contrasts between Sparkplug and
Gamal. The huge gap in their ages surely accounted for some of it,
as did the facts that they represented two distinct branches of the
equine tree, and had completely different life stories. But Sparkplug
had his own distinct personality, one that was markedly different

from Gamal's, and, I suspected, from other burros. At his age, a burro could be separated from his mother, although in the wild he would still have tagged along beside her until she began nursing her next foal. Sparkplug had not yet been gelded, and by the following spring was beginning to come into his own.

What was not in the book I read about burros, but what I learned from experience, was that there was not just a single, all-purpose bray. The one he used upon his arrival surely was to announce his presence and to find out if there were others of his kind in the vicinity. But I was to discover that Sparkplug could also let loose one bray for joy, another out of boredom. He brayed one way for food, another when he caught the scent of a female in season. He brayed one way for hello, another for goodbye. Above all, I learned that he had strong opinions on many subjects and was not at all shy about expressing them.

Sparkplug would stand by the rail of the paddock, generally in the company of Hot Britches, and, for what seemed like hours, throw back his head, lift his upper lip and catch various scents on the wind. When something excited him, or was of particular interest, he would let loose with a series of brays that went from a rapid-fire staccato that sounded like someone opening and closing a squeaky wooden door, to a more leisurely hee-haw. Often, extended dirt baths followed his vocalizing. He would flip back and forth, raising great waves of dust, then stand up and shake off half of it. He seemed happiest when I patted his rump, which produced a dusty cloud. None of this rolling was done solely for pleasure, although he clearly enjoyed the process. In nature, dirt baths help protect burros, as well as other animals, from biting flies and other pests, and offer a slight barrier from the sun.

Apart from everything else, Sparkplug was reaching adolescence. Sometimes I would watch him run in circles out in the meadow, then kick up his heels. He would pull on the tail of Britches, then run away while looking over his shoulder to see if he had initiated a friendly chase. Britches never took offense, and the two could usually be found standing side by side minutes later. Sparkplug was keen on exploring his new environment, but also wanted to know that the safety of the barn was never too far away. He was bold, but not reckless; adventurous, but not yet independent. Sparkplug liked having a person to turn to as he still needed the security of knowing there was a home base to which he could return. I was touched to discover that I was that home base. Sparkplug awakened my dormant motherly instincts, certainly more than any human ever had. As I saw him investigate his surroundings, and watched him grow and change, I wanted to encourage him, but also protect him.

One blistering August day, I asked Wendy to haul Gamal, Shiloh, and Sparkplug the few miles to my house, specifically to my acre-sized meadow that adjoined the main house. The meadow was bisected by the Aquetong Creek, which eventually made its way to the Delaware River. Railroad tracks, of what had become a tourist steam train, ran alongside one border of the unfenced property. In the 1700s, settlers from Manchester, England, established a cloth mill at one end of the meadow. Eventually, the mill went out of use, and had lain in ruins, its windows shattered by Boy Scouts perfecting their slingshot skills.

Charlie Evans, the man from whom my ex-husband and I bought the property, had owned the old mill, plus two houses and a barn. But before we came on the scene, Charlie had sold the ruins (as the mill became known) to his assistant in his set design business. The assistant, in turn, had an idea: restore the structure and transform it into a home for his wife and five children. The assistant also had another idea: that his property included the meadow. It did not. But he was an unconventional person who regarded the meadow as a common area, an empty stage waiting for his visionary design.

From what I could see, there was nothing garden-variety about the garden parties he held there. White smoke, rising from the charred flesh of fresh spring lambs roasting on a spit, billowed into the night sky; newly installed outdoor lights shone into my trees, exposing their skeletal structures; tipsy guests sprawled on the grass; and at one event, a fully inflated hot air balloon hissed and swayed as it waited to give rides to the partygoers.

But as amazing as those parties were, they could not compare to what Gamal, Shiloh, and Sparkplug experienced on that summer afternoon. All three animals were energized by the new environment, and no coaxing was needed to get them out of the van and onto the succulent meal I had previously thought of as grass. The dense carpet had never been used for grazing during my tenure, perhaps ever, and the stream kept it a deep, luxurious green. Although Wendy held both horses on a lead rope, Gamal quickly assumed the role of pathfinder. Sparkplug, who had almost complete trust in the elder statesman, followed.

For quite a while, they tore at the sweet grass and chewed with greedy abandon—the equine equivalent of letting kids loose in a candy store. Then, between bites, Gamal saw something familiar—water. He let out a whinny of excitement and wasted no time getting to the stream. I asked to take his rope, and it wasn't long before we were standing in a foot or two of water. Soon Shiloh, held by a horse-experienced neighbor girl, followed suit. Gamal not only drank the water, he blew bubbles in it. Wendy let out a whoop as she watched him lower himself into the flowing creek and flip from side to side. Shiloh, in a more restrained manner, simply waded. Sparkplug was content to observe from the shore. Half an hour later we emerged, refreshed and renewed.

As Wendy prepared to load the horses into the trailer, I didn't think it was right that Sparkplug had confined his visit to grazing. Since Gamal enjoyed the water so much, I thought it worthwhile to see if the burro had any interest. After all, how would he know unless he tried it?

I led him to the edge of the stream and gave a slight tug on his halter to encourage him to go in. He flattened his ears against the length of his neck. I cupped my hand, brought some water to his lips. He jerked away as if it was poison. Thinking he just didn't understand the unique opportunity, I persisted and splashed his legs to show him what a gift cool water can be on a hot day. That tore it. Sparkplug broke free of my grip and took off in the meadow. Wendy turned around just in time to see the catastrophe unfold, and cut me a "I can't leave you alone for a minute" look. Worse, I heard the "all aboard" whistle of the steam train in the distance, calling to tourists in town. In fewer than ten minutes, the locomotive would make its

Gamal showed a fondness for water. He waded with me
regularly in the Delaware River. With my Border Collie,
Stockbridge, named after the town where I found him,
sick and half starved. 1980.

way along the same railroad track used in the classic silent film *The
Perils of Pauline.* The grade crossing was only a few hundred yards
away from the meadow. When the engine let loose its earsplitting
whistle, the horror that might ensue would rival that of Pauline tied
to the trestle.

Burros are not known for their speed, but I discovered that if suf-
ficiently motivated, they can easily outrun the most persistent human.
Sparkplug would allow me to get within a foot of him, let out a
half bray, kick up his heels, then dart just beyond reach. After a few
fruitless minutes of chasing, I realized his goal had morphed from
escaping the water to having a little fun.

Time was not on my side. Not knowing what else to do, I copied
the little burro's performance in New York when he refused to go on
camera at *Good Morning America:* I sat down. My position seemed to
send some sort of signal to him. Immediately, he ambled over and
stood next to me. I stroked his neck and apologized for scaring him.
But before he could get away again, I grabbed the lead and hustled
him into the trailer.

Minutes later, as the train chugged past, Wendy and I were all smiles as we waved to the unsuspecting day-trippers.

That evening, it was cool enough for the horses in Wendy's barn, including Gamal, to be released into the pasture. Even though he and I had already spent quite a bit of time together at my place, I went back over to the farm to linger with him by the fence. There he was, in the distance with his friends, belly high in tall grass. The horses' languid movements indicated that nothing was more important in the world than the pleasure of grazing on sweet, moist shoots. Barn swallows and bats were similarly engaged and swooped through the thick humid air, catching their dinner on the fly. They, too, seemed to be one with their activity.

Fifteen or more horses grazed in the field, but I had eyes only for Gamal. He had plumped up nicely in my care; but more than that, he was contented and settled in a way he hadn't been a year earlier. In every way that mattered, he was my horse and our relationship was sacred to me. Technically, I did not own Gamal, but he belonged to me. I wondered if he knew that I belonged to him, too. His thick black tail swished from side to side as he ground one mouthful of grass after another in his powerful jaws. From time to time he stopped, lifted his head, and peered into the distance—seeing what I could not see, hearing what I could not hear. I could let him alone no longer.

"Gamal," I called. He lifted his head, still chewing.

"Gamal," I called again, in case he hadn't heard me.

He zeroed in and charged in my direction. He stopped short at the fence, kicking up dust and small pebbles. Gamal's display now was neither aggressive nor challenging, as it had been on that first day after the auction. This particular evening, maybe because of our adventure on my meadow, he was especially full of enthusiasm, good humor, and affection. He knew me, and in his way wanted to please me. What he didn't know, or perhaps did, is that he pleased me as no one ever had.

We went through the carrot distribution ritual and shared a few with his friends. When the bag was empty, his friends departed; but Gamal stayed. Slowly, he drew closer and closer. I draped my arm over his neck and stared into the bottomless pupil of his eye. His eyes, his nose, his ears, all so oversized. His hooves could have crushed me with a single blow, yet this huge, gentle beast wanted nothing more than to dally with me beside the fence.

Gamal never conveyed anything to me in words, but that did not mean nothing transpired between us. He communicated in two ways: by his actions, which were standard horse behaviors, and by his breathing, which was beyond anything I had read about, heard about, or experienced. Like everyone, I had been taught that breathing was involuntary, akin to a beating heart or digestion, an unconscious and automatic act. Yet what I experienced with Gamal was more like breathing "plus": there was an intentional quality to it. I cannot go so far as to say it was *his* intention, yet it was a different kind of breathing than what he did as he was grazing, or running in the field, or standing in his stall waiting for his dinner. Was this something he did only with me, or did he enter this dreamlike state alone, or when he was with other horses?

I never initiated these focused breathing sessions with Gamal, never urged him to hang his head on my shoulder and breathe into my ear, or lean against me so I could feel the full force of his great lungs as, effortlessly, they took in and expelled air. Most of my time with him was spent doing the regular things that people do with horses: walking, talking, feeding, grooming—everything except riding. Because I was so inexperienced, I didn't think I should take a chance with the Fund's horse, in case he got away from me or was injured. As a result, our relationship was side by side, not astride.

When Gamal got into a certain mood and made a point of drawing me into his meditative state, I knew enough to be ready to accompany him. Gamal had a calming effect on me and I trusted him in a way I trusted no one else, just as long ago the women who rode his back into the tank on the Steel Pier trusted him. He was a reliable mount, and I surrendered to him for the ride.

Intuition ruled: Wherever the breath took me, I followed. I never knew where, if anywhere, it would lead. There was no compass or map to help me find my way on these magical journeys, just my confidence in this extraordinary horse.

Remarkably, the outcome was different every time. Sometimes I experienced sheer bliss that I could feel this close to anyone, much less a horse. As time went on, though, my encounters with him became less about our personal relationship and more about my relationship to the world. For brief periods, I would tap into a consciousness that transcended the concerns of everyday life and revealed the unity and perfection of things just as they were.

But other times I experienced a choking sadness. Scenes from my childhood appeared almost as before-and-after images: at first, safe, secure; then abandoned, broken, struggling to belong to someone, somewhere. As the sensation expanded, I continued breathing and felt I was taking in all the sorrow of the world, my own and everyone else's. It was the sorrow of being human, the melancholy of temporal life. Gamal, the field, the other horses; Sparkplug, the swallows and bats. For now, we were part of the world, but we were fleeting. The pain of knowing that one day I would be separated from Gamal, from all of this, was unbearable and I rebelled against the cruelty, the injustice. I wanted to be at the fence forever with Gamal, the setting sun, the green grass.

I opened my eyes to regain my composure. The instant I did, I was simply a woman standing next to a horse in a pasture. Any chance for a sense of oneness, or a resolution, was gone.

I needed to understand, to make sense of what was happening while practicing the seemingly mundane act of breathing with Gamal. The search itself, the very idea that there could be something to it, unnerved me. Either I was losing my mind, or was on the verge of some sort of personal awakening. This practice was not something I sought or initiated. I was not part of a group, not a devotee of an eastern religion, not even a churchgoer. I was a child of the 1960s, so of course I paid attention when Donovan and the Beatles went to India to study Transcendental Meditation. But I never joined anything, never adhered to anything, never really practiced anything at all. I was a proud outsider, the perpetual observer. But now, although I was still flying solo, I chose Gamal as my personal guide.

Spurred by the possibilities of the process, I reverted to an old habit and researched the etymology of the word "breathe" in the dictionary, to see if language could offer some insight into the amazing power of such a simple and natural practice. Breathe led to the word "respiration," which took me to *spirare,* to breathe; and then to its Latin root: *spiritus,* spirit. Spirit, something that transcends life and death.

I began to wonder if, somehow, the breath was a pathway to something healing, something everlasting, something accessible to all.

Although Wendy was a riding teacher and an accomplished rider, she was also a student of the legendary instructor George Morris, who trained members of the U.S. Olympic Equestrian Team. Between loading her horse, driving to Morris's farm in nearby Hunterdon County, New Jersey, taking the lesson, and then repeating the process in reverse, she was gone for several hours several times a month. Gamal and I had our greatest adventures in her absence.

Wendy's farm was just steps from the sixty-mile-long towpath of the canal that ran parallel to the Delaware River, which forms the border between eastern Pennsylvania and western New Jersey. At one time, mule-drawn barges hauled coal from mining regions in northeastern Pennsylvania to industrial areas around Philadelphia. Now the canal served only one purpose: recreation—the perfect place to take in the sights of the river by foot, bicycle, or horseback.

In what would become a ritual one or two lazy summer afternoons a month, I would lead Gamal from the barn, then amble down a lane to the towpath. From there, we would walk south until we reached a place I came to think of as "our spot." It was just beyond the toll bridge that had been built a decade earlier. A few houses still clung to the shore of the river, and my spot with Gamal seemed also to have been the site of a house at one time. Perhaps the property had been claimed by eminent domain; or by the flood of '55, an event that locals still spoke of in anxious tones.

I noticed the spot first because of its low stone wall and cracked but elegant slate patio. I wondered about parties that might have been held there in the past, or the everyday comings and goings. At some point, people had called this place home. But even in ruin, it was still the perfect place to sit as Gamal took one of his frequent grazing breaks. As he ate, and crunched his meal with great satisfaction, I would point out to him the ingredients in his salad: chicory and wild carrot; bouncing bets and asters; purslane and chamomile. Here and there, a few cultivated plants, day lilies and lilacs, bore testimony to the spot's domesticated past. At river's edge, a towering, ancient sycamore tree, one badly in need of the pruning it would never get, still hung on and framed the scene nicely. This became our special time together, with Gamal loading up on fresh vitamins while I daydreamed about the new life he and I had created for the ruined house. In a way, the horse and I had made it into a home again.

Eventually, I noticed stone steps leading down to what must have been the former lawn of the house. Nature had seized the opportunity to reclaim the space, but tall, verdant grass still predominated. The steps were impassable, overgrown with poison ivy, Virginia creeper, and every other manner of root and vine. But they were the only way to get to the meadow, a place I knew Gamal would love. Later, when I would walk the towpath alone, I started bringing clippers and, snip by snip, cleared a path. Although the steps were fairly steep and shallow for a horse, I figured that since he was agile enough to negotiate a ramp and then dive into a tank of water, he would also be capable of mastering them.

Gamal executed the steps with graceful athleticism, and acted as if the untouched meadow was his fondest dream come true. When it came time to return to the farm, it was all I could do to pull him away from the lush edible carpet. He chose what section of the meadow we would concentrate on, and it was only during our fifth or sixth visit that he raised his head long enough to notice the river. His ears bent forward with interest and he gave a gentle snort. Tentatively, he drew me closer to the riverbank until we stood beneath the giant sycamore. As he edged nearer the water, I assumed he wanted a drink. He tapped the water with his hoof, as if to be sure it was the real thing. He took a small sip.

Before I could even react to what came next, Gamal waded knee-high into the river, and just as quickly, flopped down on his side. If I hadn't been quick to move, he would have crushed my feet. He rose up, shook himself off, and made for deeper water.

The only trouble was that the river was a lot deeper than the creek in my meadow, not to mention the tank that Gamal was used to at the Steel Pier. There were additional hazards: slippery rocks under-foot and a strong current that could have easily carried us the mile or so south to the wing dam and rapids. Those benign-looking ripples claimed a person or two every few years. If the worst happened and we were swept away, I knew Cleveland would have demanded an ex-planation for my incompetence, even if I was submerged in a watery grave. No, this was taking the phrase "go with the flow" too literally.

Yet Gamal was unfazed by what he seemed to regard as a delightful situation and advanced farther and farther until it was deep enough for him to swim. Until that moment, I hadn't realized fully what a strong and powerful animal he was. If he was trying to reenact Washington's crossing of the Delaware, something that took place just a few miles south, he was off to a good start. I had to stop him.

There is an old Spanish saying, "Fear runs down the reins." I was about to discover that courage does, too.

In the frenzy of the moment, I realized that the only way to stave off a tragedy was to jump on his back, something made easier by the buoyancy of the water. I leapt up, grabbed his halter, and insisted that we turn around. There was no hesitation in my voice. Soon, we were back onshore, drenched. I slid off his back, my whole body trembling, my legs quivering. He returned to grazing as if nothing had happened.

My heart was pounding, my knees shaking. How had I summoned the nerve, and why had he obeyed? Did he think I was one of his former riders from the Steel Pier? Or was it something else? Maybe the horse was testing me again, to see if I had acquired more confi-dence. Whatever the reason, I knew I had reached down deep inside myself to access an inner strength I hadn't known I possessed. Gamal responded to my firm hand and trusted that I knew best. For the first time, he followed my lead.

To me, this was a literal and figurative watershed moment, one that changed everything. I had never been interested in dominating Gamal, but I was interested in gaining his respect. Even before I met him, his value to me was indisputable. Now, at last, I felt I had proved my worth to him.

There was another change, too—one that I could both see and feel. Gamal seemed almost relieved that someone was in charge, that it was not left to him to decide what to do. Of course he was fully capable of taking the lead and making decisions; but there seemed to be a part of him that wanted someone else to do it—if not always, then at least sometimes. This was that day, and as we strolled back to the barn, the rope I held was slack, he never pulled or tugged. I was leading him.

As we walked along, something else occurred to me: Gamal not only liked water, he loved water.

That was not our only encounter at the river, but for better control, I fitted him with an actual bridle and bit for future outings, and allowed him to wade only so deep. Nonetheless, he nearly dove in every time. He pranced, danced, rolled, and, in what he seemed to find endlessly amusing, blew bubbles in the river. Gamal was in his element, and I had to admit that this fearless, water-loving horse was well suited to his former occupation.

On another warm sunny day, when I knew no one would be at the barn for a few hours, I drove over to take Gamal for another of our clandestine outings. I'm not sure why the secrecy, but I thought it would be easier, as the saying goes, to ask for forgiveness than permission. I had Gamal's bridle on when I heard a car in the driveway. I knew it wasn't Wendy's truck, but whose? To my horror, it was Cleveland's maroon Checker cab, retrofitted as his personal vehicle. He was on his way elsewhere, he said, and thought he'd drop by. When I didn't answer my home phone, he said he had a hunch I'd be with Gamal. He was right on that front, but he had no idea what I was up to—no one did.

My concern about how Wendy might react if she knew what I was doing was nothing compared to my concern about how Cleveland might react. At most, Wendy might be annoyed if I got myself into a jam that would require her assistance. But Cleveland was something else entirely. While my legal standing with Gamal (owner or caretaker?) was as murky as the water in the Delaware River, I assumed the horse belonged to the Fund. But even if I was merely Gamal's caretaker, what kind of care was I taking by exposing him to potential danger?

Gamal was oblivious to this, of course. He knew where we were supposed to be going—it had, after all, become something of an intermittent practice with us—and he was beginning to get a little agitated at the delay. He was a horse that was fond of a routine that ended in a reward, and he had no problem expressing his displeasure if he didn't get it. I certainly couldn't disappoint him by putting him back in his stall, or simply turning him out into the pasture.

I shifted from one foot to the other as Cleveland stroked Gamal's nose and chatted. Should I tell him what I had planned for the afternoon? And if I did and he agreed, was I really competent enough to handle Gamal, or had I, so far, just been lucky?

Finally, I interrupted him and said what I had been withholding: Gamal and I were headed to the river. I asked if he'd like to join us.

Of course he did, and seemed pleased by the suggestion. For my part, I was surprised by his apparent faith in me. It was more than I had in myself.

We made our way along the towpath, then down to the river's edge. As Cleveland watched Gamal in action and saw the horse's affinity for water, he raised his eyebrows.

"You don't think he misses diving, do you?" he asked with a combination of amusement and concern.

It was an astounding idea, as both Cleveland and I had taken it for granted that the diving horses were somehow forced against their will to perform. It took me a while to respond as we watched Gamal flop back and forth in the shallows. Hard not to realize that he loved the water.

"The diving part, maybe not," I said. "But the attention, the applause, I can imagine he misses that."

I paused to admire Gamal taking full advantage of his aquatic getaway.

"But," I added, "I'd like to think his new life has its compensations."

Chapter Eleven

That I still knew little about Gamal's origins bothered me. Where did he come from? Who trained him? How was he trained? Was he always drawn to water? I wondered, too, about other people he had known over the course of his life. Did they care for him? Did he care for them? And, of intense interest, did they have similar otherworldly experiences with him as I did? Over a year had passed, and I still did not have the answers I was seeking.

Eventually, I was able to track down Bill Ditty, who had worked with Gamal on the Steel Pier. He and his wife, Ruth, had since moved from New Jersey to the west coast of Florida. Our telephone conversations, although brief, led me to believe that they would be the ones who could finally satisfy my curiosity. How to meet up with them was another matter. A tight budget precluded my hopping on a plane, and my car was not reliable enough for such a long trip; but, miraculously, my parents provided the opportunity. They asked if I would drive their car to Florida. By now, they had become snowbirds, and this would save them one leg of their annual 1,200-mile winter migration from New Jersey to Florida. As it happened, their seasonal digs on the Gulf of Mexico were only a few hours from the Dittys'. At last I had my chance to delve into Gamal's past with people who knew him.

When Cleveland learned of my trip, he saw it as the perfect opportunity to combine it with work. After all, he said, I was going to be "down there" anyway. My assignment was to check on a load of burros that had been delivered to one of the Fund's first adoption centers beyond the ranch. I looked at a map and saw that the part of Georgia where the adoption center was located was nowhere near the west coast of Florida. But there was no arguing with Cleveland, who, after all, was my boss.

Now that I would be straying from my original route, I looked to see if there was anything else of interest in the general vicinity. I discovered that somewhat nearby were two horse auctions I had wanted to investigate, places to which I was both attracted and repelled. Once the trip became complicated, I invited Wendy to come along as another pair of eyes and help with the driving.

Road trips sound good on paper, especially after a couple of glasses of wine. They invoke fantasies of *On the Road,* or *Travels with Charley,* or the original odyssey, *The Odyssey.* Reality is different. For one thing, there are usually time constraints. For another, financial constraints. And for women travelers, a third issue—safety considerations. In advance of this trip, my father warned that quirky, off-the-highway detours in remote locations, just the sort of thing I was drawn to, could turn sinister fairly quickly. My parents knew about the side trip to the Dittys', but I may have neglected to mention Cleveland's assignment and the horse auctions.

An initial rush of excitement as the rubber hit the road was followed by hour upon hour of tedium, bad food, and interchangeable chain motels. Music could have been a salvation, but thanks to my father's Scottish parsimoniousness, choices were limited. Although he bought a new Buick every year, his purchases extended only to stripped-down, base models. To him, a car represented one thing: transportation. He rejected accessories such as power windows, convertible tops, or high-performance engines. His one concession: a radio, for safety.

Wendy and I headed south, in the dead of winter, in a brand-new navy blue Buick with cloth seats, nonmetallic paint, plain black tires, and an AM radio. It was so inconspicuous a vehicle that had we been on stakeout duty, we would have blended seamlessly into our environment.

· · ·

We had traveled nearly eight hundred miles south, yet far from being the springlike weather I anticipated, high winds and sleet lashed at the Buick. Once off the interstate, we passed through one small town after another and I began to wonder if we had somehow veered into a time warp. I had seen little poverty in my day, and none in this country. There were houses, mostly unpainted, some covered by tarpaper, houses I would have sworn were abandoned until I saw someone coming out the front door. There were houses with no evidence of electricity, causing me to wonder about indoor plumbing. Most houses had curls of white smoke rising from slanting chimneys, which I assumed was the source of heat. In these sleepy, backwater towns, stray dogs, and there were plenty of them, would stop in the middle of the road, hike up a hind leg, and scratch at fleas biting their bellies.

Finally, we reached a town I considered the last outpost of civilization, Athens, Georgia. We cruised past the tall Gothic-style Confederate Memorial Monument, which resembled a church steeple, while seeking a place for lunch. I remembered reading that the whole area had once been an important cotton-growing region, and early magnates built a railroad from Atlanta to Augusta, with Athens as a midpoint. That same railway shipped supplies to the Confederate army during the Civil War. We had a quick snack, consulted a map, and saw that we were only half an hour from our destination. It was midafternoon, and although we knew we should put some steam behind it, neither of us wanted to.

It was sleeting harder now, as we made our way along another local road. More tarpaper shacks, or if people were better off, permanently immobilized mobile homes. Who among the locals, I wondered, would be able to afford to care for a burro properly if they did adopt one? A terrible sadness pervaded the area, a sense of defeat. These were my impressions, my attitudes, before I even stepped out of the car. To lighten the mood, we whistled an impromptu duet of "Dueling Banjos" from the movie *Deliverance.*

Up ahead, I spotted a crooked, dented mailbox with the correct address, and turned in to the rutted driveway. Thick reddish mud splashed up and coated the sides and wheels of the Buick. From then on, things took on a hallucinatory quality.

Straight ahead lay not a shack, but an antebellum mansion, perhaps one built by a wealthy landowner, back when cotton was king.
Over the years it had fallen into what might be called disrepair. As
befitted a house outside Athens, it was in the Greek Revival style,
with Doric columns that rose to include a second story porch. Now
it was an empty temple glorifying a way of life long gone, a constant
reminder of all that was lost. Once, it must have been magnificent.
But in its present condition, it needed more than a coat of paint, or
its shutters screwed back on their hinges—the old place was in an
advanced state of decay. Even in a rainstorm, and from inside the car,
we could see cracked windowpanes and missing shingles on the roof.

Several large mixed breed dogs that had been dozing on discarded
sofas on the front porch leapt up and came at the car with raised hack-
les. As they jumped against the doors with bared teeth, their nails
gouged the new Buick's paint. Their owner emerged from the house,
and with a practiced harshness shouted, "Hush up." They cowered
and disappeared around back. I cracked the car window, introduced
myself, and asked where I should park. The man reacted as if he had
never heard so ridiculous a question.

"You're already parked, aren't you?"

I shut off the engine, got out, and prayed the dogs wouldn't be
back for round two. I noticed the man staring at my father's license
plate, and thought I saw him mouth the words "New Jersey."

We followed him into the house, being careful to avoid the most
obviously rotted planks on the porch. Inside, the wife greeted us.
She was a plump woman, as opposed to her rail-thin husband, and
considerably more personable. She directed us to the kitchen, where
one bare ceiling bulb cast a harsh light. The best you could say was
that the place was in its original condition. Over the years, no one
had slapped on an anachronistic addition, or removed the crown
molding—everything was original. We seated ourselves in rickety
chairs and I asked where the burros were. The man took offense.

"Do you think we keep them in the house?"

I gave a nervous laugh and assured him I thought nothing of the
kind—not that I could have been blamed if I did. After all, there was
no heat in the house, there was at least as much furniture on the front

porch as inside, and there was no running water. I discovered this last piece of information when I asked to use the bathroom.

"I'm attached to the university," the man said. "I'm a graduate student." It was an odd thing to announce out of nowhere. I suspected what he was really saying was that although he was living in squalor, he was connected to something grand.

I wondered about the couple's background. Was this a back-to-the-land project, fifteen years after such a thing was fashionable? Was this the last remnant of a plantation that had been in the family for a hundred or more years? Were they in over their heads on a misguided home improvement project? Or was the place all that was available in their price range? Surely the fact that they volunteered to find homes for burros meant that at least one of them had a good heart. But whatever their story, I knew it was in my best interest not to ask.

It was twilight now, and raining even harder when the husband commanded that we go out to see the burros. I had no hat, no hood to my jacket, no umbrella. Worse, I was wearing loafers. I hadn't brought boots on the trip on purpose as I wanted to avoid checking luggage on the flight home. I felt the man's critical gaze and knew I had to go outside, no matter what.

I wasn't more than a few feet into the back acreage when mud sucked a shoe right off of my foot. He doubled over in laughter. We trudged onward. In the distance I could barely make out twenty or thirty pairs of burro ears; soaking wet ears; dripping ears; horizontal, not vertical, ears. I asked where the barn was. I thought maybe the burros would follow us and we could conduct the rest of our business inside.

"Barn?" he said. "Why these critters are tough, they're from the Grand Canyon." He said it in a pointed way, as if to draw attention to the fact that I was not tough enough to suit him.

He was wrong—those burros needed shelter. They were desert creatures, ill-suited to bone-chilling, damp conditions. But for the time being, I kept my mouth shut and eventually it was he who suggested it was getting too dark, and that we should regroup in the morning.

Once Wendy and I got back into the car, we held in our comments until we were sure we were out of earshot. We wondered if someone had slipped acid into our drinks when we stopped for lunch, or if the couple was demented, or if we even dared go back the next day. But we had to, or at least I did. Not only was I inspecting the operation for Cleveland, I had to do it for the burros' sake.

Back in the relative safety of Athens, we checked into a hotel. From posters stapled to telephone poles, I noticed what seemed to be a burgeoning indie rock scene. Bands that had already made it, like the B-52s and R.E.M., would pop up in town occasionally for old times' sake and served as inspiration to the aspiring ones. Athens was not immune to the changes in the world, and if I had my way, change would also be coming to that adoption center.

My first order of business was to call Cleveland and give him my disturbing report. He was duly concerned, and asked for more information and photos after our revisit in the morning. I stayed up late, taking notes on my discoveries and covering as much as I could remember about the deficiencies: fencing, water, food, shelter. This grew organically into a second project, one aimed at avoiding these sorts of problems in the future.

Over the next several hours, I completed the first draft of a plan for how I thought burro adoption centers should be operated. At the top of the list: screening potential coordinators and their facilities before animals were placed in their care. After that, I drew on what I had learned about burros firsthand and from books, and coupled it with what I had learned from my time spent observing adoptions at the animal shelter in New Jersey that the Fund nearly acquired. Common sense worked its way in, too. The one thought that spurred me on was that animals' lives were at stake. They were depending on us to do the right thing. Before I knew it, it was well past the middle of the night and time to turn in.

The next morning, my jacket was still damp from the previous night's soaking and my curled, cracked loafers were ruined. Before I could return to what I began thinking of as the scene of the crime, I found a mall where I outfitted myself in what can only be described as survivalist gear—a heavy, hooded, waterproof jacket, flannel-lined jeans, and tall, waterproof boots with felt linings and heavy treads.

By noon the rain had let up. The puddles back at the adoption center were covered by thin, brittle ice, and the mud had morphed into semi-stiff, reddish brown meringues. As the man looked me up and down he seemed to disapprove of me even more.

The pasture holding the burros was in sorry condition. Summoning all the compassion I could muster, I told myself that the pair was well meaning, but terribly uninformed. They were, after all, volunteers. They had heard about the need to find homes for the burros and had offered their land, and their time, to help the cause. The Fund would have reimbursed them for animal feed, vet bills, and incidentals; but the know-how was up to them. Sadly, they knew little. Some of the burros seemed sick, as evidenced by watery eyes and runny noses. Others appeared malnourished. It was impossible for me to know if they had arrived in that condition, or if they got that way during their time in Georgia. Regardless, they required immediate veterinary attention.

"It would be good if they saw a vet," I said in a casual manner. "Do you have one who comes out this way? The Fund will pay, of course."

The woman looked worried, almost panicked. She deflected my question by saying, "They're all eating fine."

I looked over at the soaked, half-frozen hay. There was plenty of it, I had to give them that. But I wondered why, if the burros really were eating well, there was so much hay.

I spoke to the couple about erecting at least a run-in shed, that the burros required protection from the elements—ice and cold now, intense heat in the summer. The man didn't say a word, but his eyes narrowed with each of my suggestions.

As much to break the mounting tension as anything else, Wendy and I walked the barbed wire fence line and found many low spots where a burro would only have to step over to escape. We came upon a small stream, partially covered by a thin sheet of ice. This, I realized, was the burros' sole water source.

When we returned, the couple's body language stated the obvious: it was them against us. The man fired the first salvo.

"Just who the hell do you think you are," he said, "coming down here and telling us what to do."

I explained to the couple what they already knew: that the burros were still the property of The Fund for Animals and that I worked for the Fund. Since I happened to be traveling nearby, Cleveland asked me to stop in. I was there for support, I added.

They weren't buying, but that didn't stop me from trying to sell.

"We all want the same thing, don't we? We want what's best for the animals," I said.

I was sweating now, and not just from my subzero-rated jacket. I looked from his face, to hers, and back to his. They were inscrutable. Neither said anything until, after what seemed like hours but was probably only seconds, the man took a step closer to me. Making a low growl not unlike that of his dogs, he looked me in the eye.

"You think we're southern scum, don't you?"

Now I was the silent one. My mind was racing—was he going to hit me? Should I say anything in response, or would it only make him angrier? I knew that my purpose there was to be helpful. But while we were there, had he caught Wendy and me exchange knowing glances? Had he seen us raise our eyebrows, or roll our eyes? Maybe— although I thought we had been subtle about it.

I assured them repeatedly that we held them in the highest regard. Yet our terror of how this might escalate was so strong that we backed out the front door while still blathering about appreciation and respect.

Once we were back in the mud-coated, scratched Buick, I peeled down the road as fast as I could, short of setting off a speed trap.

"That's all we'd need," I told Wendy. "A small-town Georgia sheriff with a quota to fill."

We continued our southern trek. Two days, and two depressing visits later to Georgia horse auctions in Valdosta and Quitman, we were finally closing in on the one thing I looked forward to about the trip: meeting Gamal's former trainer, Bill Ditty. We checked in at the only place near his remote home, an old-fashioned rustic motor lodge, the kind made up of tiny, individual bungalows like the ones in the movie *Niagara*. But instead of a roaring waterfall for scenery, the view here was of scrub pines, scraggly palms, and a cracked and faded shuffleboard court. It was cheap, it was clean, and at the end of what had already been a long trip, it was sufficient. We dropped our few belongings and headed off to the Dittys'.

I was excited by the thought of meeting people who actually knew Gamal in his previous incarnation as a diving horse. Both Bill and Ruth had been very friendly and forthcoming during our several phone conversations, eager to share their experiences. I was prepared to ask them about how they trained Gamal, where he came from, and how they had become involved in such an unlikely occupation. But I also intended to address some tougher issues, such as the stories I'd heard about the abuse of the horses, or, as was rumored, that the animals were forced to dive by a variety of harsh methods.

I had visited Florida many times, but as we drove down one back road after another, it was clear that this was not the state I thought I knew, that all I actually knew were the tourist-laden fringes that hug the coasts. In fact, most of Florida is rural or semirural, and it takes a constant battle with pruning shears and pesticides to carve out the manicured oases that vacationers see. This was the first time I had ventured into the real thing.

The Dittys' house was deep in a maze of country roads, all of which seemed simultaneously familiar and unfamiliar. We had no local map, and I had to rely on the scant directions Bill had given me over the phone.

We were off the asphalt now, and the sand and crushed shell road barely supported the Buick's tires. Houses were becoming scarce. The sun was low in the sky and the acres of common cabbage palm trees that lay ahead were beginning to throw shadows across the road. Their stiletto-like leaves silhouetted against the darkening horizon seemed threatening. These were stout, sturdy, native palms with a tough crisscross pattern on their trunks, nothing like the smooth, elegant royal palms found at resorts. Surrounding them were impenetrable fields of low, dense palmettos. I jerked the Buick to a halt as a wild sow and her piglets trotted in front of us. We were each surprised to see the other, and as mother and brood made for the underbrush, I marveled at the nimble gait of these wily, bristly creatures.

Soon there were no houses at all.

A wave of anxiety began to overtake me and I considered making a U-turn and forgetting the whole thing. But straight ahead was horse fencing—at last, something recognizably domesticated. I slowed the Buick to read the name on the mailbox and realized we were at our destination.

The Dittys had been waiting, and people and animals piled out of their small prefab house, rushed the car, and seemed genuinely glad to see us. Although we had declined their dinner invitation, they told us it was not too late for dessert. We went inside and I hardly knew where to focus—the place was alive with dozens of birds in well-kept cages, and just as many houseplants, all of which seemed to be in bloom. As we sat on the sofa, several tiny dogs joined us and curled against our hips.

It was hard to keep straight who lived with Ruth and Bill— adult children, grandchildren, stepchildren. What was clear was that although they had few material possessions and were squeezed into a small house, everyone was welcome, everyone seemed grateful for what they did have. Displayed prominently amid the clutter was a Bible. Ruth told me that she was studying to become an ordained minister and hoped one day to have her own congregation.

It was clear that Bill and Ruth were perfectly content with their present life, but they became alive when talking about their Steel Pier days. Ruth was at the ready with posters and photos, scrapbooks and programs, as backup to her husband's exploits. They told stories of all of the horses they worked with: Lorgah (for Lorena Carver and George A. Hamid); Dimah (Hamid spelled backward); Dimah Junior; Powderface; Gamal; and Emir. During the time the Hamids owned the pier, many of the horses were given Arabic names, a nod to the Hamid family's Lebanese descent.

Ruth brought out a harness, a flimsy item not much larger than a couple of belts stitched together. It looked ancient, like something with barnacles dredged up from an underwater archaeological site. This relic was just as precious to me as any museum piece: it had once encircled Gamal and all the others. As I held the cracked, desiccated leather I couldn't really imagine having only that to hold on to during a plunge. Of course, I couldn't imagine taking the plunge under any circumstances.

Bill said some of the horses mugged for the audience by "answering" questions posed by the announcer, such as "Are you ready to go?" The horse would shake its head up and down for yes or back and forth for no. Bill said some horses would run up the ramp and barely wait for the woman to spring onto its back before diving off the platform. Others would spend ten or fifteen minutes gazing calmly at the ocean, then at the crowd, before Bill would resort to using a cue, a whistle, to get them off their mark. Old Lorena Carver, who had been with Doc since the earliest days, rewarded all of the horses at the end of the dive by giving them as many carrots as they wanted.

Bill brought up the subject of abuse on his own. He told of a time when the SPCA came to visit, unannounced. They told him there was no way that horses would perform such a dangerous stunt without either a cattle prod or a collapsing platform. Bill gave them a demonstration. He released one of the horses, Emir, at the bottom of the carpeted ramp. The animal galloped to the top of the tower and

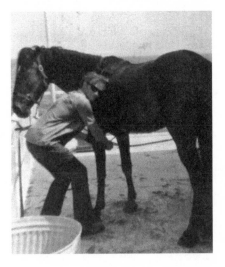

Bill Ditty removes the harness from Gamal after a dive. The thin, flimsy straps were all the rider had to hold on to during the forty-foot leap into the ten-foot-deep pool. 1970.

Lorena Carver spent most of her life with the diving horses. She was the first rider in 1906 at age twenty (billed as "The Greatest of All. The Girl in Red. The Bravest Girl in the World") and trained the horses. Here with Gamal, handled by Bill Ditty. 1970.

executed a flawless dive without any prompting, and without anyone on his back. What the SPCA thought was a collapsing platform were sheets of plywood covered in carpeting and attached vertically to the framework to protect the horses' legs in case they accidentally dove too close to the edge.

As for the training, Bill said the first requirement was to get a horse that was intelligent, curious, and unafraid. It helped, he said, if they liked water. I had to admit that the description fit Gamal perfectly. Bill also said that as much training was done on land as in the water. He would play with the horses for hours, until they trusted him and associated him with treats and fun.

Much as Walter the stable owner told me, Bill would begin diving training in earnest by literally leading a horse to water: small pools, maybe only a foot deep. Next, into water several feet deep. Eventually, the horse would be trained over jumps on dry land, and then jumps with a sand-bottomed trough of water on the far side. The first training platform, located directly beneath the performance platform, was about twenty feet high. The platform used in performances was forty-five feet high, while the pool beneath was twelve feet deep and about twenty feet across. It was lined in plastic, and made of steel panels that were slid into vertical I-beams.

I asked about what I had heard, that the pool had bags of gravel around the inside to keep the plastic in place. If a horse hit a gravel bag, it would skin its knees. Never happened, Bill said. As with any swimming pool, the weight of the water kept the plastic in place.

When I brought up Sonora Carver's blindness, Bill admitted that the act wasn't a risk-free proposition. Ruth was quick to point out that Sonora loved her job, all the girls did. The proof, she said, was that Sonora continued to dive sightless for nearly a dozen years after the accident. She also mentioned that Sonora wasn't the only sightless person associated with the act. Lorena Carver was also legally blind by the end of her tenure, presumably from her diving days. Bob Schoelkopf had told me the same thing.

After a while, the conversation turned to the man seated in front of me. How did he wind up with such an improbable career? Bill smiled. "You can blame the circus," he said.

Bill Ditty was one of thirteen children born to an impoverished family in South Pasadena, California, in 1939. When the family moved to upstate New York, his parents sent him and his younger brother to an orphanage where they were declared wards of the state. By age ten he became fed up with life in the institution. Bill said he fled and joined the circus.

"What kind of job could a ten-year-old do for a circus?" I asked.

He smiled again. "The job no one else wanted: cleaning up after the animals."

Bill said it wasn't long before he developed an affinity with the performing animals, the elephants and big cats, and eventually began to learn the rudiments of training them.

At age eighteen, he signed on with the Marines and completed one tour of duty, but afterward the circus life called to him again. "Sawdust," he said. "It gets into your blood."

Before joining the military, he had been with Ringling Brothers, but this time around he joined the smaller Hamid-Morton Circus. The Hamid family, in addition to owning the Steel Pier, also owned a traveling circus and a staffing agency that provided performers for other circuses and carnivals.

Before Bob Schoelkopf was there, Bill also landed a full-time gig at the newly opened Aquarama in Philadelphia. In warm weather, the outside pool featured a "mermaid" show; a show with Flippy the clown, who would fall into the water only to be "rescued" by dolphins bearing life preservers; seals that would honk out "How Dry I Am" on bulb horns; and the only whale in captivity at the time, Willie the Killer Whale. It was here, in this environment, with these people and these animals, that Bill Ditty discovered his calling: training animals. Philadelphia was also where he discovered Ruth Conrad, who became his fourth wife and provided him with the sense of family and stability that had eluded him.

She was working at a sports show. Ruth told me she was "a townie and circus people don't go for townies."

But Bill did go for her, so much so that it wasn't long before he proposed. Before Ruth agreed, she said there was a stipulation: she and Jesus were a package deal. Bill went home to think it over, and appeared the next day with the declaration, "I want Jesus, and I want you." Three weeks later, they were married.

By 1965, Aquarama was already experiencing financial difficulties. Impresario George Hamid Sr. stepped in and leased Aquarama in an attempt to turn it around. He assumed that what worked at the Steel Pier would work in South Philadelphia, and he duplicated many of the pier's features—weekly dances for teenagers that were broadcast on TV, boardwalk-type games, and from time to time the diving horses were brought in for special appearances. But the place never really caught on, and by 1969 it not only closed, but the striking modernist structure housing it was demolished.

Senior, as he was known, took a liking to the young Bill Ditty and the feeling was mutual. When Ruth and Bill's daughter, Susan, was born in the early 1970s, they named Senior the godfather. Things were starting to go Bill's way, and even before Aquarama closed, Senior offered him a permanent position at the Steel Pier, first as a general worker, and later as the trainer and handler of the diving horses.

Bill reminisced about Dimah Junior, who died of a twisted gut, more properly known as colic. Bill knew the horse was sick and alerted the owners, the Hamids. By this time, Senior had retired, and Bill said his heirs did not share his same concern for the animals.

"Hamid Senior was in the business for the show," Bill said. "Hamid Junior was in the business for the money."

Bill said he pleaded for a veterinarian, and eventually one was sent; but it was too late. Hours later, Dimah Junior collapsed in the barnyard while a helpless Bill held the horse's head in his lap until the animal drew his last tortured breath. Around 1969, Lorgah "just disappeared one day." He was, by then, "old and heavy" and not well equipped to dive. When Bill asked what happened to him, Hamid Junior told him to "mind your own business." How different this was from what I had read about Doc Carver's treatment of the horses. For all his faults, Doc made sure all of his horses were cared for after their diving days were over. Even those that he bought, but that didn't make the cut, enjoyed a humane retirement.

I could tell that Powderface was one of Bill's favorites. He described the horse as a big ham who enjoyed pizza and Italian water ice. "He was a real professional," Bill said. "He loved the spotlight and couldn't wait for the show to begin." When I told him about the horse's probable fate at a slaughterhouse, Bill's eyes filled with tears.

No one said anything for a while after that.

For my part, I was imagining the last hours of Powderface, a horse that had worked hard during his life by entertaining hundreds of thousands of people, and had known affection and attention in his time. On that last haul, from the auction to the slaughterhouse, did Powderface think he was being trucked to another performance? Was he frightened? Hungry? Thirsty? Was he waiting for a cue from Bill Ditty as to what he should do next? What were his final thoughts, his sensations, before a minimum wage worker in a Canadian abattoir pressed the cold steel of the captive bolt pistol against his skull to render him unconscious before slitting his throat?

Everyone involved with the act must have needed to compartmentalize some of the conditions the horses faced. Bill may have reasoned that his love for the animals, and gentle training methods, would override the shortcomings. Or that their lot in life was better than it is for many creatures. To some extent, he was right. It was a complicated issue, one made more so by the fact that the Dittys had a deep attachment to animals and, in their way, truly cared about them.

I brought out a few current photos of Gamal and Shiloh and asked the Dittys what they remembered about them.

My first surprise was when Ruth said there was never a horse named Shiloh, at least not while they worked at the pier. "If you notice," Ruth said, "all of our horses were geldings. When a female horse goes into heat, well, she'd be hard to handle, she'd excite the males and dirty the pool water." I was reminded that Bob Schoelkopf said he didn't remember Shiloh diving either, and he was there during at least part of what I had been told was the mare's term at the pier.

On the other hand, I knew that there had been several other female diving horses over the decades—including Duchess of Lightning, another named Snow that Sonora wrote about in her book, and the first diving horse, Black Bess. Regardless, the implication that Shiloh may not have been a diving horse at all was a shocking thought. If it was true, and if Cleveland found out, he'd have my head for having encouraged him to buy her. I decided on the spot to use the uncertainty to give me more incentive to find someone, somewhere, who could confirm or deny Shiloh's employment history. For the time being, I consoled myself with the fact that Gamal was the last verifiable diving horse, and definitely the last in the Carver line.

The next surprise shook even that shaky sense of certainty: Gamal was not really Gamal. For a second, I wondered if yet another of the Fund's purchases, purchases that I initiated, had ever dived at all. Was he just a ringer sent to the auction to dupe an unsuspecting buyer?

Those fears were unfounded: my Gamal had indeed been a diving horse, but his real name was Emir. Bill said the "real" Gamal was an older diving horse who worked at the same time as my boy. The tips of the real Gamal's ears turned inward slightly and he did not have a white star on his forehead. Sometimes, when Bill felt that the real Gamal had done enough diving for the day, he'd substitute Emir. He'd comb down Emir's forelock to cover the star on his forehead. I wondered if the reason my Gamal did not come to me when I called him on that first day out in the field was simply because I was using the wrong name. Regardless, I had been calling him Gamal for a year and a half and would continue to do so.

Bill revealed the history of the horse who became mine. While scouting for diving horse prospects in the late 1960s, Bill and another Steel Pier worker found him at an auction. "It was somewhere out in Pennsylvania," Bill said. "Near Doylestown."

Wendy's eyes widened. "Old Marlin France's auction?" she asked.

"Yeah," Bill said. "For a long while the Carvers had a farm in Pennsylvania. But when they sold it, we used to winter the horses in Marlin's stable before we started using Hammell's in Absecon."

Wendy told Bill she knew Marlin, that he had schooled her in basic stable management. I didn't know him, but was reeling at the thought that Gamal was now back in Bucks County, only fifteen miles or so from where his diving career began.

My Gamal/Emir, who surely had yet another name before he became a diving horse, was a Quarter Horse mix. This, I discovered, was a favorite blend for diving horse prospects as it produced small, sturdy animals. On the day Bill bought him at the auction, he was able to meet the horse's consignors and ask about his background. They told Bill that my Gamal was originally from Texas. His first job was on a ranch where he worked as a cutting horse. Cowboys ride into pastures on horseback and, with the help of their highly skilled steeds, separate and herd cattle. It's tricky work, and a poorly trained horse could cause a stampede or even risk the life of the rider.

Gamal was so good at his job that he was sent to work in rodeos. Eventually, he wound up at Cowtown. Despite being located in southern New Jersey, as opposed to a western venue, Cowtown claims to be the longest running weekly rodeo in the country. Soon, barrel racing and cutting horse trials were added to his repertoire. According to Bill, the horse was so expert that he "could turn on a dime and give change." Based on the fearlessness that sort of work required, combined with Gamal's compact stature, Bill saw potential in the horse, bought him, and hauled him to Atlantic City.

When the three Atlantic City businessmen assumed ownership

of the pier in 1973, a change in attitudes accompanied them. Bill's connection to his surrogate father and benefactor, Senior, had already been severed. Now, his more tenuous connection to Junior was gone, too. Giving grudging credit, Bill admitted that at least Junior grew up in an entertainment family, even though he was never a performer himself. But the new owners had no background in entertainment, their interest in the diving horse act extended only to the revenue it created. They were money guys, Bill said. His years of training and caring for the three remaining diving horses—Powderface, Gamal, and Emir—were as nothing to the new owners.

After enduring a miserable year and a half of indignities, Bill Ditty finally had enough and quit. At the pier, he called the shots and was respected as the undisputed master of his craft. Afterward, he took an entry-level position with an amusement ride that mirrored his own decline in status: the Plunge of Power. Bill said he was never injured while working with the horses—not while training them, nor during

Lorena (front) and Sonora, mid-1930s, astride Judas
(a name long associated with betrayal). The two women
had a tense relationship at best, but always put on a happy
face for the camera. Lorena, a woman scorned, blamed
Sonora for stealing her husband, Al Floyd (Carver).

the many times he filled in as a rider if one of the girls called in sick. But at this new job, he broke his back and neck, leaving him with permanent disabilities.

Uncompensated for his infirmities, lacking a pension, and no longer able to work, Ruth and Bill realized that getting by on meager Social Security disability checks would be impossible in New Jersey. But in parts of Florida, in the secluded and rough inland regions where the land is flat and the sun unrelenting, they could afford their own modest place with a few acres for the animals they would acquire. Besides, Steel Pier people stick together: one of Bill's former coworkers, a diving horse rider named Barbara Gose, lived in a nearby town.

As the horses' trainer and handler, Bill provided most of the details about Gamal and the others. But it was Ruth who dropped the most jaw-dropping personal remarks. For one thing, she confirmed what I had suspected: that Al was not Doc's son. He simply took on the Carver name after Doc's death as a good hook for the show. He then went on to marry Sonora. This meant, of course, that contrary to what Sonora wrote in her book, and how things were portrayed in the movie *Wild Hearts Can't Be Broken,* she was neither Doc's daughter-in-law nor a Carver at all.

"So the whole family business thing was made up? How could that be?" I asked.

Ruth said it was just how people in show business did things. As if I needed further proof, I now knew that even Gamal wasn't Gamal.

Bill Ditty may have started his life without a family, but he was no longer an orphan. The animals that surrounded him, as much as the people, were part of his clan. As I viewed the untidy, unruly scene, I realized I was not just visiting Gamal's former trainers: I was visiting his family. I was not the only one who loved the old horse; they did, too. And just as they were connected to him, that same bond connected them to me.

As Wendy said goodbye to Ruth, I knew this was my last chance to ask Bill if he ever saw signs that Gamal possessed a kind of otherworldly, all-knowing quality. My experiences with the horse were some of the most profound in my life and I had to find out if Bill had similar encounters with Gamal.

Bill rubbed his chin in thought. "You know, that horse was a natural for the job. He always loved the water and would go right in. If he had any quirk, I guess it was that he liked blowing bubbles in his water bucket."

We got in the car and Wendy couldn't stop laughing. She'd heard the last of what Bill told me, and had seen Gamal blowing bubbles, too. Some horses just do, she said.

Was Gamal really just a one-trick pony? A water-loving, daredevil of a horse that, in his spare time, blew bubbles? To me, he had become a teacher, a confidant, my best friend.

Before dropping my parents' new car at their place on the Gulf Coast of Florida I made one last side trip, this time to get the Buick washed and detailed. It helped, but a close look revealed that it had aged prematurely in the week since it left home in New Jersey. I felt equally battered, and wondered if the whole trip had been an extended dream—a dream of lives lived in ruins; of lives ruined; and of lives raised up from ruins.

Not a dream was my report to Cleveland about conditions at the adoption center. He wasted no time in assigning a Fund person in the South the job of seeing to it that the Georgia burros got the care they needed. I figured if that person had a southern drawl, they would have had a better chance of success than I. But although that fire might have been extinguished, I wanted to do what I could to ensure that nothing similar happened at future adoption sites by suggesting how adoption centers should be operated. I knew that proposing overall improvements to the program might be construed as criticizing Cleveland, but it was a risk I was willing to take: animals' lives were at stake.

I labored over each part of my self-initiated project, the first of its kind I ever attempted: bullet points to highlight the topics; expanded discussions of each section; and at the conclusion, recommended courses of action. It took some time to complete, partly because I wanted to be sure I covered everything; partly because I was such a poor typist that a page slathered with Liquid Paper sometimes required a complete redo; and partly because I questioned whether I was crossing the line between constructive criticism and condemnation. The final result was so valuable to me that I drove to New York and delivered it to Cleveland in person, rather than risk it in the mail. He raised an eyebrow as I explained what it was and handed it over, but said nothing as he placed it atop an imposing stack of papers on his desk.

Rather than address it on the spot, he updated me on the current status of the burro rescue project. Since the Fund had shown the world how such a recovery project could be accomplished without bloodshed, I asked why the government hadn't followed the blueprint and removed the animals themselves. Cleveland waved aside my question. "Would you count on the government to do it right?" He made a good point.

The Fund was now saving more than burros. Wild mustangs were in the mix, and feral goats and pigs from the navy's San Clemente Island had been added to the roster. "The ranch is bursting at the seams," he said, with a combination of pride and uneasiness.

I took that as my cue and brought up the Georgia situation. Although it had been resolved, I suggested more stringent standards be implemented for future satellite adoption centers. I put a twist on the biblical quote and told him that while many may offer to help, few should be chosen. He gave a weak smile but, again, said nothing. I told him it was all in my report, but that I thought that before any more animals were delivered to centers beyond the ranch, the prospective volunteers should be thoroughly screened, and their farms inspected, to make sure the facilities were appropriate. He looked at me as if I were someone he had never before seen. Perhaps he was deciding whether or not I was competent or if my observations and opinions could be trusted. Perhaps he was surprised at my audacity for making such suggestions. I know I was.

He turned his attention out the window, and seemed mesmerized by the people below, hustling to and from their jobs, carrying on with their little lives. I could not imagine the burden he had taken on, saving animals from those who sought to kill them, and then from those who might inadvertently kill them in the process of saving them. I left the office that day with little hope of ever discussing my adoption ideas with him again.

Chapter Twelve

Winter gave way to spring, and the multiflora roses that created a prickly barrier along the fence line of the horses' pasture let loose with tens of thousands of intensely scented blossoms. I always made a point of inhaling their fragrance deeply, as if it would provide some sort of long-lasting nourishment.

Little Sparkplug was coming into full bloom, too. He was a year and a half now, his jawline was beginning to show a more mature roundness, and he'd added a few inches to his height. As if I needed any more reminders that he was indeed growing up, he responded to the sashaying of Shiloh's swaying hips with a hearty hee-haw every time she walked past his stall. Although he and Hot Britches still spent much time together, the llama was no longer Sparkplug's sole companion. The burro had graduated, and now spent part of his time turned out with the geldings. Although they chased him once in a while, there was no meanness involved, just horseplay.

Yet while Sparkplug's animal family had expanded, I was still his human family—a role I took on gladly. I could tell from the way he swished his broomlike tail when he saw me, or sniffed my cheek, or held his ears at attention when he heard me approaching, that I occupied a special place in his world. I never felt my attention to Gamal was cut in half by Sparkplug's presence. Quite the contrary: my capacity for caring had doubled.

. . .

It had become my habit to stop by the barn either first thing in the morning, or at dusk. Early in the day the animals were alert, fully charged from a night of rest, and eager to get on with their lives. By dusk, they were calm, satisfied, ready to turn in. Midday, they tended either to be dozing, or were far out in the pasture and too busy to come over to see me. Just as this was their routine, so, too, did it become mine. One day led to the next and the next, varying little. It was so unvaried, in fact, that when the slightest thing was different, it stood out as being very, very different.

This, I imagined, was how animals sensed the world—they compared their picture of normalcy with anything at odds. If staying alive is paramount in the wild, then being on the alert for anything that could jeopardize that state is paramount. Those predators at the top of the food chain—animals like humans, sharks, tigers—have less to worry about than do animals at the bottom, such as rodents, rabbits, insects. In the barn, if the horses were always fed at five but were still unfed at six, the most apprehensive among them would kick their stall doors or whinny or tighten their guts with anxiety and wonder if starvation could be far behind. If the sky had been cloudless but a shadow passed over the sun and lingered too long, some might sense that a thunderstorm was coming and would lead the herd closer to the gate and the relative safety of the barn. If their regular path through the pasture was smooth, but one day a horse happened to notice a slithering snake, it did not accept this as benign. It might refuse ever again to set one hoof on that path. Survival was the name of the game, and difference equaled danger.

On that one summer day when I entered the barn—it could have been the fiftieth day, or the third day that month, but certainly the same early morning hour as always—I knew without knowing that everything was as it had always been: the animals had eaten and were itching to go outside; someone was refilling the water buckets that had been drained during the night; someone else was in and out of each empty stall with a long-tined rake, separating the manure from the sawdust bedding, and piling it in a wheelbarrow that would then be taken outside and added to a steaming mound in varying stages of decay. Flies buzzed, spiders wove their invisible webs.

I came to Gamal's stall first. He was a little more antsy than usual, perhaps because it was already hot and humid and he knew from experience that his hours in the pasture would be cut short and he would be brought back inside if the temperature rose too high. He wanted out, and he wanted it now. I patted his neck and told him he had to wait his turn, that he didn't want to cause a stampede, did he? His look told me he didn't care. He just wanted out.

Sparkplug's stall was next. I always saw the tips of his ears before I saw him. The stall doors were built for the height of horses, not burros, so Sparkplug could not drape his neck over the top, as did the other boarders. And as I took those two or three steps to Sparkplug's stall, and did not immediately see the tips of Sparkplug's ears, I was gripped with a flash of anxiety. Some animal instinct in me had been awakened and warned of danger, as alarming as if there had been a snake in my well-worn path. This did not rise to the level of words or conscious thought, but something alerted me that all was not as it had always been. It was over in the blink of an eye, a millisecond, for the brain kicked in immediately and reassured me that the burro could have been standing a few steps to the side, or leaning down to take a drink from his water bucket and that everything was fine.

I trusted the brain, and as I looked over the stall door, I expected to see the round bright eyes, the ears upright and tilted forward, and thought I might even get a good morning bray. And when I was not met with any of those things, there was another millisecond of disbelief, of thoughts coming in a rush, promising that of course everything was as it had been, why wouldn't it be, how could it be otherwise in this summer of endless sunny days, when everything in my life was finally coming together, and when this one little burro was coming into his own. How could it be any other way?

Sparkplug was not even facing the stall door, but had his back turned to me. I called his name and one ear swiveled slightly in my direction. I thought I saw a slight heaving of his ribs. I was reminded of Shiloh's cough a year earlier and how my concern about her proved unwarranted. This had to be something like that, the brain said. My gut, however, was saying something else entirely.

Just as I was about to look for Wendy, she appeared. I tried to read her demeanor, but she was a woman who generally gave the impression of having things under control. And if things were veering out of control, it was unlikely she would reveal it to me.

"I've already called the vet," she said, anticipating my question. "He'll be here as soon as he can."

This was a good thing, for just as in human medicine, the sooner Sparkplug was examined and treated, the better. But this was also a bad thing because, like any well-seasoned horse person, Wendy could treat all but the most serious conditions herself.

I did my best to hide my mounting hysteria and asked what she thought the problem might be, if she had ever seen symptoms like this before, and if she thought Sparkplug was going to be all right.

"Let's not speculate," she said. "Why don't we see what the vet has to say?" Wendy was far too intelligent, and too experienced, to get my hopes up, or to dash them.

I believe she also meant to calm me, but her words had the opposite effect. I went into Sparkplug's stall and felt his forehead with the back of my hand, as one might feel a child to check for a fever. He seemed hot, hotter than Gamal's neck had been. Not only were his ribs heaving, but his nostrils flared a bit as he drew each breath. He did not want the carrot I offered, he did not want water when I led him to his bucket. I had nothing to offer but my presence, and I wasn't sure he even wanted that. Wendy didn't have to tell me: Sparkplug was gravely ill.

The vet finally arrived, but I don't know how long it took. While waiting, I went into a kind of fugue state, oblivious to the time of day or the activity around me. All I could do was wait, worry, and wish there was something I could do to make things return to the way they had always been.

The vet, the more personable partner of the one I usually saw, went through the usual questions for the medical history: when did you first notice the symptoms (Wendy said just that morning); has he otherwise been eating and drinking normally (Yes); has his energy level been normal (Yes); is anyone else in the barn experiencing the same thing (No). Sparkplug's other history, the part that had always been so precious to me—his rescue from the Grand Canyon, his time at the ranch in Texas, his trip to New York for a TV appearance, and especially his attachment to the animals on the farm and to me—all of that was irrelevant. All that mattered now were his inner mechanical workings, the vessel that made the rest of his life possible.

The vet looked Sparkplug over from a distance, and had him trotted up and down the aisle. The burro did not become noticeably winded. Then he examined him up close. He put his stethoscope to the burro's ribs and listened to the mysterious goings-on in his chest, first on one side, then the other. It seemed to take a very long time. He put his hand over his nostrils and listened again. He looked in the burro's eyes and up his nose for signs of discharge (there was none). He took his temperature (it was normal).

Just as I was about to latch on to these last two findings—no discharge and no fever—as a sign that I had overreacted, that I was wrong when I thought Sparkplug was hot; just when I was about to switch back into business-as-usual mode, the vet said to Wendy, "I don't like some of the noises I'm hearing in there. I'd like you to bring him in to the hospital for some radiographs." I was still adjusting to the fact that there was such a thing as a horse hospital when he added, "Sooner rather than later."

As Wendy readied the truck and trailer, I pressed the vet for more information.

"Could it just be allergies?" Although it seemed an absurd suggestion even as I said it, I didn't care. All I wanted him to tell me was that, yes, allergies were a distinct possibility, or that maybe Sparkplug was just having an off day, or anything but what I feared was a serious condition. But he did not, could not, relieve my anxiety.

"I can tell you for sure, it's not allergies. But until we do some tests, get some pictures of his chest, that's all I can tell you."

I knew he wasn't going to give out any more information, so that left me alone with my imagination.

Sometimes these things just happen," the vet said to me at the hospital. He turned his attention from the dim glow of the X-ray on the light box to me, then back to the X-ray. To him, the ghostly images on the film meant something, something recognizable, perhaps even treatable. To me, cobwebs, clouds, chaos.

More than the diagnosis of acute interstitial pneumonia, it was that phrase "sometimes these things just happen" that haunted me. The random hand of the universe was at work. While that randomness might present someone with a winning lottery ticket, it might also allow a stray bacterium to lodge in a lung.

How was pneumonia possible, I asked. Sparkplug was only eighteen months old and had come from hearty stock that had survived the Grand Canyon. Adding to my case, or maybe to get him to reconsider the dire diagnosis, I reminded him that the burro had been inoculated. In theory, that should have offered some protection. Yet even while saying these things, I knew that there is no absolute protection in this world, no safety. You do the best you can and hope that random hand passes you by.

The vet struggled to offer an acceptable explanation. Stress of handling and travel can be causes, he said. But since Sparkplug had been here a year, that did not apply. Perhaps, he suggested, the burro was simply born with a compromised immune system, a weakness, a deficiency. I nearly took offense: there was never a more perfect specimen than this beautiful boy.

"We've already started him on IV antibiotics and fluids," the vet added. "If you'd like to wait around until he's done, you can go back to see him."

"How serious is his condition?" I asked, violating Wendy's dictum of not asking a question if you don't want to know the answer.

In as gentle a manner as possible, he told me the next twenty-four hours would be critical.

As I waited for Sparkplug, I wandered the huge barn that served as a horse hospital. The vet and his partners were in the process of building a new facility, but in the meantime had leased an entire barn, one of several on a large horse farm, to use as a temporary hospital. Skylights in the roof kept the place bright, and giant fans, built into the walls near the ceiling at either end, kept the air moving. There were separate sections for exams, for surgeries, and treatment rooms with slings and hoists, the type one might use to pull an engine from a car. For a building that housed animals, it was remarkably clean and looked almost as if it had been vacuumed.

I assessed the other patients, mostly Thoroughbreds. Not only were they twice the height of Sparkplug, but were also considerably taller than Gamal. They were different in another way, too: none seemed as sick as my burro. I could tell from their charts, which hung from stall doors, that quite a few had common sports-related injuries. Others had fertility problems, the inability to breed or to bear more expensive, leggy offspring. I did not wish any of them ill, but wondered why Sparkplug had not contracted a simpler, more benign condition like theirs. They had all the advantages, I thought. It wasn't fair.

A technician informed me that Sparkplug had completed his first treatment and ushered me into a room where they were disconnecting his IV line. We had only been apart for a few hours, but already he seemed a little better. If fluids had created such a dramatic effect, maybe once the antibiotics had a chance to work, his condition would reverse itself. I told Sparkplug this, and that everything humanly possible was being done for him. I did not add that humans were not omnipotent.

On my way home, a new concern overtook me. What if Sparkplug had acquired pneumonia not because of a personal immune deficiency, but one shared by all of those who came from the canyon? What if it was similar to when Native Americans succumbed to smallpox because they had no natural defenses? If that was the case, it would mean the end of our adoption program.

When I called Cleveland that evening to let him know about Sparkplug's illness, I expressed my concern about the possible broader implications. Before I even finished the sentence, he interrupted with an uncharacteristic disregard for expense.

"Just have them do everything they can for him," he said.

I didn't tell him that I already had.

As much as I rebelled against the possibility that Sparkplug had any inherent deficiencies, that was the theory I came to accept.

It was not something endemic to others of his kind: by then, burros had already been adopted from Arizona to Texas to Georgia, and there were no other reports of respiratory problems. While this was good news for the program, it was distinctly bad news for Sparkplug.

The next morning I called the hospital and received the dismal report that there had been no change in Sparkplug's condition. The vet added that I could visit the burro later that day, that my presence might cheer him up. This was especially hard to hear. Sparkplug was one of the jolliest beings I had ever met, but now he was in no condition to play any pranks. It also meant that the connection we had together was real, and not just my imagination. The vet had noticed how the little guy wanted to stay with me, rather than go along with the technician.

Sparkplug looked tiny and very much alone in his big, bright stall. The bedding was nearly up to his knees, his water bucket was filled to the brim, and a fresh pile of bright green hay lay untouched in a rack. As much as you could say under the circumstances, he had very nice accommodations.

Sparkplug did not hear me approach, which was uncharacteristic for him. Back at Wendy's he seemed to know the sound of my car's engine and was always ready for me at his stall door. Now, he was oblivious to his surroundings, standing in the middle of the stall with his head hanging low. When I looked closely, I could see he was having trouble breathing. When I called his name, though, he pulled himself together. He gave a weak half bray, just a snort of recognition, and took a step or two in my direction. I was overcome that he recognized me.

Once again, I was reminded of how young Sparkplug was. My relationship with Gamal had a very different tone. Gamal had insinuated himself into my life by his defensiveness—it was a challenge to get the tough old guy to accept me. But the hallmark of my relationship with Sparkplug was the opposite: he looked to me as his surrogate mother, his protector.

I put my hand on his large fuzzy head and realized he was still abnormally warm. His eyes were not as bright as usual and, despite his efforts to steady his head, it began to droop. Although it looked as if storm clouds were gathering outside, it was still a pleasant early evening. With the staff's permission, I led him out onto the grass. We didn't go far, we couldn't really. Sparkplug became winded after only a few hundred feet.

I sat down with my back against a tree and pulled my knees up to my chest. There was barely a reason to hold on to Sparkplug's rope, he was that weak. A light breeze, one that carried the scent of an impending storm, provided some relief from the midsummer humidity. But Sparkplug had little interest in whatever stories were on the wind and for the first time I recognized that he might very well die.

It seemed wrong that we could have succeeded in rescuing him from being shot by the Park Service, or even from starvation on the floor of the canyon, only to have him taken by this invisible enemy. My plan was that Sparkplug would live to be thirty or forty, as some burros are known to do. Now I was unsure if he would make it another day.

As hot tears etched their way down my cheeks, I became aware that Sparkplug had been inching closer and was now standing in front of me. He rested his head on my bent knees and simply stood there. At first, I wondered if he was doing this because he could no longer hold up his head, but as he stared into my eyes, I knew he was doing it because he wanted to. I was his home base and he was looking to me for comfort.

I could not lie to him, could not tell him that everything would be all right. I realized that the only thing I could do was to be with him, undistracted by my own needs or my arguments with the universe about the way I thought things ought to be.

I brought a few things for him in my pack, and began with his favorite, sugar cubes. It took him a long time, but he licked them, then finally bit and swallowed them. He no longer had the strength to crack off a chunk of carrot, so I broke off small bits which he chewed without enthusiasm.

He seemed to enjoy it when I brushed him. Gently but deliberately I began at his head, just below the ears, and worked the brush in a circular motion down his neck. All the while, I spoke to him softly and told him what a perfect and handsome boy he was. Certain parts of his shoulders or side were especially sensitive, and as he leaned into the sensation he stretched his neck, which seemed to ease his breathing.

I had just about finished grooming him from head to hoof when we were pelted by rain. Sparkplug's dislike of water had not diminished with his illness, so I led him back inside. Soon the rain became a real midsummer soaker that pummeled the metal roof of the barn and sounded like discharging machine guns. Sparkplug was uneasy, and I tried to calm him by explaining that we would stay dry as long as we were inside. But the real cause of his anxiety was not a fear of getting wet, but the violent cracks and crashes from the electrical storm that swirled overhead. I tried not to let on, but I was just as fearful as he was. Making matters worse, some horses in the hospital were even more distressed by the storm than Sparkplug. They whinnied, they panted, and at least one kicked his stall door repeatedly. Our recent heavenly experience outside had become something of a hell inside, and I was hard pressed to know what to do.

Language would not serve me now, nor would food. I had to find another way to communicate. Just a short time earlier the grooming session seemed to ease him, so I decided to continue. This time, though, I did not use the brush, but, instead, my hands. I had no formal instruction in massage, or any kind of bodywork, so I relied on what felt right. The spine seemed like a good starting point, and I began kneading the skin on either side. The results were dramatic. Within a few minutes he was noticeably more relaxed. My hands felt guided by an invisible force as I moved over his body. When I began to get the sensation that a particular spot needed attention, I would concentrate on that area until the tension had disappeared. Once I shifted my focus from suppressing my fears to calming his, my fears disappeared. Through the catalyst of the storm, I was able to achieve a closeness and a connection with Sparkplug that I would have never experienced otherwise. And in the process, he was able to relax and feel better.

I don't know how long we were at it, but when I once again became aware of my surroundings, the storm had passed, the sky was dark, and I was alone in the horse hospital with Sparkplug and the other patients. Either the staff forgot I was there, or perhaps they didn't care. Using my knapsack as a headrest, I leaned against the wall of the stall and hunkered down for the night.

By morning, Sparkplug seemed brighter, and was certainly breathing easier. I gave him a kiss, told him I'd be back later. He looked at me, and gave a full bray, rich and deep. I left the barn believing the crisis was over.

I was wrong.

Sparkplug's last bray was, in fact, a farewell. I wasn't home for thirty minutes before I had a call from the vet.

"I don't know any other way to tell you this. Sparkplug died."

"He can't have died," I said into the phone. "He was fine. He was better. I know he was better."

"I'm really sorry," he said. "We did everything we could, but sometimes these things just happen."

Chapter Thirteen

As I entered Wendy's barn the next day, Gamal was not there to greet me as he usually was. Before I even had time to panic, a girl noticed I was looking for him. She had started mucking the stalls in reverse order, she said. Gamal was already in the pasture.

On my way outside, I ran my fingers over Sparkplug's name on the hand-carved wooden sign attached to his stall door. The sign was still there, but Sparkplug was not. His full water bucket, now covered by a thin film of dust, still hung on the wall; and the hay, left for him on the morning he went to the hospital, was untouched. Like my grandfather's coffee cup that was washed and put back in the cupboard the morning after he died, the stall gave the impression that Sparkplug, too, was just gone momentarily—perhaps out in the pasture, or in the cross-ties getting his hooves trimmed—and would be back any minute.

Outside, the dense aroma of the multiflora roses trapped in the humid summer air, something I had previously experienced as delightful, now struck me as cloying, tinged with decay. All of life seemed fetid, pointless.

This was how grief descended on me: the things that once held comfort and meaning were now sources of pain.

Of course, I turned to Gamal. Who else in the world would understand? Besides, for all I knew, he might also have been sad and needed consoling. Many animals had passed through the farm during his tenure, but Sparkplug had been there almost as long as Gamal. Surely he counted on the little burro and was attached to him. Why wouldn't he have been affected?

I called his name, and gave a whistle. Gamal responded like a well-trained field Setter and raced to the fence. He certainly showed no sign of grief or mourning.

Gamal was robust, well muscled, and his dark mahogany coat gleamed in the early morning sun. During our fifteen months together, and as his health improved, he had, in a sense, become younger. Ordinarily, I would have found this pleasing; but not on this day. Today I faced up to the fact that, despite appearances, Gamal was old. Had he collapsed then and there, right in front of me, people would have said he had a good, long life. I would not have said that, or even thought it; but others would.

This new perception of Gamal as nearing the end of his days left me unnerved, shaken. Sparkplug's death, and the many ways it dampened my enthusiasm and shattered my confidence, was bad enough. But I could not bear to think about Gamal leaving me, too, since being unnerved might lead to being unhinged. One trauma at a time, I told myself. At some point, though, I knew I needed to come to terms with Sparkplug's sad fate because, like red wine spilled on a white tablecloth, the stain was spreading.

During the weeks that followed, I visited Gamal more often than ever to make the most of whatever time I had left with my beloved horse.

I began not by telling Gamal that I was distraught about Sparkplug—that was too much to broach in the beginning. Instead, I stuck to the quotidian: updates on the Fund's various projects, even the weather, anything to distract. He accepted this news, as he did all of my chatter, with equanimity.

Some days later, I revealed I would no longer be going to horse auctions. Seeing so much suffering only increased my own and I could not endure more. Besides, what was the point? For every horse I rescued, twenty or fifty or a hundred would take its place.

More than a week passed before I revealed the awful thing I had withheld from him: Sparkplug was dead. The strapping little burro, the one I thought might even outlast me, was gone forever.

There was something else I told Gamal: Sparkplug's death had me second-guessing my involvement with animals. After all, if I couldn't protect one young burro, what hope did I have of being able to help any others? My belief that things had finally fallen into place, that I was making a contribution, had been delusion, fantasy.

My face flushed as I remembered my temerity, my egregious over-stepping, in giving Cleveland (Cleveland!) my advice on how to run his adoption program. Who was I to tell Cleveland anything? He probably had a good laugh with Marian after I left our meeting in New York, then tossed my adoption suggestions into the trash along with the day's junk mail. It was a wonder he didn't fire me on the spot. Perhaps, I told Gamal, I should save him the trouble and submit my resignation.

I assured Gamal, though, that the one thing, the only thing, about which I was not deluded was the value of our relationship. Unlike friends or family, people who, upon hearing the news about Spark-plug, invariably delivered platitudes like "You can't blame yourself" or "You did all you could," Gamal consoled simply by being with me, fully present in a way in which no emotions were encouraged or discouraged.

After Sparkplug's death, I lay low. I didn't call Cleveland to check in as I usually did, nor did he get in touch with me. For my part, I needed time to get some clarity on where my life was headed. For Cleveland's part, he was probably just busy with other things. One of his many strengths was that he did not allow setbacks to stop his plans. He focused on the big picture, the greater good. That was something I aspired to, but had not mastered.

In the middle of my crisis in confidence, a small miracle arrived in the mail. Several months earlier, I had submitted an article to the horse magazine *Equus*. It was based on the horse auctions I had attended and concerned the shocking number of horses that were being sold for slaughter across the United States. The ubiquitous meat trade was not only threatening the very existence of serviceable, trail-riding, companion horses, but the associated cruelty was unjustifiable. I highlighted the mare and foal I purchased at a large auction in Front Royal, Virginia, who I named Royal Virginia and Amazing Grace. Their story was even more dramatic than most of the horses I bought, and made the best example. In order to show the magazine's readers how they might experience the rewards of rescue and rehabilitation, I included graphic photos of the mother and daughter that I took at the auction itself, then documented their progress from living skeletons to plump, happy horses. I listed the associated expenses, and suggested that the magazine's readers might want to buy one or two themselves, to save an animal from a cruel fate.

With everything that was going on, and with the amount of time that had elapsed since I submitted the piece, I had forgotten about it. Now, I opened the envelope with little enthusiasm, assuming it would be a rejection. But it wasn't: it was an offer to publish, under the title "The Horses Nobody Wants." That I would be paid was just icing on the cake.

That acceptance letter didn't change everything for me. I still mourned Sparkplug's passing. I still mourned the other horses at auctions that were not as lucky as those I had rescued. But it was a reminder that, little by little, progress was being made. And I was beginning to see that my contribution to helping animals, however small, had to do with writing and photography—even if my style, my ability, or my particular concerns did not mirror Cleveland's.

Eventually, Cleveland made the first move and called me. I braced myself, assuming either that he was going to fire me or that I would beat him to it and quit. In the moment, I didn't know which was worse. But instead, he started off by informing me that a load of forty burros would soon be heading my way (forty being the number of burros the trailer could hold).

Just as when he sent Sparkplug to appear on TV, he attached no great significance to what he was announcing now. It was simply the next logical step in his ever-fluid plan: there were too many burros on the ranch, and not enough homes in the immediate area. I, apparently, was the one with the most experience to handle the assignment. Given my track record—one burro who did not survive—it occurred to me that Cleveland must really have been desperate. But he went on in his usual offhand way about how it would be up to me to find a site large enough to serve as an adoption center; and then to find homes for the forty animals. When that was accomplished, he would send forty more.

Despite the overwhelming nature of what he was saying, I knew this assignment was a turning point, a defining moment when I could either flee or, as Gamal might have recommended, dive right in. The old horse would never steer me wrong, and surely even little Spark-plug would, in his way, have urged me to help his brethren.

For a moment, I hesitated.

But after I caught my breath, I realized that if I'd learned nothing else from Gamal, from the many characters in his past, and even from the diving horse act itself, it was the value of taking risks to achieve what was thought to be unachievable, even unthinkable.

Although my mind was racing at the enormity of the assignment, I told Cleveland I would get started.

The first forty burros did indeed arrive, but not to Wendy's place. The pasture she rented adjacent to her three-acre farm was not large enough to accommodate them, nor did she have sufficient indoor facilities. Cleveland assigned me the unenviable task of informing her that in order to consolidate operations, Gamal and a few others— Hot Britches, Shiloh, and Prince Nelson—would be moving out. She wasn't happy about it, but came to accept that the project had grown beyond her farm's capacity.

The next couple of years were spent welcoming load after load of burros, hundreds in all. There was an enormous response to the press coverage, and having an adopted burro became a must-have on farms everywhere. R-D-R Farm, just across the river in New Jersey and owned by Rolf and Dale Bauersachs, was well equipped to handle a large influx of animals. Their huge indoor riding ring served as a staging area, while the farm's extensive pastures, which included small barns and run-in sheds, were fenced in such a way as to make them perfect for separating males from females while ensuring shelter for all.

An unexpected bonus was George Millar, owner of a neighboring horse farm, who, decades earlier, had been a rodeo rider. Rolf knew George's background and called him to ask if he'd help herd the burros. Contrary to what I expected, this middle-aged cowboy with mischievous blue eyes was not born and raised out west, but back east in northern New Jersey. Yet George turned out to be just the man for the job. His rodeo experience, his roping skills, as well as his knowledge of Border Collie training, was invaluable. With nothing but a whistle here, and a hand signal there, he and his dog, Missy, acted as a team and were able to persuade the burros to do just about anything. I, in turn, persuaded George to help transport the animals to their adoptive homes, in between his stunt work for the film *Witness*.

For months straight in the beginning, then off and on for years, we would cruise along in his pickup truck, delivering burros all over the East Coast. Unbeknownst to him, I wrote the words "We Haul Ass" in the dust on the back of his trailer. People in passing cars would smile and wave to a puzzled George, who couldn't understand why everyone was suddenly so friendly. To pass the time on longer hauls, he'd sometimes challenge me to a competition of naming breeds of horses or sheep or goats. I'd never win, of course, but I learned a lot. In passing, he'd impart nuggets of wisdom like "Water is the best medicine" or would describe the relative nutritional value of a season's first, second, or third cutting of hay. As if it was his personal theme song, he'd crank up the radio and slap the steering wheel with his callused palms whenever he heard Waylon Jennings belt out "I May

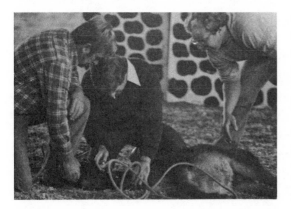

George Millar, left, and Rolf Bauersachs, right, at R-D-R Farm assist veterinarian Dr. Pete Bousum with an incoming burro. While the majority of the animals arrived in good health, many were afflicted with parasites and malnutrition. 1983.

Be Used (But Baby I Ain't Used Up)." He seemed to know every waitress in every two-bit luncheonette within fifty miles—or would after we'd stop in for a bite; and he could fix just about anything with a penknife and baling wire. It is not an exaggeration to say that the project would not have been nearly as successful, or as fun, without George's help.

The first load of burros arrived on a memorable date: October 6, 1981. It was the same day Egyptian president Anwar Sadat was assassinated, and coverage of that event threatened to eclipse a large press conference I had scheduled a few days later at the farm. Instead, in some ways it almost helped. The media seemed to have decided that the public needed relief from the turmoil in the Middle East, and representatives from every network and newspaper within a hundred-mile radius converged on the Bauersachses' farm to cover the refugees from the Grand Canyon. Even Cleveland seemed impressed with my efforts.

The night the burros arrived—invariably they showed up in the middle of the night—one grizzled veteran, with a bite-sized piece missing from the tip of one of his ears and a crescent-shaped scar on his nose, stepped out of the herd, ambled up to me, and stared into my eyes. By now I knew what that meant: he was mine. After all, with Hot Britches, Shiloh, and Prince Nelson going to Texas, I reasoned that Gamal needed a companion at R-D-R. For an animal whose only contact with humans had been during his rescue from the Grand Canyon, the ancient burro was immediately, and strangely, affectionate and friendly—as if he had always been someone's pet. I named him Cairo, after the city dominating the news. The veterinarian estimated he was somewhere north of thirty years old. His overall condition was poor, as was the case with many of the burros. Cairo's teeth were either broken off at the gum line, or rotted. His hooves were badly in need of trimming, and he was stick thin. Even without dodging the Park Service's bullets, Cairo's health was a reminder that life at the bottom of the Grand Canyon was a harsh existence and was yet another reason to rescue the animals.

Finding homes for the burros amounted to a tough crash course in animal adoption. When I suggested in my report to Cleveland how the adoption program should be operated, it was based on logic and limited experience. But later, I became convinced that the section on how to screen potential adopters, or the bizarre things people might do or say, was something that required extensive, firsthand experience. For as much as I learned about burros, I learned even more about human behavior, and not all of it was savory.

There was a run on the younger animals, as if they would stay cute and babylike forever. Some people thought nothing of asking to adopt a nursing foal—without its mother. Needless to say, they were turned down. Several people tried slipping me a crisp hundred-dollar bill to get first pick. Others were insistent on a particular color, or derided the appearance of some animals with less-than-perfect conformation. They, seemingly, had forgotten the purpose of the project: saving lives. One man stole a burro under cover of night. An adopter, someone I knew to be financially secure, wrote a bad check for an adoption on which I was never able to collect. Sometimes I worried that the burros had become like those other fads of the era, Pet Rocks and Rubik's Cubes. I worked diligently to find the best homes with the best people. Inevitably, I made rookie mistakes; but never, ever, did I knowingly place an animal in an unfit home.

Overall, my interactions with adopters exposed me to people with

At one of the Fund's satellite adoption centers in the Blue Ridge Mountains of Virginia, 1986. A Grand Canyon burro who I named Calvin was immediately friendly. Many so-called wild burros are affectionate, even to strangers, dispelling the notion that they are good only as pack animals.

big hearts who would stop at nothing to make sure their new charges were living a life of luxury. There were children who were to grow up with a burro as a pet, the way others might have a cat or dog. There were families whose humane endeavors expanded once they realized the value and benefits of rescue. And the deep, lifelong friendships I developed with some of the adoption center coordinators made me feel less alone in my work.

It took barely a month before the original forty burros were adopted. Cleveland sent forty more, then another forty. Eventually dozens upon dozens of wild mustangs joined them. Soon, my local area was saturated. Since people across the country had volunteered their farms as satellite adoption centers, Cleveland began sending me to prescreen the people and their facilities; and when the animals arrived on these far-flung farms, I would return to direct the publicity and show the farm owners the ropes of the adoption process. Through the Fund's efforts, over six thousand burros and four thousand mustangs, plus hundreds of goats and pigs, were saved from certain death on public lands, and then placed into adoptive homes.

Despite my frequent work-related absences, I was a regular presence at R-D-R Farm. While the publicity about the burros and Gamal had died down, that didn't mean the adventures were over. For one thing, Gamal had a new friend—Cairo. It was only fitting that the two mature gentlemen, both of whom had led long and colorful lives, should buddy up together. As I had hoped when I was given permission to keep Cairo, the two old equine cousins bonded. I often found them standing side by side in an enormous field—something they did by choice.

For several years in a row, Cairo made local appearances in a role he was born to play—the burro in the manger at live nativity scenes at Christmastime. Gamal was more of an action character. Once, when a reporter came to the farm to do a follow-up story, Gamal broke loose from a farmhand who was bringing him outside. Out of the corner of my eye, I noticed a dark shape dart by while the reporter was interviewing me. It was Gamal. He was, after all, used to being

Old grizzled veteran of the Grand Canyon, Cairo, took a liking to Wooly Bully, right, a burro from Death Valley that was decades younger, stronger, and larger. It was not uncommon for burros to buddy up with others, as they are, after all, herd animals. A solitary burro is a sad burro.

the center of attention and perhaps was jealous that the focus at that moment was not on him. While the reporter chatted on, the photographer snapped away at the admittedly impressive Gamal, his mane flowing in the wind. Neither reporter nor photographer had any idea he was out of control, and it was all I could do to keep my composure. Gamal's dash for freedom was short-lived, though, and he was corralled within minutes. With no one the wiser, the shot of him on the run wound up in the accompanying newspaper article.

But Gamal and Cairo's biggest adventure took place together, in New York City, on the Feast Day of St. Francis of Assisi. An acquaintance who was organizing the first Blessing of the Animals at the Cathedral of St. John the Divine asked me if the pair might like to participate. With Cairo's nativity scene experience, and Gamal being a seasoned showman, I thought the gig was made to order.

The ceremony was meant to encourage respect for all life-forms, including the earth itself. The Paul Winter Consort was scheduled to perform its *Missa Gaia* (Earth Mass), the cathedral would be overflowing with plants and flowers, and a silent procession of animals, ranging in size from a giant African elephant to a bowl of algae, would make their way up the aisle to the nave, where they would be blessed by the dean of the cathedral. Those in the congregation were encouraged to bring their well-behaved pets, anything from cats and dogs, to hamsters and parakeets, to rabbits and goldfish. After the service, those animals, too, could be blessed—outside in the garden. This was a solemn yet celebratory affair, one marked, above all, by dignity.

Gamal was plump, shiny, and fit, well into his
thirties. He enjoyed galloping in a pasture—
often in competition with King, my retired
racing Greyhound. 1987.

Wendy agreed to transport Gamal and Cairo and, as in the old
days, we headed off together. We had instructions to maneuver the
trailer and truck into a side lot of the cathedral, which doubled as
a stone yard. Construction on the Gothic-style structure, one of the
world's largest, had been ongoing for nearly a hundred years and
wasn't expected to be completed in any of our lifetimes.

In a scene that could have been straight out of the Middle Ages,
huge blocks of granite and half-finished gargoyles were stacked in
piles awaiting the chisels of expert stone masons, many Italian-
trained. As I looked up, the spires of the cathedral seemed to reach
the heavens and I could only imagine the awe such a sight would have
engendered in illiterate medieval peasants. It was doing something
similar to me.

The side yard was also where the processional animals would be
unloaded and festooned with garlands of flowers, while the animals'
handlers would be issued a white robe. Wendy and I slipped into
our vestments and marveled at the scene. It isn't often that you have
a chance to get up close and personal with such a wide variety of

creatures. The camel (or was it a dromedary?) reminded me of Hot Britches the llama, and I wondered briefly how he was doing at the ranch in Texas. Especially impressive was an Irish Wolfhound, who, I was told, was *Guinness*-certified as the tallest dog ever measured. All was going smoothly and I looked forward to leading Gamal to the cathedral's front entrance on Amsterdam Avenue, then up the granite steps and through the cathedral's massive bronze doors. Meanwhile, photographers from news outlets around the world were already gathered on an elevated platform, ready to snap photos of Gamal, Cairo, and the others, to give the event the coverage it deserved.

Gamal had no problem with the algae or the snake, the emu or even the eagle. But he drew the line at the elephant. Just as at the Battle of Heraclea in ancient Greece, when King Pyrrhus unleashed his twenty elephants and overcame thousands of startled Roman horses, Gamal panicked at the sight of the enormous pachyderm, pulled away from my tenuous grip, and ran wild around the grounds of the cathedral. The gate leading to 113th Street was open, and there was no chance of closing it in time. If he escaped the side yard, he would face city traffic and it would pretty much be over for Gamal—and for me, too. Not only would I be devastated, but there would be no explaining it to Cleveland.

Gamal was truly agitated, and what moments earlier seemed like a festive, even spiritual event was now a frightening scene of potential horror. The blocks of granite, I realized, were not so much stacked as strewn. Gamal could easily break a leg if he tripped over them. And then there were the other people and animals, milling around in their costumes and holding their respective creatures. Few were aware of the potential disaster. It didn't take much imagination for me to realize that they could be trampled by the out-of-control diving horse. And if the other animals sensed danger, the anxiety could become contagious.

In the end, old Cairo saved the day. He saw immediately what was happening to his buddy, and knew what to do about it. In an instant he let loose with the loudest bray I had ever heard. Gamal was instantly affected. The former diving horse stopped "on a dime," as Bill Ditty once said of him. Wendy ran with the willing burro to Gamal, grabbed his lead rope, and as if it was all in a day's work, led the two back into her trailer. An on-site veterinarian checked on Gamal and pronounced him scared, but fine—nothing that couldn't be cured by a long drink of water, and a cool-down walk—that is, once the dreaded elephant left the yard.

But one problem remained—the two noticeable gaps in the carefully planned procession, one for a horse and another for a burro. As it happened, someone handed me a spare horse (much like Noah's Ark, there were two of almost everything), which I led reluctantly into the cathedral. Someone else followed us with a spare burro.

Meanwhile, Wendy, Gamal, and Cairo sat out the celebration in the trailer, having already been more blessed than anyone could imagine.

Chapter Fourteen

Y ou want a job?" the old guy asked.

He barely looked up as he coiled a hose and headed back to a trailer. What I had just said to him must have prompted his offer, although angling for a job was the last thing on my mind.

I was in Florida again—staying with my parents for a brief winter escape. My visit coincided with the annual Florida State Fair held in Tampa, and my mother, ever the innocent, asked if I'd take her. My father had no interest in such outings and preferred, always, to stay home with a book. I agreed, partly out of obligation, and partly because it seemed like a kitschy adventure might be just the ticket, maybe even similar to the time she and I visited the Steel Pier.

We strolled the midway, shoulder to shoulder with leathery Floridians, and sweaty, sunburned tourists. Every type of agricultural exhibit and homegrown food imaginable was on display: enterprising kids showed off immaculately manicured 4-H animals that would later be sold; and rosy-cheeked women proffered equally rosy strawberry pie. There were the "Hurry, hurry, hurry. Step right up" games of chance; and gravity-defying thrill rides accompanied by music so loud and disorienting that it could bring on vertigo even before you bought a ticket. As for food, there were the usual corn dogs and funnel cakes. Or you could go for more regional fare like boiled peanuts, deep-fried frog legs, or alligator bites ("Tastes just like chicken"). To top it off, perhaps indulge in a swirl of ephemeral cotton candy that vanished into nothingness with each tap of the tongue.

Derivative diving horse acts plagued Doc Carver almost from the moment he introduced his spectacle, leading him to copyright the term "diving horses." Here, in 1982, a diving mule performs at the Florida State Fair in Tampa.

Ultimately, though, the midway was too middle America for my taste. My interest lay elsewhere. I had a new camera and was in my Diane Arbus phase. Here, I thought, would be the perfect place to capture candid shots of so-called circus freaks. I dragged my mother behind the tents to an area clearly marked "Employees Only."

But instead of doing what I came to realize was making fun of people, I encountered scenes of unexpected tenderness and unlikely beauty: a man carefully, kindly, hosing down an unchained, compliant elephant; a carnival worker sleeping on a tattered lounge chair beneath a giant canvas banner featuring a scantily clad woman. I had to admit, this was a more touching experience than I anticipated. The "Employees Only" sign was right: we didn't belong in their world. Humbled, I led my mother back out front.

It was there, in the mainstream and in broad daylight, that I saw something truly odd. Straight ahead was a sign: "Jonny Rivers' Diving Mules." Next to it, a tank and a ramp with a platform on top. Could it be?

In a scene eerily reminiscent of the Steel Pier, there were indeed diving mules, but also diving dogs, and even a diving monkey clinging to the collar of one of the dogs. It was a free-for-all, as one animal after another took flying leaps, more like exuberant cannonballs than graceful swan dives, into the tank.

Granted, the platform from which they jumped was lower, maybe thirty feet instead of forty. And the variety of animals lent a comical note to the sight (but not that comical: I worried, in particular, about the monkey, so small and fragile). But what was not at all reminiscent of Carver's diving horse act was any sense of anticipation or awe. It was akin to getting nutrition via a feeding tube, rather than by eating real food.

Nonetheless, I went over to the men working the act. After all, we had something in common, even if we were at opposite ends of the diving horse spectrum. Without making any small talk, I started right in by telling them I had Gamal, the last of Carver's Steel Pier diving horses.

And that's when it happened. The older of the two men offered me a job. He didn't ask me how I acquired the horses, or why; but he didn't need to. My credentials were superb: I possessed the equivalent of an Ivy League–educated horse, veritable diving horse royalty.

He needed help with the act, he said, and asked if I was available. Not for diving, he stressed (although I had a feeling it wouldn't have taken much to persuade him); but for help with caring for the animals. I glanced over at a groom toweling down the tail-wagging dog and the monkey with nervous, jittery eyes. The placid, plump mule was in a portable pen, air drying in the warm Florida sun.

Not for a full second, but perhaps a millisecond, I considered how freeing it might be to run away with the circus (or the equivalent), to join a community of carnies who had their own code of honor, their own secrets, their own world. I had always considered myself an outsider. With them, I surely would have been an outsider among outsiders. But the millisecond passed as quickly as it arose. I begged off politely and, without revealing who I worked for, told him I already had a job. I would have been glad to chat about how long he had been involved in training animals, if he knew the Dittys, or where he learned his unusual trade. But while he, too, was polite, he went back to work once he found out I was unavailable. After all, as I now knew, he was short-handed.

The diving mule act had an unexpected consequence: it reawakened my interest in the act's history. As I left the fair that day, I wondered if Doc Carver's troupe had ever played the venue. I found out later that it had, numerous times. In fact, from what I gathered, they were on the road almost continuously, heading south in the winter, north in the summer, on both coasts, in Canada and Mexico, and abroad. Doc's horses, like the diving animals that day in Tampa, were never featured acts in a circus or carnival. They struck out on their own—sometimes sharing a venue such as a state fair or rodeo, sometimes as the sole attraction.

Before the internet, uncovering the history of people from the purposely secretive world of circuses and carnivals was nearly impossible. The stories they sold to an unsuspecting public about their individual backgrounds, or their familial relationships, were wild, fantastic, and, in their way, charmingly deceptive. In Doc's case, the stories were not so much lies as whoppers—exaggerations to bolster the appeal of the act.

Doc, like his contemporary P. T. Barnum, was not only a great publicist, but was also possessed of what was known as a silver tongue. But unlike Barnum, Doc was also a great performer. One true part of Doc's overall narrative was that he was a world champion exhibition shooter. But his innate gift was honed to perfection not under the mentorship of Indians (as he often claimed), but through hours of solitary practice.

Playing fast and loose with names was practically a pastime for Doc, such as changing his favorite horse's name from Babe to the more dramatic Duchess of Lightning. But he didn't stop with horses. There were also the various ways he billed himself in the early days—Evil Spirit Carver, Wizard Carver, Spirit Gun of the West.

Diving horses became a thriving business, but also something of a mixed blessing. Copycat acts sprang up across the country,

By the early 1900s, Doc Carver, every inch the prosperous businessman, found both fame and fortune with his diving horse empire.

along with criticism from those who were concerned about the act's safety.

To fend off imitators of his act, Doc had the term "diving horses" copyrighted.

To counteract claims of inhumane treatment, Doc's poster reassured patrons that the horses were "Trained with Sugar and Kindness. Treated as Companions and Friends." Soon, there were five diving horses: Powderface, Cupid, Little Powderface, the Clown Horse, and Silver King. The Clown Horse was also touted as being able to kiss "like a human being."

The years following Doc's death weren't always good ones, but they were busy ones for the diving horses and those involved with them. Lorena trained both horses and riders, scouted for new human and equine talent, and took the act on the road. Sometimes, that road led abroad, most notably as far as Egypt.

Meanwhile, Sonora continued to dive while Al handled the act at the Steel Pier from 1929 until they retired in 1942 and moved to New Orleans. The diving horses continued with Louis Perillo handling the horses with his wife, Betty, one of the riders. But in 1944, Louis was drafted into the army. With Louis gone, one of the horses,

Lorena Carver, known also as Lorena Lawrence, Lorena Lorenz, and Lorena Floyd, was probably the first girl rider of the diving horses in 1906. Despite traveling around the world with the diving horses, she longed for a career that never materialized: as a Hollywood actress. With Red Lips, circa 1925.

John the Baptist 2nd, was so distraught he refused to dive, and would barely eat. Betty Perillo petitioned the army to give Private Perillo a special ten-day leave to see the horse. Incredibly, it was granted. John immediately perked up and performed beautifully—until Louis left again. There was nothing to be done but to put John's career on hold until Louis Perillo returned for good.

In 1946, a hurricane destroyed the horses' diving ramp and platform. The spotlight was extinguished, and the act might have become just another quaint memory of a bygone era but for the pier's new owner, George Hamid Sr. Hamid, a Lebanese immigrant, was a former tumbler with Buffalo Bill's show. Show business was in his blood, and Senior knew that nothing drew a bigger crowd than the diving horses. He rebuilt the tower, and in 1953 brought them back.

Sixty-seven-year-old Lorena was also brought back, but this time only to manage the show, not as the owner of the act or the horses. After traveling the world with the horses, she had returned to America down on her luck. Becoming a hired hand again must have been a tough pill to swallow, but a job was a job.

Still, Lorena rose to the challenge. She fashioned herself the grand doyenne of the pier, even though her empire was reduced to an eight-foot-by-six-foot combination office and storage room, one that she shared with sequined bathing suits for the diving girls, and tubs of carrots and sugar cubes for the horses. Between performances, and always with her black Miniature Poodle, Babette, close by, she played hand after hand of solitaire.

But by 1973, her imperial facade was wearing thin. If Lorena learned nothing else from her many decades in show business, it was how to read a crowd; and by 1973 the crowd had also thinned. Fifty onlookers at the end of the windswept pier would have been considered a lot. It was time to hand out the last of the carrots and sugar to horses who came to expect the reward from their mistress. It could not have been a coincidence that 1973 was also the year that George Hamid Jr. sold the pier to the three local businessmen.

Surely it was a wrenching moment when Lorena said her final farewell to the last of the Carver diving horses whom she had worked with side by side, some for decades—Emir (my Gamal), the "real" Gamal, and Powderface.

Lorena, the former "Girl in Red. The Bravest Girl in the World," had to draw on that bravery when, at age eighty-seven, she moved to Miami. She knew the town well from her touring days, when the diving horses had a regular engagement at Aquafair, another Hamid-owned amusement park similar to the Steel Pier, but with a distinctly Floridian twist—alligator wrestling.

Just five years after Lorena left the pier, Terrie McDevitt became the last rider on the last horse for the last performance, on Monday, September 4, 1978. In a magazine interview, she brought up Shiloh's name and allayed my concerns once and for all about whether the mare had ever been a diving horse. She reminisced about that last night on the Steel Pier. Shiloh was supposed to have been used, but McDevitt made a last-minute change. What McDevitt may not have known is that by substituting an original Carver horse, Powderface, for Shiloh, the act had come full circle.

McDevitt was quoted as saying, "I remember my last dive. Everybody knew by then the act was over for good. We were out here drinking champagne, squirting it all over ourselves and the horses. Powderface had done the last two dives and I was supposed to ride Shiloh. But I wanted Powderface for the last dive.

"He didn't want to do it. It was just bitter cold out and the water in the tank must have been under 50 degrees. There was hardly any audience, just workers from the pier. All I could think about was the hot shower when it was over, the little electric heater down in my dressing room.

"Powder didn't want to go. He knew it wasn't his turn. But I made him go. We went and it was perfect. A perfect dive."

A perfect dive, just the kind of professionalism Doc would have respected.

Chapter Fifteen

The now-exemplary ranch inevitably had growing pains. The Texan, the man who delivered Sparkplug to me four years prior, and who ran the ranch, finally went too far.

What I had thought of as his little weakness—exaggerating his contributions—was actually something worse. His tall tales had grown too tall, tall to the point of challenging Cleveland's authority. Being some 1,500 miles from New York, calling the shots locally, and occupying a house on the property led someone who already had a questionable relationship with the truth to feel like the animal sanctuary was his idea, his property, his domain. And for a time, it seemed like it was—until 1984, when Cleveland took action and showed him and his family the door.

While his exit solved one problem, it created another. The ranch could not function without someone in charge. For one thing, it was full of animals—mostly burros, but also mustangs and goats and pigs and assorted other creatures—and they needed constant, uninterrupted care. A few ranch hands, men Cleveland thought were loyal to him, took over the day-to-day feeding operations, but Cleveland knew another slot needed to be filled—by someone from home base who did not view animals as livestock (no matter how tenderly treated); and who understood and embraced the Fund's overarching philosophy. Until a permanent replacement was found, someone resembling that description needed to be put in place immediately.

Cleveland's first choice as interim director was one of his two current heirs apparent. Unbeknownst to the other, both men had been led to believe they were being groomed to take over Cleveland's position one day. Dangling the "someday all of this will be yours" carrot in front of talented, enterprising young men (never women, to my knowledge) was a common practice of Cleveland's. Even the Texan was in the running at one point. One of the current hopefuls, a sincere, blue-collar Jersey guy, was already employed full-time else-where, but was attending college at night with a major in zoology. He was looking forward to an early retirement from his current job, after which he would devote his life to his real passion: animal protection. The other heir, already a Fund employee, was brilliant, witty, and Ivy League–educated—a southern gentleman who lobbied as effectively in Washington as any corporate suit. He was the one tapped for Texas.

He made it clear in advance that he could only fill in at the ranch for a week or two, no more. With a wife and children back in D.C., he could not spend too much time away from home. At least that's what I was told. Once again, whether out of confidence or despera-tion, Cleveland's gaze fell on me to step in temporarily.

I can't say I ever grew accustomed to Cleveland's surprise assign-ments, but I was no longer as shocked by them as I had been. Of course my mind raced even as he was outlining his plans for me. While I was gone, who would take care of my animals—Stockbridge, my dog, and half a dozen cats? What about my house? I had a pretty good idea that my parents would agree to move in and manage what they thought of as their surrogate grandchildren. But most concern-ing to me was Gamal. Of course he would be fed and watered and turned out; but would he miss me? Pine for me? Even though I hadn't left yet, I already missed him. But, I reminded myself, it wasn't for-ever. Surely, I hoped, my stay would not exceed a week or two, tops.

For several reasons, I couldn't say that I looked forward to the assignment. My narrow view of America closely paralleled Saul Stein-berg's *New Yorker* magazine cover. New York City and select East Coast locales, combined with a few locations on the West Coast, were, to my way of thinking, the only ones of interest, or even value, in the country.

Making matters worse was the ranch's setting, rural Texas. Even though I had never been to Texas, it didn't stop me from putting the state on my must-never-see list, especially during the hottest time of the year. There was the whole "bigger is better" part of that oxymoron, "Texas culture" (hair, plates of food, boobs). It was the state, after all, where breast implants were invented. And, as a vegetarian, I was repulsed by their love of barbecue and meat in general. Finally, that other pesky little detail: Kennedy's assassination in Dallas. And, insult to injury, the subsequent reign of LBJ. Was I the only one, however wrongly, who held it against the entire state?

But the main thing dampening my enthusiasm was a lack of confidence: I doubted my ability to handle the assignment. As soon as Cleveland brought it up, the weight of being responsible for hundreds upon hundreds of animals hung heavy.

Reluctance and resignation morphed into abject terror during my conversation with the heir apparent the day he left the ranch, and the day before I arrived.

"Do you have a gun," he asked.

It would not have been unlike him to tease me, so I played along.

"Of course not," I answered with the kind of laugh that showed I was in on the joke. The subtext, of course, was that my sort of people, his sort of people, didn't have guns. We eschewed guns. But my laughter rang a little hollow when I realized he wasn't laughing.

"Well, you might want to think about getting one. There are some strange things going on down here."

He proceeded to fill me in on certain details that Cleveland had neglected to mention. Details like the fact that although the Texan had been dismissed, he was still in the area. In fact, he was living only a few miles from the ranch. Or that on most nights, portions of the wire fencing along the ranch's borders were cut, and considerable energy would be spent every morning rounding up any animals at large, escorting them back to safety, and patching the wire. He said it was not unusual to hear gunshots in the middle of the night, either, although he never discovered the origin. And, he concluded, he wasn't entirely sure the remaining ranch hands were quite as loyal as Cleveland thought they were.

The heir apparent's report reminded me that along with exaggerating, another of the Texan's little weaknesses was carrying a gun, like the huge .357 Magnum he brought north when delivering Spark-plug. He moonlighted, after all, as a local deputy sheriff—something that, when I first heard about it, sounded quaint, even comical, in a Barney Fife sort of way. Now it wasn't quite so amusing. And then I remembered something else: the ranch's very location was at the recommendation of the Texan. Somehow, back in 1979 and '80, when Cleveland was deciding where to buy land on which to put the res-cued burros and horses, the Texan was able to convince him that his part of the world, northeastern Texas, was heaven on earth. In fact, the enormous temperature fluctuations, from sweltering in the summer to freezing in the winter, made it more challenging for both animals and people than would a more temperate climate. But being on his home turf, not climate, was at the forefront of the Texan's mind. As if that wasn't enough, the heir apparent and I were almost finished with our conversation when he added, "Oh, one last thing. Be careful of Nim. He's a lot stronger than he looks."

Nim! I had forgotten about him entirely. Sadly, that could be said to be the story of his life.

Nim, also known as Nim Chimpsky, was a world-famous chim-panzee born in a research laboratory. His name was a twist on the name Noam Chomsky, an eminent linguist. At just a few days of age, Nim was pried from the protective clutches of his mother, as were her ten previous infants. Nim was to be raised as a human as part of an experiment to determine how language develops, and it would be years before he saw another chimpanzee again.

Project Nim, as the study was called, was meant to validate an earlier chimpanzee study called the Washoe Project, named for Washoe, a female chimpanzee. She, like Nim, was also raised as a human. Since chimpanzees are physiologically incapable of mak-ing the same vocal sounds as humans, both animals were taught to communicate via American Sign Language. Washoe learned over 350 signs, and, without prompting, even taught some signs to her son.

B. F. Skinner, in his book *Verbal Behavior,* cited the Washoe Project as supporting the theory that nonhuman animals can indeed learn language, even though it is not an innate skill. Dr. Skinner's book was criticized by Dr. Chomsky, which in turn raised the ire of Columbia psychology professor Herbert Terrace, a former student of Skinner's. Terrace's graduate studies had, after all, involved extensive work with pigeons, and perhaps because of all that time observing birds, he had a heightened sense of pecking order. To his way of thinking, his mentor, Skinner, and not Chomsky, had to be right. And so began a case of scholarly one-upmanship that, for all intents and purposes, destroyed Nim's life.

Both the project, and Nim, were doomed from the start. Nim spent the first months of his life with a human family who, while affectionate and caring toward the infant chimp, knew only the most basic signs themselves and so were in little position to teach him anything. When Nim was moved to a Columbia-owned facility, his schooling was conducted in a barren eight-foot-by-eight-foot room with one graduate student acting as teacher, while other graduate students took notes behind a one-way mirror—hardly an ideal environment for learning, or for raising any living being. There was a revolving door of students, with many having different ideas about how Nim should be taught, cared for, and disciplined. Finally, there was no one person in his life to provide emotional support.

Four years later, and to the dismay of many of the graduate students, Terrace declared abruptly that the days of mincing words with a chimpanzee were over. Chomsky was right, he pronounced, and Project Nim was over. That meant Nim himself was over, too. That Terrace's own study was flawed seemed never to have occurred to the professor. In the end, it was a miracle that Nim learned as much as he did—two hundred signs.

After axing the project, Terrace returned Nim to the concrete confines of the place where he was born, the Institute for Primate Studies at the University of Oklahoma. Except for his first few days of life, Nim had never seen other chimpanzees, much less lived in a cage. By now, he was neither man nor beast, making this new chapter of his life all the more inhumane.

One year into his brutal confinement in Oklahoma, Terrace paid Nim a visit, trailed closely by a videographer to capture the momentous occasion. Nim had a strong reaction to the man he had known his whole life, and perhaps even thought of as family. He went from being in a stupor to jumping up and down, signing wildly, and trying to hug Terrace through the bars of his cage. Based on this desperate display, one might have expected the scientist to experience remorse of conscience and work out an arrangement to relocate Nim to a more caring environment. Instead, Terrace left without looking back and never visited Nim again.

After the visit, the chimpanzee descended into a deep depression. From Oklahoma, he was sent to an NYU-operated medical research laboratory in New York State where he was heavily sedated and used for drug testing. It is unlikely he would have survived without the Fund's intervention.

By then, word had spread about Nim's fate and animal defenders were up in arms. Cleveland took the lead and persuaded Nim's legal owner, Dr. William Lemmon, director of the Oklahoma center, to bring Nim back as a way to avoid the mounting criticism of the animal's treatment. Once Lemmon agreed, Cleveland went a step further and persuaded him to sell Nim to the Fund so the animal could live out his days at the ranch. Cleveland promised to build a first-class enclosure for Nim and, in a kind of arranged marriage, asked that a female chimpanzee beyond breeding age be provided as a companion. Eventually Lemmon agreed to that, too, and even traveled to the ranch to give suggestions on how to design an ideal compound for Nim and Sally, the chimpanzee chosen to become his life partner. In 1982, nine-year-old Nim and his old lady, thirty-two-year-old Sally, moved into their new home at the ranch.

The addition of chimpanzees to the roster of ranch residents nearly put me over the top, and, for the first time, I called Cleveland to express my doubts about whether I was really the right person for the job. He assured me I was, and that I would not be responsible for feeding the chimpanzees or cleaning their enclosure, only for overseeing the whole ranch operation. I know this was meant to calm me, but, really, what could he say? The heir apparent had already left and I was to fly to Texas the next morning.

A woman seated on one side of me on the airplane was affable enough, but as the trip wore on, and as she drank more, she also became more talkative. She was a native Texan, she said between slugs; but changing planes in Dallas was just the beginning of her journey, not the end. She was a registered nurse, heading to Manaus, Brazil, deep in the Amazonian rainforest, to care for patients with tuberculosis. My slight familiarity with Manaus was from the Werner Herzog film *Fitzcarraldo*. So I told her what I learned from the movie: Manaus was a city built on rubber fortunes and the improbable site of an opera house.

Her eyes widened. "Herzog?" she asked.

For one optimistic moment, I thought we might launch into a discussion of German filmmakers.

Instead, I realized too late that she had no idea who I was referencing.

Ditching Herzog altogether, she asked where I was going in Texas. When I told her it was a small town roughly halfway between Dallas and Shreveport, Louisiana, she quipped, "Ah, Shreveport. The syphilis capital of America." Did she know this from her capacity as a nurse, or personal experience? (I didn't ask.)

One of her jokes: "Question: How do you know when a Texan is lying? Answer: When his lips are moving."

She told me that every lake in Texas was man-made. (Could that possibly be true?) She said Texans love catfish, nearly all of it farmed. "But don't eat it," she warned. "It's toxic." (I had no interest in eating catfish, or any other fish.) She claimed the fetid hatchery ponds, combined with the antibiotics they feed the fish, created, as she put it, "monsters."

As she dozed off, she mumbled, "I'd rather be in the jungle than in Texas." And this was when the jungle was the jungle, not the rainforest.

.   .   .

When I pulled in to the ranch, I expected to see burros, horses, maybe even some herding dogs, looking to make themselves useful. Instead, I was confronted by the bizarre sight of three giant red piles, the tallest being some fifteen feet high. Before I even had a chance to wonder what they were, I was confronted by something that, to me, was equally surprising: the business card of the ranch's head honcho. As we introduced ourselves to each other, he handed me his card. In giant letters, larger than his name, were the words "Peas and Watermelon." Now maybe my surprise was because I was jet-lagged, although I'd crossed over only a single time zone. Or maybe it was because my social intelligence lagged behind most people's, but I almost laughed out loud when I read the card. Peas and Water-melon? I realized just in time, though, that in this part of the world, specializing in peas and watermelon was as legitimate a specialty as corporate law or dermatology might be elsewhere. Like almost every-one involved with the Fund, the head honcho, by financial necessity, had a sideline.

My eyes wandered back to those piles. What could they be? I threw caution to the wind and asked.

"Well, those there would be cranberry hulls," he asserted.

That explained their color, although the three piles went from bright red in the tallest, to reddish brown in the medium, to the smallest pile being really no color at all.

I took a guess. "Fertilizer?"

The honcho bent over laughing.

"Oh, that's a good one," he said. "No, it's feed. Full of vitamins, just full of 'em."

I'm from New Jersey, a state famous for its cranberry bogs, so I knew that cranberries contained vitamin C. But was there more to them than that? Maybe the honcho was on to something—although I did wonder why they weren't used for animal feed in my part of the world.

Being in this foreign land left me with a hollow, uneasy feeling. It was too late in the day for a grand tour of the ranch, but as much to get my bearings as to reconnect, I asked to see my old friends that had been in my care up north: Shiloh, Prince Nelson, Stanley, and Hot Britches. Surely these familiar faces would be a balm for my jagged nerves.

Of the three horses, I was closest to Shiloh and I hoped she'd remember me. Although we spent over a year together, we had not seen each other in more than three years. Next, Prince Nelson. I had been with him almost as long, but I doubted he'd recognize me. His attention was always focused on Shiloh. And then there was Stanley, a retired New York City Park Ranger horse. I imagined I would be a stranger to him since our time together, while six months or so in length, was somewhat lacking in depth. Finally, there was the inscrutable llama, Hot Britches. I never did know what went on in his mind, and had no reason to think it would be any different now.

We hopped into the honcho's pickup truck and drove to a distant pasture. At that time, 1984, the ranch was only about four hundred acres. In that part of Texas, four hundred acres isn't much more than a large backyard; but to me it seemed nearly as big as the whole state of New Jersey.

From far away, I could see my old friends in adjoining runs, each with an ample turn-out shed: Prince Nelson and Stanley were together in one; Hot Britches and a companion llama the Fund had acquired for him in another. And in the third, the gleaming, robust Shiloh, still as bright as a newly minted penny, and with a young horse by her side. As we approached, I couldn't help but notice that the dark bay-colored colt bore a striking resemblance to Prince Nelson. The honcho watched my eyes go from the colt, to Prince, and back again. He confirmed what I suspected: Prince Nelson was the father. The stallion had since been gelded, but before that, somehow, he consummated his love with Shiloh. The honcho blamed it on the Texan's mismanagement, a theme that would be repeated often. While I wasn't in favor of breeding animals, especially since so many already needed homes, I couldn't help but give a silent "atta boy" to Prince.

Despite what Terrace may have opined, I knew in my bones that, to varying degrees, all three horses remembered me. Shiloh was the most demonstrative. After giving my hands and face a good sniffing, she whinnied once or twice then galloped a bit. She nudged her boy forward, as if to introduce him to me. I was careful to make a big fuss over him, and to compliment her on what a fine job she did. Prince Nelson, too, made quite a production of sniffing me. He concluded by bobbing his head up and down, showing that his wavy, blue-black mane was as gorgeous as ever. While the fire in his eyes was no longer as intense as it had once been, he continued to cut a remarkably handsome figure. And there was dear Stanley, who, during his working life, patrolled Prospect Park in Brooklyn with a mounted police officer. The day I picked him up in the city, I was appointed an honorary Urban Park Ranger. Stanley looked me over, and eventually nuzzled my cheek. He appeared fit and happy. As befitted a former ranger, he was a true leader, fully in charge in a quiet, capable way. All three horses, from entirely different backgrounds, had made a seamless adjustment to their new lives on the Texas ranch.

As for Hot Britches, he was still the Britches I used to know. When we pulled up to the llama area, he and his companion ambled over to the fence in an extremely leisurely way. His ears swiveled antenna-like when I called him by name. It took a little longer for him to respond to the word I was told that he knew on the day I picked him up in Vermont: "kush." After a couple of tries, he sank to the ground. It gave me a small thrill to realize that I had penetrated his strange, alien mind. Perhaps an even greater thrill: he didn't spit at me.

As we headed back to the main house, where I would be staying, I wondered if I had done the right thing by denying Gamal the experience of living a freer, more natural life. God knows his life as a performer, both as a diving horse and when he'd worked in rodeos, had been highly regimented. Now, although nothing was asked of him, it was still a life of stalls and feeding time; of orderly turn-outs and returns; and of lights on and lights off. While all of his physical needs were met, he did not have the luxury of galloping on the range, living with a small herd of horses, establishing his place in that herd, and having those equine relationships be the central focus of his life.

I knew from the beginning that when Cleveland said Gamal could stay with me permanently, I was getting the better part of the deal. But how much better? As I thought back to when I was angling to hold on to him, I was keen that he not be an anonymous member of a herd, I wanted him to be one of one. Had he been shipped to the ranch, he, like Shiloh and Prince and Stanley, would have been one of many. They certainly didn't seem to mind it. Would Gamal have been happy there, too?

Just as I hoped, my relationship with Gamal had evolved into being the main thing for both of us. Our lives revolved around each other, and to a certain extent we relied on each other. Now, I hoped I hadn't done him a disservice. I wanted to think that his loss, if that's what it was, was balanced by the personal attention I, and others at the farm, gave him. But was our connection as important to him as it was to me?

Gazing out at the ranch through the pickup's windshield, imaging the life Gamal might have experienced there but for my interference, brought unexpected tears to my eyes. I knew I was too attached to him, loved him too much, but what could I do? I was in too deep, and had been from the start.

There were two other animals at the ranch that I needed to see right away, but for an entirely different reason: the chimpanzees, Nim and Sally. It was something, really, that I wanted to get out of the way. They represented my biggest challenge—and fear. It was imperative that I establish a rapport with them and ensure that as long as I was on the premises, they were safe and healthy. I wasn't exactly sure how to do it, but I knew it had to be done.

Nim made an enormous fuss when we met, not of recognition, of course, but of excitement. He pounded his chest, made screeching noises, and spread his lips broadly, revealing an impressive and fearsome set of pale yellow teeth with sharp, prominent fangs. I had no doubt about what those teeth could do if Nim decided to put them to work. He also showed off by swinging from various ropes in the enclosure. I had never been one for zoos, so my exposure to chimpanzees was limited. But even I could tell that Nim was quite a specimen: muscular, shiny, and seemingly in peak physical condition.

In a tender moment, he extended his hand through the bars of the enclosure, not to shake my hand, but to connect fingertips, like God and Adam on the ceiling of the Sistine Chapel. I marveled at how alike our two appendages were, and yet how different. His hands were raw power and possessed a strength far beyond mine or even the mightiest bodybuilder's. His nails were a thick opaque black; his palms, smooth and leathery. The backs of his hands were covered with tufts of coarse, wiry, coal black hair that thickened as it ran up his arm.

Sally stayed in the background and expressed her excitement by riding around and around and around in tight circles on a tricycle, like a dotty maiden aunt. Although she wasn't wearing clothes, it was easy to imagine her dressed in a gingham dress and straw hat adorned with daisies. I found out later that Sally had been captured as an infant in Africa, then sold to a circus where she was taught to ride a tricycle. Clearly, it was a trick that stuck. She seemed to enjoy performing, something I found touching—and sad.

The honcho said I arrived just in time to watch the chimpanzees' evening feeding. From inside the compound's kitchen, one of the Hispanic farmworkers brought out trays laden with an enormous array of fresh fruits and vegetables. He slid them into the area where Nim and Sally were accustomed to eating. Hard not to draw a parallel between that and the feeding of inmates in solitary confinement. Thank God, and Cleveland, that at least the two had each other.

Nim lunged for the yellow watermelon (the first I'd ever seen of that variety), then the strawberries, the bananas, and what the honcho referred to in Texish (that language I hadn't heard since the original Texan left Bucks County) as "maders" (tomatoes). Sally grabbed a few pieces when Nim wasn't looking, then retreated with them to a corner. While she didn't appear remotely underfed, the dynamics in the enclosure were obvious: in Nim's mind, he came first and second. Little old Sally, a distant third. I made a mental note to discuss it with Cleveland. For all I knew, this was the way things went in chimpanzee society.

My concern for the chimps' welfare did not take into account the reverse: my welfare. That first night, I was awakened by a loud pounding on the back door. Then the sound of someone pulling so hard back and forth on the knob that I thought the door might be torn off its hinges. I remembered the heir apparent asking me if I had a gun and telling me that Nim was stronger than he looked.

Soon, there was the same pounding and pulling on the front door. Mercifully, both doors were locked. As in a bad dream, I wanted to act but was paralyzed with fear. I couldn't even get out of bed to hide beneath it, which was my first impulse.

As suddenly as the pounding began, it ended. I looked at the clock: 3 a.m. Who, or what, could it have been?

There was no more sleep after that. I got up earlier than usual and, to my surprise, found the honcho waiting just outside the back door.

"Have a good night?" he asked in a flat tone that could have been interpreted either as sympathy or sarcasm. He gave a halfhearted apology for "the ruckus" during the night and said the culprit was Nim, escaped from his enclosure. As he said this, he casually but pointedly ran his finger over some freshly cut grooves in the back door, created by what seemed to be nails—or claws.

"At three in the morning? How?" I asked.

"Well now, I cain't say for sure but, you know, the former manager . . ." His voice trailed off, leaving me to assume the Texan did it. Somehow, though, that didn't make sense. How would the Texan have gotten that far onto the property? Wasn't the chimp enclosure locked with a key? Surely someone changed the locks when the Texan left, didn't they? And finally, how would the honcho have known that Nim was loose? He lived nearby on his own farm, but not within earshot.

I came to suspect that it was not Nim, pulling and gouging the doors, but someone pretending to be the chimpanzee. Someone was trying to scare me. Whoever it was did a damned good job.

It was barely seven but already hot. By midday, and for the duration of my stay, it would be well over 100 humid degrees. Maybe the animals, the head honcho, and the ranch hands were used to it. I was not. I realized that down here I'd actually need one of those broad-brimmed straw cowboy hats I saw for sale at every convenience store on the way to the ranch.

Only the honcho was around in the mornings. His crew, he said, was out rustling the animals that had escaped during the night. I didn't let him know I was already familiar with that situation. Better to let him talk. He concluded his explanation with the same phrase he used to emphasize almost everything: "I guarantee it," with the syllables expanded as "gare-un-tee." I thought of the woman on the plane and her joke asking how you can tell if a Texan is lying. Another variation could easily be "When he says I guarantee it."

This time, "I guarantee it" followed his theory that the Texan, the former manager, was the one causing trouble. After what he had told me about Nim, I had to wonder who the real perpetrator of the fence cutting was, and if the honcho himself had something to do with it. After he took me on a tour of the property, some by truck, some on foot, I saw it wouldn't be hard to nip a section of fence here and there, shoo out a couple of burros, and then take credit for returning them.

But maybe the heat had addled my brain. Maybe I was being paranoid.

I had to admit, the rolling hills dotted with ponds (man-made?) were beautiful. Hundreds of burros, mustangs, goats, and pigs— animals that otherwise would have been slaughtered—grazed peacefully in the fields, or dozed beneath the live oak trees. I wondered if Sparkplug's mother was among those still on the ranch, or if she had been sent to an adoption center. I may even have found a home for her, never knowing who she was.

All the animals on the ranch were there only because they faced peril elsewhere. I realized soon enough that for some, animals like Nim and Sally; or a small gentle horse named Cody, who was purposely shot in the leg by his vicious owner; or Peg, the three-legged cat maimed by an encounter with a leg-hold trap, much irreparable damage had been done. Yet while these animals had experienced the worst of humanity, they seemed to bear up well despite their tragic histories. Others, like the majority of the burros, horses, pigs, and goats, had no idea they were ever even imperiled. Regardless of how any of them got to the ranch, it was now time for us to show them the best that humanity had to offer.

. . .

That first full day on the ranch fell naturally into what would become a routine. I'd be up early before the worst of the heat, and would follow, or sometimes even help, the ranch hands round up animals, or feed them, or clean and fill their water troughs. Midday, while they were still hard at it, I'd retreat inside, where I'd do paperwork, make phone calls, or run into town to do errands. As the sun dipped into the sky and things cooled off slightly, I'd be back out again.

At least weekly during my six-week stint, if not more often, the local veterinarian would stop by, providing a nice break in the schedule. He was a straightforward, reasonable person, one without ulterior motives. He never spoke ill of anyone, never gossiped, but if asked, would answer truthfully.

Once, early in my stay, we approached the goats' area, and I wondered aloud why quite a few were standing with their heads down but were motionless. Without a word of explanation, the vet got out of his vehicle and freed them. Their horns had been stuck in the wire fence. He explained that the wrong type of fencing, meant for sheep, had been installed. The larger squares allowed goats to slide their narrow heads through (probably in an effort to get at the greener grass on the other side). But when they tried to pull back in, their horns ensnared them. From then on, I made a point of checking the goat enclosure several times a day. I also made a note to discuss the fencing with Cleveland.

I looked forward to accompanying the vet from pasture to pasture, often riding in the back of his pickup as it was easier than getting in and out of the cab. Besides, I liked getting the wider view of the ranch and playing the role of a cowgirl. I was flattered when, right off the bat, he assumed that I was competent (rather than the reverse) and asked me to assist him. I'd sometimes be asked to hold on to truculent animals while he dewormed them or administered vaccines. Other times, I'd hold a bag of IV fluids above an animal's head while the vet inserted a needle into a sick creature's vein. Once, I witnessed the birth of twin goats. The mother was overdue and bleating in distress.

With Darwin, a stray Beagle who
wandered onto the Black Beauty
Ranch. 1984.

Thankfully, the honcho had noticed and called for professional help.
The vet palpated her abdomen, gave her an injection, and a short
time later not one but two perfect little goats slid out into the world
beneath the hot Texas sun.

The veterinarian played a key role in another situation on the
ranch. The day after I arrived also marked the arrival of a stray Beagle.
Maybe it was a coincidence, or maybe someone knew I was there and
dropped him off. The dog was emaciated, covered with ticks, and
nearly eaten alive with what can only be described as herds of fleas.
He bore no identification. A call to the local animal shelter and the
police revealed that no one had reported him missing. I was told I
could bring him to the pound, but, of course, who knew what might
become of him there?

I felt more in my element with small animals, so I loaded the filthy
dog into the front seat of the Fund's pickup and set out for the vet.
This move horrified the honcho. I learned later that many Texans are
highly protective of their trucks, perhaps more than they are of their
animals.

After the usual exam, blood work, deworming medicine, and flea
control, the vet asked what my plans were for the dog. I had no plans,
it was just my second full day at the ranch. I told him I'd play it by
ear. The dog, whom I named Darwin (inspired by Charles Darwin's
ship *Beagle*), needed time to recover and, truth be told, I needed him.

Of course, Darwin and I became fast friends. He had no idea I had
just arrived at the ranch. For all he knew, I had always been there
and always would be. He became my farm dog, a role for which he

was ideally suited. Leash-free, he would stick by my side as I walked the fence line, looking for breaches; or, unasked, would make the considerable leap into the back of the vet's pickup to join us on a job; or would roll onto his back and demand belly rubs. He had not yet been neutered, but never once soiled the house. And sometimes in the morning, upon hearing the distant yipping of coyotes, this domesticated representative of the canine tree was stirred enough to throw back his head and answer them with a soulful howl. Darwin was a very good boy indeed.

I became close to only one local during my stint: a salty-tongued woman who described herself as "an old broad." She showed up one day at the ranch, introduced herself, and planted herself at the kitchen table. The old broad was what you might call a "full-figured gal." Her hair was dyed bright orange, and that first time, and every time I saw her afterward, she wore what I believe is called a housecoat— something between a nightgown and a bathrobe. Within a few min- utes, I learned she was a native Texan, but certainly not the standard variety. She was well traveled, seemingly well fixed financially, and liked nothing better than to tell stories. Whether or not her stories were true was irrelevant. At no time did I get the impression that she was either building herself up or taking credit for things she didn't do. She was just one of those people who knew how to capture the funny edge of life and describe it perfectly.

She had had several husbands. The first she called "gimlet ass"; and she ran away with him on a bus bound for California when she was seventeen. She confided that she never had any physical attraction to the second one, who she called "chicken legs"—leaving me to wonder why she married him. But before I could ask, she was on to the next husband, her third. She loved him, she said. Loved him dearly. He, of course, was the one who died prematurely. But she was content with her life, her memories, and her farm.

The old broad had no children, but did have a herd of pet steers, Polled Herefords, and they seemed to fill a similar niche in her life. One day, she asked if I'd like to come out and help her feed them. By then, I had become used to feeding the horses and burros. How much different could a herd of twenty or thirty steers be? In short, very different. They knew her truck and rushed toward it. Each one was enormous—almost as big as her truck. I feared leaving the safety of the cab until I realized that she, a seventy-something-year-old woman, was right in the thick of the fray pushing bales of hay from the truck onto the ground. I had to join her.

The animals had simple names like Carl, Bobby, and Elmer, and she knew each one. She'd scold them if they got out of line or pushed each other around; and would encourage the shy ones to come forward. These animals were not being fattened for the kill—she was a vegetarian. I became a weekly visitor to her kitchen, where she would serve things like okra prepared in three styles, stuffed summer squash, black-eyed peas, stewed tomatoes, and bread she had baked herself. Who needed meat?

I was not without mixed feelings, that last morning at the ranch. After all, I had been there much longer than the one or two weeks I had anticipated, and I knew that leaving animals I had grown close to was going to be tough. But the bright side was the thought of returning to my animals at home, particularly Gamal.

I wasn't going to miss being Cleveland's watchdog. On the surface, the honcho and I were cordial, yet distant. But I lived in fear that he knew that I was on to his shady financial dealings and who knows how that might have ended?

Over time, I had seen things at the ranch that just didn't add up. There was the man from Oklahoma who showed up a few times with a big gooseneck trailer and, with the honcho's help, loaded only the flashiest burro specimens, the white ones with gray patches; or the even more rare pure white ones; and always, many more females than males. I knew he wasn't running a satellite adoption center, and he certainly wasn't adopting that many pets for himself. I could only surmise that he was selling or breeding them. Bolstering the theory that something was off: I saw him paying the honcho in cash.

There was another time that a different man showed up late one night. From the house I could see some sort of financial transaction taking place by the glow of truck headlights and, again, it was a cash deal. And then I had a look at the books, and I saw payments hand-entered into the ledger for loads of grain or hay that had never been delivered.

I packed what I considered evidence carefully: notes, photographs, amateur forensic accounting, and a nutritional report on those cranberry hulls. A week or two earlier, I had collected samples from the three ever-present cranberry piles and took them all the way to an agriculture testing service in Nacogdoches, some ninety miles distant. I wanted to be sure I was well beyond the local good ol' boy network. The results revealed moisture and fiber in the freshest sample, some moisture and fiber in the middle sample, and no nutritional value whatsoever in the oldest, sun-bleached sample. The cranberry hulls were the equivalent of junk food.

I wasn't going to miss the heat or the fire ants or the stares of the locals, either. I know my appearance puzzled them. My hair was very short, I wore no makeup, yet I was female. Their suspicious stares would follow me in stores or restaurants with an expression that was not "who" is she, but "what" is she. Being scrutinized, being forever the interloper, dashed any (very) fleeting idea I might have had of staying on and blending in. I came to appreciate certain things about the area, but ultimately I knew I could never really be accepted as one of them, nor did I want to be.

As for Darwin, while it was hard to say goodbye, and I shed more than a few tears, I knew he was going to a handpicked, veterinarian-approved, loving home. After he was fully rehabilitated, and after his neuter surgery, the veterinarian told me he had found the perfect place for the dog—one with a younger retired woman. She needed him, he said, as her previous dog, also a Beagle, had died. And so I let him go. Darwin did me a great service, practically saved me by providing canine company when I needed it badly. Now I returned the favor by facilitating his physical restoration and seeing to it that he was set for life.

Although I had known them longer, saying goodbye to Shiloh and her male harem was less complicated. They were very happy, even joyful, with their arrangement at the ranch—something that had been the goal for them all along. I felt certain Shiloh would forever

Burros, rescued from the Grand Canyon by The Fund for Animals, in a more hospitable environment, with pond, at the Black Beauty Ranch. In the background, left, the llama Hot Britches. 1984.

be blowing kisses to her geldings, and they would forever be catching them.

What I would miss, and still do:

The dawn chorus of coyotes, yipping in unison, as if to celebrate each new day. I never saw them, but they made their presence known vocally.

I knew it was unlikely that I would ever again look around anyone's land and witness the miracle of hundreds of wild burros and mustangs grazing innocently and safely. Maybe the original Texan was right, maybe in some ways this was heaven on earth.

I'd miss the simple pleasure of driving down a dirt road in a pickup truck, listening to country singers George Jones or Merle Haggard, Gene Watson or Don Williams, on the radio, and knowing that I was experiencing the real deal, not a slicked-up, rhinestoned, mullet-haired, pop version of either the music or the life it reflected.

I would certainly miss visiting the old broad and her steers on her eccentric farm. The idea that such an anomaly existed in the middle of what I thought of as "barbecue land" gave me hope that other peaceful preserves might be out there somewhere.

Nim, the chimpanzee, learned two hundred words in American Sign Language as part of an ill-conceived, inhumane psychology experiment until he was rescued by The Fund for Animals. Nothing pleased him more than brushing his teeth—which he taught himself. At the Black Beauty Ranch, 1984.

Mostly, I would miss the wide vistas of the ranch, the seemingly endless pastures, the sense of expansiveness in land and spirit. I imagine that Doc Carver was similarly influenced by the open range and that it heightened his sense of self-determination and curiosity. Surely it inspired him and opened his mind, if not always his heart, to the vast possibilities of the world.

Just as it was imperative that I greet one animal in particular as soon as I arrived, it was now equally imperative that I bid him farewell: Nim. Of all the animals I anticipated meeting at the ranch, he was the only one I feared in advance. I never thought he would become the one I came to admire and adore.

By now Nim knew me, and my presence did not engender as much excitement as it once had. Sally, on the other hand, had become bolder and more demonstrative. She came right over to see if I had brought any treats. I slipped her a banana—in part as a gift, but in part to distract her so I could focus on Nim. I gave him one, too, but I knew he would stay to chat at the bars of his enclosure. He looked at me with his deep brown, nearly dark red, inquisitive eyes. I always had the feeling he was not looking at me, but was somehow looking into my soul. It was impossible to hide any emotion from Nim, and so on this last day he seemed to sense there was something different about my visit.

In the interest of safety, I never extended my hand into the enclosure, but always placed it flat against the bars. As I did it this time, he stroked my palms delicately with his fingers, more so than usual, and almost made me cry. I knew that I was about to become just another person passing through his life.

Maybe to lighten the mood, he rubbed his index finger across his front teeth. The honcho told me on my first evening that this was a sign that Nim wanted to brush his teeth, something he did for fun. I had come prepared and gave him a brush preloaded with a small knob of paste. He was delighted, and did a job that would have made any dental hygienist proud.

I could linger no more, but there was one last thing I needed to say to Nim.

A few days after I arrived at the ranch, I went to the county library to look up some phrases in American Sign Language in the encyclopedia. I always spoke to Nim in words, but since he knew two hundred expressions in ASL and I knew none, I wanted to expand the way we communicated. One sign I learned was "I love you." It involved extending the thumb sideways, putting the two middle fingers against the palm, raising the index and pinky fingers, and shaking the hand back and forth horizontally. I had done this with Nim before this last day. Some days he responded, some days he didn't. This time he signed back, and it nearly broke my heart because I knew that what might have meant something closer to "love ya" in the beginning had grown into something true for both of us: real love.

As I was about to leave, he raised one hand, drew together the tips of his fingers, placed them to his lips, and then touched them to his cheek. It was the sign for the word "kiss." I signed back the same way.

Chapter Sixteen

Despite my desire to keep Gamal at the same barn permanently, he had to move—several times. When he went from Wendy's place to the much larger R-D-R Farm, it was to consolidate the Fund's various animals, and accommodate the hundreds of incoming burros and mustangs seeking homes. But that was not to be his final residence, either. After the Fund rescued tens of thousands of animals across the Southwest, it was in dire straits financially. I was given to understand that every penny made a difference. Shiloh, Prince Nelson, Stanley, and Hot Britches the llama had already gone to live in Texas on one of the return hauls, so that helped the bottom line, but further cuts were needed. One year, just before Christmas, I had to pack Gamal's blanket, unscrew his nameplate from the door of his stall at R-D-R, and move him to a less expensive venue.

This, Gamal's third barn, was run by Harold, a wiry World War II veteran with forearms the size of Popeye's, but with a distinctly gentler demeanor. Harold was retired, but as someone who didn't enjoy having time on his hands, he rented the barn and pasture from the owners of the estate on which it was located. His half dozen or so boarders covered his expenses, giving him a little spending money left over. Harold fed and groomed the horses and, since he was also a trained farrier, kept everyone's hooves in peak condition at no extra charge. As with Gamal's previous move, the horse surprised me once again by taking his change in residence in stride.

Yet apart from the blessing of Gamal's smooth adjustment, the holidays were shaping up like the trite plot of a made-for-TV movie.

I had just broken up with a boyfriend, and while I didn't second-guess my decision, it occurred to me that choosing a less festive time of year to pull the plug might have been a better approach. Delaying the split by a week or two would have relieved me of the tiresome question asked by every hairdresser or dental hygienist or post office clerk, "What are your plans for the holidays?"

I had no plans for the holidays, none at all.

There were a few "charity" invitations I could have accepted, but being the awkward extra person at a dinner party or on the receiving end of consolations seemed worse than being alone.

Not that I was totally alone: the company of my cats, my dog, and, of course, Gamal, was preferable to that of any human I knew at the time. I had become living proof of something my father would say, not entirely in jest, of certain couples in our church whom he referred to as "childless": the trouble with Protestants is that they love animals more than children. I had veered far from my Presbyterian roots, had just rounded the corner of thirty, was what I considered child-free, and was the current adopter or caretaker of more animals than most people have in a lifetime.

By now, Gamal and I had been together for several years. Contrary to what I had expected in the beginning, every day with him was a celebration. No matter how often he saw me he high-stepped, bobbed his head, shook his mane, and pranced. If he was in an even more expressive mood, he'd nuzzle my cheek with his whiskers, giving me goose bumps. I never presumed that it was all about me—after all, carrots or apples or pears were always part of our interactions. But I knew at least some of his ebullient antics were his way of greeting a treasured friend. Unlike how, over time, most people become habituated to the status quo, Gamal never took me for granted.

It was only late afternoon on Christmas Eve, but already the sun had nearly finished its descent. Outside, the temperature was also dipping, to just 28 degrees. I knew that the barn where Gamal now lived was well insulated. He held his weight, had plenty of bedding, and never showed any sign of discomfort. Still, my impulse tended toward the impractical, such as wishing I could install central heat, or fit him with an electric blanket.

Something I hadn't thought of in years came to me: my mother's fruitcake. It was the dreaded confection she considered a Christmas delicacy. She'd spend hours in the kitchen combining candied fruits, raisins, nuts, and other ingredients that, separately, might have been edible; but combined, produced rock-hard, toothachingly sweet bricks. Recipients of her gift would give a wan smile and place the cake somewhere out of sight. My mother never seemed to notice, and cranked out the same recipe year after year.

The memory of her fruitcakes led me to the idea that there was something special I could do for Gamal: warm him from the inside. I could make a pot of oatmeal, enough for him and the other horses in the barn. Why not host my own holiday party with an equine-only guest list?

Perhaps because I would be cooking a special Christmas treat, I was reminded of something else I associated with those early fruit-cake sessions. As I would sit on a kitchen stool and watch my mother mince bright green candied pineapple, or dice walnuts, she would tell me the story of how, at "the stroke of midnight" on Christmas Eve, barnyard animals would acquire "the power of language." I was never sure whether or not she believed it, but I was as transfixed by the idea of animals speaking (presumably in English) as I was by the phrase "the power of language." I peppered her with questions for which she had no answers. What power, exactly, did language hold? Would the animals speak only to each other, or to whoever happened to be within earshot? Was the ability to speak confined to barnyard animals, or did all creatures acquire this fleeting skill?

I was not the sort of child to accept things at face value. As with questioning the reality of Santa Claus, I was also skeptical of the talking animals story. But since we had neither barnyard animals nor access to a barn, I couldn't prove or disprove its veracity. Now, decades later, I realized that not only did I have access to a barn, but at least one animal I was desperate to converse with. Midnight was fast approaching. I decided to show up at the barn at the appointed hour with a pail of oatmeal. I was not so delusional as to expect Gamal or the other animals to speak, but it was an amusing angle on which to focus my visit.

I hurried out to stock up before the supermarket closed, and went shoulder to shoulder with others getting last-minute holiday supplies. I even succumbed to a little impulse shopping with caramel popcorn balls wrapped in brightly colored cellophane, sugar cubes, and the obligatory five-pound bag of carrots finding their way into my cart.

On the way home, the announcer on the car radio said the station would be playing Bach's *Christmas Oratorio* in its entirety, starting at midnight. To me, Bach's intricate, incandescent music came as close to what I could imagine was the music of the spheres. Surely it would enhance, even elevate, what I was hoping would be a heavenly experience in the barn. Now my party would have a soundtrack.

I was pretty good at cooking for humans, but a neophyte at cooking for horses. I had a large speckled enamel cauldron, the kind intended for use over a campfire, and got to work. I could have passed for one of the witches in *Macbeth* as I toiled over the porridge. Since I had no recipe, no idea of the proportions, I winged it with two boxes of oatmeal, salt, and enough butter to lubricate the glutinous mess. I soon discovered that without what seemed like gallons of water, the sludge solidified like cement. I steered clear of candied fruit, but added raisins and brown sugar, things I hoped the little herd would enjoy.

As I lugged the steaming pot to the car, I realized the contents had swelled to many times its original volume. I had heard about something called a "mash" that could be used to relieve constipation in horses, and hoped that just a little taste of my concoction for each animal wouldn't produce an unwelcome Christmas gift for Harold the next morning.

The half-frozen bluestone gravel made a satisfying crunch beneath my Jeep's tires as I shifted into neutral and glided down the lane to the barn. There was a fork in the lane, with one path leading up to the house, the other leading down to the barn. The buildings were far enough apart so that it was unlikely I would disturb the house's occupants. Besides, they were probably either asleep, or deep into preparations for the next day's festivities—something that seemed to occupy everyone in the world except me.

As I flicked on the barn lights, the horses squinted against the harsh brightness. A few yawned, exposing long, yellowed teeth. But all seemed interested, both in my presence and my presents. For an amuse-bouche, I unwrapped the cellophane and handed a sticky pop-corn ball to each animal. Within seconds, they polished them off. I followed it with a sugar cube palate cleanser. Next, the salad course, a carrot. Finally, the *plat du jour,* warm oatmeal proffered on a long-handled, stainless steel spoon. There was no mistaking the alacrity with which they ate.

It was just about midnight and, as expected, there was not the slightest hint that the horses might soon transform into chatterboxes. I wiped everyone's face with wet towels and slipped Gamal a few extra carrots. A couple of horses took a long, cool drink of water, turned their backs to me, and called it a night. Others bobbed their heads up and down over their stall doors on the off chance that there might be a bit more food. Soon, even they retired. But Gamal stayed with me and was rewarded handsomely for his loyalty.

I became so engrossed in tending to him—feeding, petting, but mostly chatting—that I forgot about Bach. It was now quarter past "the stroke of midnight" when I realized I'd missed the oratorio's opening cantata. I ran over to Harold's dusty Bakelite radio that he listened to while doing his chores and turned it on. He was a little hard of hearing, and, as I was to discover, compensated by setting his radio's volume to high. With just a click of the On button, it came to life with a choir belting out "Hark! The Herald Angels Sing" as if it were a show tune. I struggled to find my classical station only to discover that Harold's radio only had an AM band.

I spent another ten minutes rifling through the tack room looking in vain for another radio, while cursing myself for not having brought my own. I ran out to my Jeep to see if the sound from its radio would carry into the barn. It did not. The perfect scenario I envisioned was ruined. It was half past midnight and I had heard neither Bach nor talking animals.

I was about to write off the whole night as a good idea gone bad when it came to me that there was something obvious I had over-looked: Gamal. He stared at me with an unusual intensity and alerted me to what I had been missing. In his way, he had been talking to me all along, but I had not been listening.

I had squandered some of my midnight visit by grousing about Harold's radio, deciding there would be a void without Bach's music, and especially, by trying to suppress the nagging sense that I was alone in the world.

But the night wasn't over, I could still make amends.

I ran down the aisle to Gamal and was determined to listen—not to what was said out loud, but to what wasn't. To connect, we needed a literal silent night, not the Christmas carol version.

As he leaned into me, I shook sawdust from his mane, took the brush to his neck, and made sure every bit of sticky oatmeal was gone from his face. If a horse could purr like a contented cat, he did. But the bond between us that night went beyond mere creature comforts or my ability to read his body language.

Soon, his eyelids began to droop, and my first thought was that he was falling asleep. But when I whispered his name he came to instantly, fully present. I knew from experience that he had drifted into that meditative, here-but-not-here, state of mind.

As had become my habit, I started to breathe in rhythm with him. Although I continued to brush him, I did not think about brushing, or about anything else. I simply brushed. This, I realized, was how Gamal approached the world. He became one with whatever he was doing, anything from diving, to eating, to greeting.

Soon, there was a merging between us that was beyond words, beyond touch. Through silence, we bridged the gap between indi-vidual and universal spirit. That he was a horse, and I was a human, made no difference.

That night, Gamal and I experienced the "power of language" not from putting thoughts or feelings into words, but from *being* those thoughts and feelings. Gamal's wordless language was available to me whenever I experienced life as he did, not just at the stroke of midnight on Christmas Eve. To make it happen, I needed to be quiet, and awake to the present moment. Gamal was expert at this. I was still learning.

A dozen years later, and having placed thousands of animals, I no longer worked for The Fund for Animals. The burros and mustangs, the wild goats and wild pigs, were either in adoptive homes, or were at home on the ranch. Going back to the ill-fitting positions of lobbying, or organizing protests, or even working on the Fund's publications was no more appealing than it had been originally. It was time to try something new. But my ties to the Fund were not severed entirely. Much as before, Cleveland and I still saw each other regularly, chatted often on the phone, and he would call on me for the occasional special assignment.

On the surface, it might have looked as if I was back to pre-1974, before my association with Cleveland began. Once again I was freelance writing and advocating for animals as a private citizen. But I knew it wasn't the same, nor was I the same. Gamal deserved credit for much of the change. That I saw him as a teacher with valuable lessons to share had been borne out over the years. His quiet, nonjudgmental way of listening, and the way he taught by the example of his own courageous life, had a profound effect on me. While I may not have morphed into someone as brave or confident as he, I was light-years ahead of where I had been when first we met.

As for how I affected Gamal, I'd like to think he had transformed, too—and for the better. He must have known, and been even comforted by the fact, that although he switched farms several times, I was the constant in his life. Too, there was a calmness about him not present when first we met. He became less guarded, more affectionate. My confidence became his confidence, and vice versa. We had become a symbiotic pair, with each giving the other what was needed.

. . .

The seeds for what lay ahead for me, for how my strengths and my interest in animal welfare might intersect, were sown nearly ten years earlier when I adopted a stray Border Collie that I found wandering the streets of Stockbridge, Massachusetts. I took him to the police station, and found at the front desk the chief himself, William Obanhein, also known as Officer Obie of "Alice's Restaurant" fame. When I realized who the man was, I had a moment's concern that he might want to haul me in on a trumped-up charge of some sort. Instead, he was entirely sympathetic to the dog's plight and gave me the number of an old man in town he referred to with affection as "an animal nut," Ben Roeder.

Ben and I joined forces and worked diligently to find the dog's owner, to no avail. Ben concluded that the dog was the victim of a somewhat common occurrence in the area, common enough that there was a name for it: an antique dog—one dumped by vacationers who discover that both their dog, and their newly purchased antique, do not fit in the car. These heartless tourists, who were sometimes caught in their act of perfidy, chose to assume that in an affluent town like Stockbridge, any stray dog would land on its paws.

I paid to have the dog vetted and brought back to health, since he was suffering from fever, parasites, and malnutrition. Ben arranged for him to be boarded in the little two-run dog kennel he had established for the town. I returned home, and Ben continued his search for the dog's owner by placing ads in newspapers and on the radio. The in-limbo arrangement could not last forever, though. Weeks later, when it became clear that no one was going to claim him and no one wanted him, I drove back to Stockbridge to retrieve the dog who would become my first dog ever, the one I wanted ever since I was a child, but had been denied.

Our wonderful relationship lasted for eight years, eight years of living proof that having a dog as a companion was just as rewarding as I imagined it would be. But it came to an end in April 1987. Stockbridge died.

During the two weeks that followed, two weeks that seemed like two months, sadness hovered, depression threatened. Yet because the pain of losing Stockbridge was so intense, I vowed never again to have a dog. I would be fine, just fine, I told myself, with my cats and Gamal.

I'd recently made a new friend, Dan Manning, at Harold's barn where Gamal was being boarded. He recognized my sadness about Stockbridge, took pity on me, and persuaded me to attend a local street fair, Lambertville, New Jersey's, Shad Fest, to lift my mood. He did not know me well enough to realize it would take a lot more than that.

As I trudged from booth to booth, feeling anything but festive, I bumped into a former acquaintance. Ruth Klastow had been a reporter for a weekly newspaper where I worked as a copy editor. We barely knew each other, but I remembered vaguely that, for a time, she found homes for retired racing Greyhounds. With the sharp, specific type of memory of one involved with animal adoption, she remembered my association with Gamal, my burro work, and my love of animals in general. She inquired about Stockbridge, who I must have mentioned at the office. I nearly broke down in the midst of the crowds when I explained that he had recently died.

Her immediate response was both the solution and the problem: "Want another dog?"

Of course I wanted a dog, but I wanted Stockbridge. To me, taking in another dog would cheapen his memory, trivialize our time together. But before I had a chance to explain this, Ruth was well into her pitch.

She relayed the heartrending tale of a retired racing Greyhound named King. The saddest part of his life, she explained, took place not during his racing career, but afterward, during his long search to find a permanent home. Although Ruth was no longer facilitating adoptions, King had been one of her placements that became what is known as a "bounce"—a dog whose adoption was not successful and that needed to come back into the program. Trouble was, there was no program, and nowhere for the dog to bounce back to.

On the Massachusetts track, where his registered name was Low Key Two, King raced in Grade AA, the highest level of achievement.

His owner, who had a few dozen racing dogs as a hobby, decided that King had been good to her and she would be good to him in return. As I was to discover, she was known for ensuring homes for all of her former racers, champions or not.

She enrolled King in a Massachusetts track's adoption program, and before long the nearly six-year-old stately brindle dog with a coat that looked like burled wood seemed to be a winner again—he was adopted almost immediately. But apparently potential adopters were not screened carefully because the man wanted King as a guard dog. Despite his imposing size, his competitiveness on the track, and the determination with which he chased the artificial lure that sped tantalizingly just out of reach around the racing oval, King was the mildest, gentlest of creatures. After a week, when for the first time in his life King was deemed unfit, he was returned to the adoption program.

Not much time elapsed before he was placed in another home, which was great—while it lasted. A year later, when the adoptive couple divorced, neither wanted custody of King. Once again, he was back in the adoption program—now nearly seven years of age, with a graying muzzle, and two strikes against him.

Ruth had started a satellite Greyhound adoption group in New Jersey and wound up taking in King as a foster dog until she found his third home. Soon, she succeeded—with a single man who doted on the dog. He came home from lunch daily to let King out, took King for long walks in the park opposite his house, and, if you had asked him, would have said that King was his best buddy. But that didn't last, either. Enter a woman, one who became the man's fiancée, then his wife. Not only was she not an animal lover, she was not even marginally humane. The only way she would deign to share a house with a dog was if the dog was kept in the basement, never allowed upstairs, and never in her sight. The man agreed, and for some time the arrangement persisted. Then King stopped eating and the man had a decision on his hands: stand up for his former best buddy, or return the dog. He chose the latter.

Nine-year-old King, a former champion, was now a three-time loser—old, unwanted, and beaten down by life. Ruth told the man he'd have to wait for a home to materialize since she was no longer involved actively with Greyhound adoption. If a home wasn't found soon—for King was still in the basement—Ruth told me the man threatened to "do what needed to be done." No one had to explain what that meant.

At that moment, I realized I also had to do what needed to be done: toss aside all notions that it was too soon for me to adopt again. The next morning, I was on my way to pick up King, a dog I never met and a breed about which I knew nothing. I did know one thing, though: I needed him and he needed a home.

Unlike my immediately perfect relationship with Stockbridge, King and I had a rough start. He never made eye contact, never wagged his tail, never played with the many toys I piled in front of him. The only good news I had to report was that he showed no interest in harming my cats. I had to assume that King had been seriously traumatized by his many adoption experiences, and who could blame him? Why should he dare extend himself again, trust anyone again, much less love anyone again, when, in all likelihood, he would be betrayed?

I continued to pine for Stockbridge, and King's lack of enthusiasm did little to boost my spirits. I may have saved his life, but what kind of life was it? He seemed not to care at all that he had been rescued from the basement and finally had the proper retirement he deserved. Still, I did the things I thought might comfort him: I spoke softly, I reassured him, I fed him the choicest of meals. But this produced little effect, and I was at a loss for what else to do. I had saved him, yet he still needed saving. Ever so faintly, I began to hear old ghosts whispering in my ear that, once again, I was failing.

I may not have known how to help King, but Gamal did.

I began taking King on my frequent visits to Gamal—not as a remedy for the dog, but because that's what I always did with Stockbridge. Horses and farms and dogs go together and are part of the joy of rural life. But after a few weeks, I noticed that, as we neared the farm, King would stand up in the back of my Jeep and look out the window. As we drew closer, he would begin to whimper—not mournfully, but with a tone of recognition or, and I barely dared think it, excitement. Soon it was obvious—King was excited, excited about seeing Gamal.

The post and rail paddocks were lined with wire, which meant I could release King safely. Greyhounds, if allowed to run loose, are unstoppable and would likely never be seen again.

Both Gamal and King were tentative when they first met. King sniffed Gamal's face hesitantly through the fence, but kept his distance. For his part, Gamal seemed preoccupied and kept looking at my vehicle, perhaps to see if his old pal Stockbridge was around. Eventually, Gamal turned his attention to this different sort of dog, this smooth dog, pointy dog, skinny dog, tall dog, and, as he was about to discover, fast dog.

It wasn't long before Gamal decided to do one of the things he enjoyed most—run. Whether or not he knew it, Gamal was speaking King's language—something I had been unable to do. Instinct kicked in, and King took up the chase. Soon the two were running side by

Retired racing Greyhound King (racing name Low Key Two)
was largely victorious on the racetrack, achieving Grade AA,
but his post-racing history began less successfully. It took five
years after his retirement for him to find a permanent home.
I was his fourth adopter, he was my first Greyhound.
He became the inspiration for me to find homes for other
retired racers, more than 5,500 and still counting; and,
through books and speeches, to promote the ethical adoption
of former racing dogs worldwide. 1987.

side, and back and forth along their common fence line. Gamal may not have been a former racehorse, but he was no slouch. On most days the result was, as they say at the racetrack, a photo finish. Both animals seemed happy to have someone to compete with, and both had a good workout.

But that enthusiasm was just the beginning of the changes in King's behavior. After a few weeks of interacting with Gamal, King's interactions with me changed, too. One night after dinner, I retired to the living room to read, and maybe even to write. King, who had already staked out his spot at the opposite end of the sofa, evinced no interest in me when I joined him. But after a while I noticed that he stood up and, in doglike fashion, circled around a few times before repositioning himself. A few minutes later, he did it again, but this time was a bit closer to me. The circling and repositioning went on half a dozen more times until the ex-racer was within a few inches. I looked over at him and, for the first time, he allowed his eyes to meet mine. Slowly, he extended his long, lean foreleg and placed his paw on top on my hand. We held that position for a long time, as if making a pact. From then on, King was no longer just living with me: he was my dog and I was his person.

I am convinced Gamal's steadying influence helped King emerge from his depression. Just as the diving horse had, in his way, bolstered my confidence and helped me rebound from Sparkplug's death, Gamal was also successful in urging King to give life another chance.

I was glad to see Virginia again, although I wished the circumstances had been different.

Even though it had been a little over a year, I believe the mare recognized me. She whinnied repeatedly and pawed the ground with her hoof. Compared to her formerly emaciated self, she was now plump, verging on too plump. Her coat gleamed bright white in the sunlight, and there was a confidence in her bearing not present when I first met her. She held her head high and had a certain glint in her eye, an almost sassy look.

What a contrast to the way she looked when first we met several years earlier at a horse auction in Front Royal, Virginia. The haggard mare and her starving foal had been purchased by two different meat buyers earlier in the day—ironic, since there was no meat on them. The foal repeatedly butted her mouth against her mother's udder, desperately and instinctively seeking milk; but there was no milk. The mare, whose winter coat sloughed off like sheets of cotton batting, was nearly too weak to stand, much less produce milk. Of course I had to buy them back from the brink.

As depressing as that first day had been, it was followed by months of joy while rehabilitating the pair. I'm sure I shed a tear the first time I saw the foal, Amazing Grace, actually get milk from her mother. Or the first time Virginia had the strength to kick up her heels. The process of clearing them of their many ills (ringworm, internal parasites, various infections) took nearly a year. But they were never meant to be mine permanently, they were to enrich other people's lives.

Grace, who developed a beautiful strawberry roan coat, did not inherit her mother's Missouri Fox Trotter gait. She was taller, too, reaching 15.1 hands, compared to her mother's 14.2. She went to a good, responsible farm where she would be trained for riding and would eventually give lessons.

I gave Virginia to the niece of a friend, believing it would be a lifetime proposition. But now, a year or so later, the niece returned the horse, citing financial hardship.

I was hardly on firm financial footing myself. As a freelance writer, my income was hit or miss. Even when I hit, it was certainly insufficient to pay Virginia's board for long at Harold's farm where the Fund paid Gamal's expenses. However, when I take an animal, either for myself or to rescue it from a desperate situation, I consider myself responsible for its life. The heat was on to find her a new home, and this time, by God, it would be a permanent one.

Not long after Virginia returned, my friend Dan, a regular at Harold's farm, suggested we take her out for a ride since she had become accustomed to frequent outings in her previous home. He thought Gamal might enjoy a change of scenery, too.

During the time Gamal had been boarded at R-D-R Farm, I signed on for a series of English-style riding lessons with the very patient

Dale Bauersachs and her gentle lesson horse, Te Amo. My goal was modest: to become acquainted with the basics. I was surrounded by horse people and wanted to get a feel for what they were doing, and how they were doing it. Eventually, I became minimally proficient— capable of a walk, possibly a trot. A canter was iffy. A flat-out gallop was out of the question. But a trail ride seemed doable.

Given my limitations and trepidation, Dan and I decided Virginia would be a suitable mount for me. Since she was even smaller than Gamal, she was also that much closer to the ground—comforting to a tentative rider such as myself. Her Missouri Fox Trotter heritage virtually assured a calm and safe outing. The breed is known for having a gait so smooth that it is said you can sip a cup of tea while riding one. As I was later to learn, the breed is also known for stamina and endurance. Dan, an accomplished horseman, mounted Gamal effortlessly and we set off.

Our excursion began with the two horses walking side by side at an unhurried pace. I left my jitters behind and began to experience the obvious reason why people ride horses—it's pleasurable to get in touch with nature and bond with an animal. We walked along in silence, the only sound being the comforting squeak of the saddle's well-softened leather. Now and then I'd give Virginia a pat on the shoulder and admire how far she had come from the days when she cut a tragic figure.

It all came to a halt, or rather its opposite, when we reached a small rise. Before I had time to appreciate the greensward, Virginia paused and scanned the broad field. She let out a squeal, and took off. Not only was I unprepared for the abrupt change in speed, I was not nearly an advanced enough rider to know how to control her. I was overcome with terror as she threw herself into hot pursuit of God knows what. I don't know how smooth her gait was, and sipping tea was the last thing on my mind. I was focused only on hanging on. Pulling on the reins had no effect on slowing her down, so I did the opposite: I leaned into her jockey-like, and went with the action. But as any experienced rider would have known, that only quickened her pace. The whole thing was too much, too fast, and I reverted to panic. I tensed up, and the next thing I knew I was airborne, my fate likewise up in the air. I came down hard on the ground in a sitting position, then fell to my side.

Gamal and Dan caught up and asked if I was okay. I had no idea if I was okay, or dead. I think Dan may have had to ask me twice before the question sank in. When I was finally able to speak, I asked about Virginia. Where was she, and her empty saddle? Was she in trouble? I sent Dan to fetch her, immediately.

He tried, but Gamal had other plans. The horse would not move. Dan made the giddy-up, click-click sound. Nothing. He tapped him lightly with his heels. Nothing. Stalwart Gamal stood firm.

By now, tears were rolling down my cheeks, but they were not tears of pain (that would come later). My burst of emotion was gratitude. I knew exactly why Gamal wouldn't move. He recognized that I was in trouble, and nothing on earth could make him abandon me. He was my protector.

Dan dismounted, helped me stand, and propped me against Gamal. As he ran off to find Virginia, I rested my head against the horse's shoulder. Between breaths, I told him he was the best friend, the best everything, I'd ever had. Like the Queen's Guard, Gamal never moved. He focused his eyes on the spot where Virginia's rounded white rump disappeared into the distance. Steadfast, he held that position until Dan and the unrepentant Virginia returned.

Dan, a big bear of a man, hoisted me onto Gamal's back as if I was a rag doll. Slowly, carefully, my horse carried me back to the barn.

Chapter Seventeen

Gamal and I were roughly the same age, about twenty-six, when we met in May 1980. While I was still young, Gamal was already what is known in the horse world as "aged." Had he died within a year, or less, from when I acquired him, only I would have been surprised. Horses who receive good care can live anywhere from twenty-five to thirty years, sometimes even longer. Of course, Gamal did not always get the best care during the course of his life, but he certainly responded to it well when he did. Always, as I promised him years

With Gamal. His compact size, courage, and love of water were the very traits needed to be a successful diving horse. 1980.

earlier, he was treated as a member of my family. I saw him often, fed him carrots and apples and pears and, his favorite treat, sugarcoated shredded wheat. Every year on the anniversary of the day we met, we shared a carrot cake. He continued to blossom, to gleam, to take full advantage of all that his new life had to offer. His frequent fence races with King became a routine.

By now, and again because of the Fund's finances, Gamal had moved on to yet another farm. George Millar helped me find a small family place with a tidy barn that housed two of their own horses, plus one boarder to help defray expenses. It was a storybook environment, with a couple and two children who showed Gamal as much love and affection as they did their own animals. The two resident horses accepted Gamal immediately and he became a full-fledged member of the mini-herd.

Gamal, King, and I took leisurely walks together down a seldom used country road to an abandoned apple orchard, with the former diving horse on a lead rope and the former racing Greyhound on a leash. It was a life so enchanted that it was as if a spell had been cast on the three of us, and that our time together would be like the prayer that concludes, "As it was in the beginning, is now and ever shall be. World without end. Amen." All of this led me to forget that Gamal was, in fact, old. In August 1989, we were both in our mid-thirties, but Gamal was ancient.

One day I had the call that horse owners are never prepared for but, on some level, always dread. I was told there had been an accident, a serious accident. In a case of horseplay gone terribly wrong, Gamal had been kicked in the jaw, unintentionally, by one of the horses. He was having trouble eating.

Life without the old horse was unthinkable, but I tried to persuade myself that top-notch veterinary care would be able to fix his injury. After all, it wasn't as if he had a disease, or was a racehorse with a broken leg. I somehow managed to call Wendy to ask if she was available for a hauling job: picking up Gamal and delivering him to the same veterinary practice that had treated Sparkplug.

A few hours later, I was standing next to the same veterinarian, Dr. Bousum, and was once again looking at an X-ray. Gamal's jaw was not simply broken, the vet told me, it was shattered. Grinding and chewing food was impossible. For now, he would get fluids and nutrients intravenously, but that was not a permanent solution. The vet did not have to tell me the one thing they could do for him. I knew the only way to relieve his suffering was to still his brave heart.

Gamal was dozing when I entered his stall in the hospital. His eyes widened when he realized it was me and not just another person poking or prodding him. Although it had only been two days since I last saw him at the farm, he was already different. He seemed shrunken, stooped. And while he recognized me, I could tell he was no longer entirely in this world—part of him was exploring the other side.

This would be my last visit with Gamal, my Gamal. Just as I hadn't wanted him to retire to the Fund's ranch in Texas those many years earlier, I also did not want him to leave me now, especially to a place where I could not join him. I stroked his nose and felt the tickle of his whiskers on my hand. I placed my palm flat against his chest and felt the steady thump-thump, thump-thump, thump-thump of his mighty heart. As much as I tried to keep my composure for his sake, hot tears streamed down my cheeks and onto his neck.

It had been nine years since we'd first met. That night after the auction, it was all flashbulbs, swarms of reporters, and crowds hoping to catch a glimpse. Now, it was just the two of us, saying our goodbyes. I leaned against his side, eyes closed, and, as had become my habit, began breathing in unison with him. Awakened were thoughts, impressions, sensations, perhaps similar to how animals perceive the world. I felt as if I was catching a current in a gently flowing river and riding it downstream. There was no struggle, no tension, no bucking of the course. My movement, Gamal's movement, seemingly the movement of the entire universe, was played out in the expansion and contraction of the breath. In this state of equanimity, there was no beginning, no ending. All that existed was spirit.

The hour was upon us. This was his life and these were his final hours, not mine. I asked him if he wanted to go home. His eyes brightened a bit as he sensed that I was proposing something good: home.

The word "home"—for me, for him, for all of us—is one laden with multiple meanings.

To me, going home meant taking him back to the little farm where he had been so happy. Gamal was not to spend his last moments of consciousness in a veterinary hospital. The farm's owners had a landscaping business, and the equipment necessary to prepare his burial in the corner of a pasture. His veterinarian, who would meet him there, assured me that adrenaline would carry him through the short drive. Back at the farm, his last sensations would be of reconnecting with his friends, both human and equine, and inhaling the scent of the fresh green pasture and the distinctive aroma of the earth. He had loved it there, and they loved him being there.

I kissed his soft horse lips but could not bear to say the word "Goodbye." Instead, I whispered, "Au revoir," till we meet again.

I drove home from the horse hospital in tears, barely able to see through the windshield and as impaired as if inebriated.

Even back then, I had already been present for countless animal deaths, everything from goldfish and rabbits, to dogs and cats, to horses and burros. As I was to discover, the more animal lives you come into contact with, the more animal deaths you witness. Yet never before, not even with Sparkplug or Stockbridge, had I been as shaken by an animal's imminent passing as I was with Gamal.

My goal for Gamal was that he should go back to the farm and feel that everything was returning to normal, that his pain would cease, that he would feel restored. My distraught condition, weeping, would have ruined his chance for that.

Dr. Bousum called later and calmed any lingering doubt I may have had about Gamal's last moments on earth. He was with his horse friends, he had time to look around and see familiar surroundings, and as he was led to his final resting place, he did not suspect that it was final.

.   .   .

Once I got inside my house it took a few minutes for me to realize that King had not appeared to greet me, as he always did. I went upstairs to find him. The colonial-era house was built into a hillside with a door leading to a fenced yard off of the second floor. It was there that I found King, standing in the middle of the yard and looking distressed. I had been so flustered when I left the house that I neglected to close the back door—something I had never done before. King was safe, but he was a sensitive dog and knew that something was wrong. It took some encouraging words to lure him back inside.

Gamal had never been in my house, yet now it seemed empty, lifeless. I believe King felt it, too, as he pushed away his dinner bowl with his muzzle. After dark, we went outside onto the meadow. This was the same meadow where those early settlers from Manchester established a mill; the same meadow where a house restored from ruins was now broken again—much like the family who once lived there. This meadow had been the scene of flamboyant, theatrical parties; and was the same one that Gamal and Shiloh and Sparkplug frolicked on many years earlier. On that long-ago afternoon, the meadow had been a treat, a change of pace for them. But on this night, it was a place to escape the unwelcome quiet of the house. A few feet away, creek water rushed over rocks, just as it always had. This was the same creek where Gamal showed me for the first time how much he loved water, and was the same one that had so frightened little Sparkplug. Yet while the flow of water was unending, both of those animals were gone.

King and I settled on the grass and leaned against each other as I looked up at the star-studded sky. I wondered if Gamal's death would lead to another setback, as it had when Sparkplug died. Back then, I experienced a crisis of confidence and was ready to abandon my work with animals. It took Gamal's encouragement to put things in perspective, to remind me that I did have something to offer the animal world—starting with my interactions with him. Who would encourage me now?

Consciously, I brought the diving horse act to mind. An image appeared: a scene from 1964, when I saw a gray horse leap from his platform into the darkness. For reasons I did not understand at the time, I cried at the sight. Now I experienced it in a detached way.

In my mind's eye I am drawn to the silhouette of a diving horse. The salt air rushing in from the ocean awakens my senses and stings my eyes. Secondary lights on the pier dim while spotlights are trained on the horse. The announcer's voice booms above the din of the crowd, "Ladies and gentlemen, prepare yourselves for the thrill of a minute. We present Carver's Steel Pier High Diving Horse!"

The horse's handler sets him loose, and just as it happened those many years earlier, the animal ascends the ramp at a near gallop. The diving girl springs onto his back and we expect them to dive.

But the horse pauses. She pats his shoulder, but he stands firm. He does not tremble or attempt to back down the ramp but seems instead to be savoring the moment. He looks out into the ink-black darkness of the sea. A few whitecaps curl in the near distance, but his eyes are fixed on something beyond, something we can neither see nor imagine. Slowly, he turns his head and regards his audience. Some people whistle, wave their arms, urge him on; but he pays no attention. He scans the crowd, taking stock, looking for something or someone. In my dreamlike state, I imagine his eyes lock onto mine.

There is a message he wants to impart, a transmission of some kind. Once he has my attention, he looks down into the pool, readies his body, and pushes off.

In unison, the crowd gasps and jumps back to avoid getting wet, but I am rooted to my spot. My eyes sting again, this time with tears. My mother wipes my face with a handkerchief, but I can barely feel her. Something more than water has washed over me: the horse has altered my view of the world.

That night on the meadow I began to solve the puzzle set before me twenty-five years earlier: the diving horses played out our fear of change, our fear of the unknown. My great and entirely human error was wanting to suspend the horse in midair, to stop time and keep things as they were on that August night in 1964, just as now I wanted Gamal to be alive, to never die. But time cannot stand still, the horse must complete its dive. It is the natural order of things.

As I sat in the darkness with King, I remembered some of the things Gamal taught me—be quiet; listen; stay open to the unexpected; breathe. I was beginning to see that my deepest bond with Gamal was one linked by spirit. Remarkably, it still was. We were just as connected now as when he was alive.

Gamal was not solely in my heart or my memory. He was, and would always be, in that invisible sacred place that others cannot see, but which each of us carries within ourselves.

Epilogue

Recently, an apartment in Manhattan sold for a record $238 million, making it the most expensive residence in the United States. The building is on the site where Cleveland's apartment building once stood. Hard to imagine that Cleveland's combination bachelor pad/crash pad, the one with the impressive south-to-north view of Central Park, is gone. His building was demolished a few years earlier to make way for the current behemoth, so tall that it casts long shadows well into the park.

Cleveland's apartment hosted countless up-and-coming animal rights activists; was where, before such a thing was commonplace, he had a special outdoor area constructed for Polar Bear so the cat could safely sunbathe on the balcony; and was where, on that fateful night in the spring of 1980, I contemplated how my life, and the life of a singular diving horse, would soon converge.

Cleveland himself is gone, too, having died alone in 1998 in that very apartment. In a move that would have pleased his Puritan forebears, he did so only after putting in a full day's work at the office. His memorial service was held at the Cathedral of St. John the Divine, the same place where Gamal nearly participated in their first Blessing of the Animals—that is, until he was spooked by the elephant leading the procession.

Not long before Cleveland died, he called me with an anachronistic proposition. A new herd of feral western burros had been discovered, and the ranch in Texas was once again filled to overflowing. He wondered if I might consider taking in a trailer load or two. By then, I had moved to a house only a few miles away, on twelve acres with a small barn. Although I had been out of the burro business for a decade or so, I was still doing adoptions, but now it was former racing Greyhounds that needed homes, and they were upon me by the thousands.

Out of habit and affection, I nearly said yes. I had honed my adoption skills and knew I could carry out his task even better than before. But practically speaking, it would have been difficult. The barn was packed with odds and ends, including items I was storing long-term for Cleveland. And fencing that had once contained the horses of my property's previous owners was in severe disrepair.

But I knew, and I think Cleveland knew, too, there was another obstacle: I had moved on. I now answered only to myself, and while it was often scary, it also felt right.

For the first time, and with some regret, I told him no. He took it well and, I'm certain, was already contemplating Plan B before we finished talking.

Doc Carver died in California in 1927. He was buried at the Rock Lily Cemetery in his hometown of Winslow, Illinois. At one point, his headstone carried his favored, but inaccurate, date of birth, 1840. It has since been corrected to read 1851.

After Al Floyd (Carver) died in Louisiana in 1961, Sonora Webster (Carver) moved back to New Jersey and died in a nursing home in 2003 at the age of ninety-nine.

For the last eight years of her life, Lorena Carver and her little Poodle, Babette, lived together in Miami in a mobile home park. In 1981, at the age of ninety-five, Lorena finally succumbed to what was described in one obituary as "a lengthy illness." Babette, herself ancient and in poor health, was euthanized and cremated. A local priest was quoted as saying Lorena was "destitute." Another obituary noted, "Friends said Miss Carver had lived alone in recent years. She

outlived her family and could not afford to keep her horses." Upon
hearing that Lorena's and Babette's ashes were unclaimed, Ruth and
Bill Ditty buried them on their property.

As noted in his obituary, Bill Ditty "joined his Lord and Savior
Jesus Christ" in 2015. His ashes are interred just a few feet from
Lorena's.

There is still an amusement pier in Atlantic City named the Steel
Pier, but apart from the name and location, it bears little resemblance to the original, the remainder of which was destroyed by fire
in 1982. Once reaching 2,300 feet in length, it is now a thousand
feet of poured concrete, and offers attractions such as a giant Ferris
wheel and roller coasters.

In 1993, the Catanoso family, which, at the time, leased the pier
from Donald Trump, brought back a diving horse act, but it, too,
bore little resemblance to the original. These were diving mules, the
same mules I saw in Florida more than a decade earlier. Animal rights
activists protested, with some carrying signs reading "Make Trump
Jump." The act was shuttered before the summer season even ended.
Undeterred, the Catanosos, who by then owned the pier, suggested

Gamal never lost his enthusiasm for life's
small pleasures. 1988.

bringing back diving horses again in 2012. Public outcry was so great that the idea never came to fruition.

In 1989, Gamal, the last of Carver's Steel Pier High-Diving Horses, died around the age of thirty-five. He was buried on the grounds of the small New Jersey farm where he spent his last years living in comfort, eating fresh hay and sweet feed, and grazing free amid the green open fields that stretched far away.

Acknowledgments

Profound gratitude to Victoria Wilson, vice president and senior editor at Alfred A. Knopf, for keeping me on the straight and narrow story path. With equal parts grit and grace, she dispensed sage advice that extended beyond the written word. Her understanding of animals aided my interactions with her immeasurably, and I am honored to be a writer in her stable.

Victoria Wilson's assistant, Marc Jaffee, never missed a beat and made everything easier by keeping the project humming along efficiently. I appreciate that production editor Nora Reichard caught all errors, great and small. The alacrity with which publicist Emily Reardon approached the book made working with her both productive and enjoyable, while publishing assistant Morgan Fenton handled the marketing admirably.

I am awed by the boundless energy and unbridled enthusiasm of my agent, Jeff Kleinman of Folio Literary Management. He pounced on my unsolicited query as if he had been waiting for it and, with steady hand and unswerving confidence, knew exactly who might be interested in publishing my manuscript.

I am forever indebted to Cleveland Amory for taking a chance on me and especially for allowing me to keep Gamal. Even in memory, he remains a guiding force and an inspiration.

Deepest appreciation to my mother, Elizabeth, who instilled in me the importance of the heart; and my father, Francis, who stressed the importance of the mind.

Kudos to Deborah Burnham, Lynn Levin, and Kitsi Watterston, of the English Department at the University of Pennsylvania and accomplished authors all. Their expertise and encouragement "has made all the difference."

Many thanks to those who augmented my research. Foremost among them, Bill and Ruth Ditty, and Lynn Ditty. Also very helpful: Nancy Boeck, Winslow (Illinois) Historical Society; Aimee Pattison, Quakertown (Pennsylvania) Historical Society; Robert Ruffalo, Rev. Ruthann Seibert; Bob Schoelkopf, Marine Mammal Stranding Center; Lorena Fretz Short; and Jacqueline Silver-Murillo, archivist, Atlantic City Free Public Library.

A tip of the hat to the many who, in various ways, aided my progress: George Banks; Dale Bauersachs; Rolf Bauersachs; Brenda Bowen Hesson; Dr. Pete Bousum; Thomas Cunningham; Andrew Holland; Ann Jones; the Lewis family: Peggy, Mike, Nora, and Ogden; Dan Manning; Jon and Wendy McCook; Frank and Ginny Napurano; Anita Parente; Daniel Stern; Mary and Rob Truland; Millard and Nancy Rich; the Wettstein family; Donna Zdepski; and especially to my dearest friend George Millar, deeply missed and fondly remembered.

Love, always, to a man worth waiting for, my husband, Charles.

Index

Page numbers in *italics* refer to illustrations.

Aesop, 126

All Creatures Great and Small series (Herriot), 79

Amazing Grace (foal of Royal Virginia), *143,* 195, 248

American Sign Language, research on chimpanzees and, 216–17, 233

American Sportsman, 10

AmFran (Thoroughbred gelding), 119, 137, 143

Amory, Cleveland, 7–10, 106, 156, 194, 241, 258–59

apartment of, 19, 20, 24, 258

background of, 3, 109

beliefs and concerns regarding money, 16, 17, 135, 136

Black Beauty Ranch and, 109, 213–14, 215, 218–19

Branigan's initial meetings with, 8, 10–12, 13–14

Branigan's report on adoption program to, 178–80, 194, 198–99

burros sent to Branigan to adopt out, 195–96, 200

on care of burros, 123

The Cat Who Came for Christmas, 18, 19

death of, 258

founding of The Fund for Animals, 7, 8

with Gamal and Branigan at the river, 157–58

in *Good Morning America* segment, 110, 121, 133–34

heirs apparent to, 213–14

Hot Britches and, 137

job offer to Branigan, 14–17

Man Kind, 8, 9, 46

New Jersey animal shelter and, 104, 105

on not sending Gamal to Black Beauty Ranch, 115–17

photographs of, *9, 18, 106,* 109, *110*

physical description of, 8, 9

Polar Bear and, 18, 19, 55–56, 258

on purchasing Gamal, 56, 57, 77

in rescue of feral burros from Grand Canyon, 108–9, 110, *110,* 130

in rescue of Nim, 218

Amory, Cleveland (*continued*)
 in rescue of Prince Nelson, 139,
  141
 sending Branigan to check on
  burros in Georgia, 159–60, 164,
  166
 during Sparkplug's illness, 187
 in swaying public opinion, 109,
  110, *110*, 121, 133–34
 work for Cunard Line, 18
 work schedule of, 17, 258
 writing career of, 3, 8, 9, 17,
  19, 46
Animal Farm (Orwell), 59
Aquafair, 211
Aquarama, 95, 172
Atlantic City
 boardwalk of, 27–28, *28,* 31, 32
 decline of, 26, 52, 93, 99–100
 Democratic National Convention
  of 1964 in, 24, 26–27, 28–29,
  30–31
 Steel Pier of, 31, 52–53, 99–100,
  175–76, 260
 as a vacation destination, 24, 25,
  26, 27–28, *28,* 52
Atlantic City (movie), 93

Babette (Lorena's black Miniature
 Poodle), 211, 259, 260
Bach, Johann Sebastian, 238, 239
Bandelier National Monument in
 New Mexico, 109
Bauersachs, Dale, 196, 249
Bauersachs, Rolf, 196, 197, *197*
bay horses, 72
Beatles, 30, 32, 36, 153
Beautiful Boy (horse from auction),
 143
Bernhardt, Sarah, 47

Black Beauty Ranch, 57, 215, 226
 animals at, 141, 217, 226–29, 232,
  232
 firing of Texan from, 213–14
 naming of, 109
 purchase of, 104, 109
 selection of location for, 216
Black Bess (first diving horse),
 51–52, 174
Botstein, Leon, 12
Bousum, Pete, *197,* 252–53, 254
Branigan, Cynthia A.
 and adoption centers for burros,
  159–66, 195–96, *197,* 200
 after leaving the Fund, 241,
  258–59
 animals in early life of, 6–7, 22, 37,
  39–40, 44
 at Atlantic City diving horse act,
  22, 23, 24, 34–36, 77, 87, 93,
  94, 255–56
 in Atlantic City in 1964, 22,
  23, 24–36, *28,* 77, 87, 93,
  255–56
 attachment to rescue animals,
  122–23, 146
 at boarding school, 22, 38–39,
  40–44, 58
 bonding with Gamal, 76–79,
  101–4, 110–17, 134, 144–45,
  145, 151–58, 192–94, 222–23,
  236, 240–41, 250, 251–52
 Cairo and, 198
 catsitting Polar Bear, 19
 cats of, 14, *18,* 22, 37, 39–40, 44
 childhood of, 22, 24–44, *28,* 58,
  255–56
 Christmas Eve with animals,
  237–41
 Darwin and, *228,* 228–29, 231

Dittys and, 159, 160, 166–67, 168–78
education of, 6, 11–12, 22, 38
English-style riding lessons taken by, 248–49
father of, 3, 6, 7, 20, 22, 25–32, 33, 36, 37–38, 39, 44, 87, 159, 205, 236
filling in for Cleveland at the Fund, 17–18, 20–23
at Florida State Fair, 205–8
at Franconia, 11–14
as freelance writer, 194–95, 241, 248
Fund job offer to, 14–17
as Fund volunteer, 14, 15
grandfather of, 22, 33, 37, 44
at horse auctions, 57, 59–67, 119, 143–44, 160, 166, 193
Hot Britches and, 137–38, 222
King and, 243–47, 246, 255, 256
meeting Cleveland, 8, 10–12, 13–14
in Morocco, 121–22
mother of, 6, 9, 22, 24–26, 28–29, 31–34, 36, 37, 159, 205, 237
at New Jersey animal shelter, 104, 105
Nim and, 216, 223–24, 225, 233, 233–34
overseeing operations of Black Beauty Ranch, 214–16, 218–19, 220–22, 223–34
personal life of, 14, 144–45, 148, 215, 236
photographs of, 28, 71, 120, 145, 228, 251
Prince Nelson and, 139–41, 222
report to Cleveland on adoption program, 178–80, 194, 198–99

research on burros, 123–26, 129–30
research on history of diving horses, 45–46, 53, 87–88, 90, 93, 94–96, 98–99, 170
research on horses, 71–73
retired Greyhound racers and, 246, 259
Royal Virginia and, 195, 247–50
Shiloh and, 114–15, 116–17, 118, 134–36, 148–49, 174, 255
Sparkplug and, 128–30, 132–34, 148–50, 181, 183–94, 195, 255
Stockbridge and, 69, 150, 214, 242–43, 245
Texan's interactions with, 131–32
Branigan, Tommy, 37
Brookshier, Frank, 123
Burro, The (Brookshier), 123
burros, 123–26
abandonment of, in the West, 106–7
at Black Beauty Ranch, 217, 226, 229, 230, 232, 232
braying of, 128–29, 147
characteristics of, 125–26, 128–30, 150
Fund's adoption centers for, 163, 164, 165–66, 188, 196, 197, 198–200
lifespan of, 146
NPS extermination campaigns against, 107–8
religion on, 125
rescue of, from Grand Canyon, 106, 108–9, 110, 130, 232
varieties of, 124–25

Cairo (burro from the Grand Canyon), 198, 200, 201, 201, 202, 203–4

Calvin (burro from the Grand
  Canyon), *199*
"Camptown Races" (Foster), 72
Captain Bob and His Dolphins
  show, 95
Carnera, Primo, 52
Carver, Al Floyd, *see* Floyd, Al
Carver, Jonathan, 48–49
Carver, Lorena
 death of, 259–60
 departure from diving horse act,
  114
 Gamal and, 88
 as legally blind by end of diving
  career, 171
 management of diving horse act,
  210–11
 photographs of, *51, 176, 210*
 retirement of, 211, 259
 rewarding of horses after dives,
  169, 211
 Sonora's relationship with, 176
 surnames used by, 51, 91
 training of diving horses, 170, 209
Carver, Sonora Webster, *see* Webster,
  Sonora
Carver, William Frank "Doc," 233
 background of, 3, 46–50, *48,* 90,
  208
 contradictory information about,
  87–88
 copyrighting of term "diving
  horses," 206, 209
 death of, 52, 93, 259
 diving horse act and, 3, 46, 50–51,
  54, 55, 88, 91, 173, 177, 208
 photograph of, *209*
 reaction to Lightning's death, 92
 as a tough taskmaster, 90
Catanoso family, 260–61

Cate, Dexter, 105–6
Cat Who Came for Christmas, The
  (Amory), 18, 19
Cervantes, 126
chestnut horses, 72
chimpanzees
 at Black Beauty Ranch, 218,
  223–24
 research on American Sign
  Language and, 216–17, 233
China Lake Naval Weapons Center
  in California, 109
Chomsky, Noam, 216, 217
Christianity, on mules, 125
Christmas Oratorio (Bach), 238
claiming race, 140
Clown Horse (diving horse), 209
Cody (horse at Black Beauty Ranch),
  226
Cody, William "Buffalo Bill," 45,
  46, 47, 48, 49
cold-blood horses, 73
Conrad, Ruth, *see* Ditty, Ruth
Cosmo (Branigan's cat), 22, 37,
  39–40, 44
Cowtown, 59, 175
Crockett, Davy, 126
Crosby, Bing, 52
Cunard Line, 18
Cupid (diving horse), 209
Custer, George Armstrong, 47

Dallas, 126
Dampier, Alfred, 49, 50
Dante Alighieri, 104
Darwin (Beagle at Black Beauty
  Ranch), *228,* 228–29, 231
DeAngelis, Josephine, *35*
Death Valley, rescue of burros and
  wild mustangs from, 109

Deloro, 35
Democratic National Convention
   of 1964, 24, 26–27, 28–29,
   30–31, 94
dentists, training of, 47
Dimah (diving horse), 100, 168
Dimah Junior (diving horse), 168,
   172–73
Ditty, Bill
  Branigan and, 159, 167, 168–78
  burial of Lorena's and Babette's
   ashes, 260
  career of, 96, 100, 114, 170,
   171–73, 176–77
  death of, 260
  on diving horses' personalities, 169,
   173
  family background of, 11
  on Gamal/Emir, 174–75, 177–78,
   203
  marriage to Ruth, 172
  move to Florida, 159, 177
  photographs of, 169, 170
Ditty, Ruth
  on Al Floyd, 177
  Branigan and, 159, 167, 168–69,
   171, 172, 174, 177
  burial of Lorena's and Babette's
   ashes, 260
  marriage to Bill, 172
  move to Florida, 159, 177
  on Shiloh, 174
  on women in diving horse act, 171
Ditty, Susan, 172
Divine Comedy (Dante), 104
diving horses act, 21, 21–22, 29, 30,
   34–36, 35
  at Aquarama in Philadelphia, 95
  Branigan's research into history of,
   45–46, 53, 87–88, 90

Carver and, 3, 46, 50–51, 54, 55,
   88, 91, 173, 177, 208
creation of, 46, 50–51, 52, 88, 208
criticism of, 91, 209, 261
dangers to divers in, 89, 90, 91,
   171
dangers to horses in, 91–92
under Hamids, 95, 97, 168,
   172–73, 210
during hurricane of 1962, 100
at Lick's Pier in Ocean City, 92
naming of horses in, 89
Perillos' handling of horses in,
   209–10
popularity of, 53, 88, 211
Resorts International's ownership
   of, 97–98, 211
sale of, 20–23, 77, 93–94, 96,
   98–99
training for, 96, 97, 170
treatment of horses in, 4, 95,
   169–71, 172–74
see also specific diving horses
diving mules, 206, 206–7, 208, 260
Dolan, Patty, 101
dolphins, 106, 172
donkeys, see burros
Duchess of Lightning, 91–92, 174,
   208

Emir (diving horse), 168, 169–70,
   174–75, 176, 211
see also Gamal (formerly Emir;
   rescued by Branigan)
Equus, 194
Ericsson, Dave, 130
Evans, Charlie, 148

Fez, Morocco, 121–22
Fitzcarraldo, 219

Florida State Fair, 205–7, 206
Floyd, Al, 52
  death of, 259
  diving horse act and, 52, 90, 209
  Lorena and, 176
  marriage to Sonora, 90, 177
  photograph of, 89
  retirement of, 209
  telegram to Carver about
    Lightning, 92
Floyd, Lorena, see Carver, Lorena
Fontana di Trevi (restaurant), 15
Forest Hills Hotel, 12
Foster, Stephen, 72
France, Marlin, 175
Franconia College, 11–12
Fund for Animals, The
  activism expansion of, 105–6
  Black Beauty Ranch of, 57, 215,
    226
    animals at, 141, 217, 226–29,
      232, 232
    firing of Texan from, 213–14
    naming of, 109
    purchase of, 104, 109
    selection of location for, 216
  finances of, 235
  founding of, 7, 8
  mission of, 104
  satellite adoption centers of, 199,
    200
  see also Amory, Cleveland; Branigan,
    Cynthia A.

Gamal ("the real"), 103, 146, 168,
  174, 176, 211
Gamal (formerly Emir; rescued by
  Branigan), 74, 102
  bonding between Branigan and,
    76–79, 101–4, 110–17, 134,

  144–45, 145, 151–58, 192–94,
    222–23, 236, 240–41, 250,
    251–52
  Cairo's friendship with, 200, 203–4
  Christmas Eve with Branigan,
    237–38, 239–41
  death of, 254, 261
  diving horse career of, 89, 100,
    158, 168, 174–75, 176, 222
  at farm after Harold's barn, 252
  at Harker's horse auction, 22, 23,
    56, 57, 59–62, 63–67, 99
  at Harold's barn, 235, 236–37, 243
  health of, 71, 79–83, 84–86,
    111–12, 151, 193, 252–53
  history of, 3, 87–88, 175
  King and, 202, 245–47, 255
  love of water, 149, 150, 157, 158,
    170, 178, 251, 255
  in meadow by Branigan's home,
    148–49, 255
  newspaper articles about, 61, 67,
    75, 94
  personality of, 69–71, 75
  photographs of, 64, 71, 101, 120,
    145, 150, 169, 202, 251, 260
  physical appearance of, 68–69, 72,
    77–78, 193
  public appearances after rescue,
    141–42, 201–4, 258
  at R-D-R Farm, 196, 200–201, 235
  Shiloh and, 119–21
  Stockbridge and, 150, 246
  veterinarian examinations of,
    79–83, 110–14, 115, 116,
    252–53
Gamboling Farm, 139
Girl and Five Brave Horses, A
  (Sonora), 90
Goldwater, Barry, 29

Goodman, Benny, 31, 52
Good Morning America, 110, 121, 133–34, 150
Gose, Barbara, 177
Grand Canyon, history of burros in, 106–7

Hamid, George, Jr., 97, 173, 176, 211
Hamid, George, Sr., 95, 171, 172, 173, 176, 210
Hamid-Morton Circus, 171
"hands," applied to measuring a horse's size, 71–72
Happy (goat), 89
Hard Day's Night, A, 30, 32, 33
Hare Krishnas, 5–6
Harker's horse auction, 57, 59–66
Harold (landlord of barn and pasture), 235, 239
Hartman, David, 133, 134
Herman's Hermits, 52
Herriot, James, 79
Herzog, Werner, 219
Hickok, "Wild Bill," 48
hinny, 123
Holliday, Doc, 47
Homer, 126
horses
  auctioning of, 22, 57, 58–64, 143–44, 194–95
  breeds of, 73
  carriage, by Central Park, 19–20
  colors of, 72
  defense against predators, 58
  "hands," as applied to measuring the size of, 71–72
  hooves of, 84–85
  hot-blood *vs.* cold-blood, 73
  lifespan of, 146

slaughter of, 22, 58–59, 194
Standardbreds, 73
teeth of, 85
Thoroughbreds, 72, 73, 75, 107
see also diving horses act
hot-blood horses, 73
Hot Britches (llama), 137–38
  at Black Beauty Ranch, 146, 198, 203, 221–22, 235
  move from McCook's farm, 196
  naming of, 137
  photographs of, *138, 232*
  rescue from boarding school in Vermont, 137–38, 222
  Sparkplug's friendship with, 138, 147, 181
Hotel du Village, 130
Houdini, Harry, 52
hunter-jumper set, 75

I, Claudius, 84
Islam, on mules, 125

Jennings, Waylon, 197–98
Jersey Devil, 25
Johnson, Enoch "Nucky," 29
Johnson, Lyndon B., 27, 30, 36, 94, 126, 215
John the Baptist 1st (diving horse), 92
John the Baptist 2nd (diving horse), 210
Jonny Rivers' Diving Mules, 206, 206–7
Judaism, on mules, 125
Judas (diving horse), *176*

Kennedy, John F., 30–31, 126, 215
King (Branigan's Greyhound), 202, 243–47, *246,* 252, 255, 256

Klastow, Ruth, 243, 244–45
Kopertox, 83–84

language, research on chimpanzees
    and, 216–17
Lawrence, Lorena, *see* Carver, Lorena
Lemmon, William, 218
Lick's Pier, diving horse act at, 92
Lightning (diving horse), 91–92,
    174, 208
Lillie, "Pawnee Bill," 48
Little Powderface (diving horse),
    209
Live from the Steel Pier, 52
Lorenz, Lorena, *see* Carver, Lorena
Lorgah (diving horse), 100, 168,
    173
Luck of the Irish (horse from
    auction), 143

Major (dog), 89
Malle, Louis, 93
Manaus, Brazil, 219
Man Kind? (Amory), 8, 9, 18, 46
Manning, Dan, 243, 248, 249, 250
Marine Mammal Stranding
    Center, 94
Mastiffs, 125
McCook, Jon, 79, 144
McCook, Wendy, 78, 79, 139, 144,
    154, 175, 186, 196
as aiding Branigan's horse
    education, 123
AmFran and, 119
barn of, 74
Gamal and, 66, 68, 70, 71, 72, 76,
    82–83, 84, 85–86, 102, 142,
    148–49, 202–4, 252
Hot Britches and, 137, 138
photograph of, *120*

Prince Nelson and, 139, 140, 141
Shiloh and, 119, 135, 148, 149
Sparkplug and, 128, 129, 130,
    148, 149, 150, 183–84, 185
trip to Florida with Branigan,
    160–61, 163–64, 165, 166, 175,
    177, 178
McDevitt, Terrie, 211–12
Millar, George, *197,* 197–98, 252
Miller, Glenn, 31, 52
Miss America pageant, 27
Morris, George, 154
mules
diving, 206, *206–7,* 208, 260
as hybrids, 123

National Park Service (NPS), 106,
    107–8, 109
New Holland auction, 143–44
New York's Hippodrome, 53–55, *54*
New York Times, 47
Niagara, 167
Nim Chimpsky (chimpanzee)
American Sign Language and, 216,
    217, 233, 234
Branigan and, 216, 223–24, 225,
    233, 233–34
Fund's rescue of, 218
photograph of, *233*

Oakley, Annie, 46
Obanhein, William, 242
Old Joe (horse), 58
Orwell, George, 59

Paul Winter Consort, 201
Peg (cat at Black Beauty Ranch),
    226
People, 109, *110*
Perillo, Betty, 209–10

Perillo, Louis, 209–10
Perils of Pauline, The, 150
Phantom (diving horse), 100
pigs, 125
Poitou mules, 124
Polar Bear (Cleveland Amory's cat),
    18, 19, 55–56, 258
Powderface (diving horse sold at
    auction)
  as diving horse, 23, 77, 173, 176,
    211–12
  sale of, 22, 63, 94, 98, 173
Powderface (diving horse, one of the
    first Powderfaces), 91, 209
Prince Nelson (former Standardbred
    racehorse)
  at Black Beauty Ranch, 141, 146,
    198, 221, 222, 223, 235
  move from McCook's farm, 196
  photograph of, *141*
  as a racehorse, 139
  rescue of, 139–41
  sale of, 140
  Shiloh and, 141, 221
Project Nim, 216, 217
Proper Bostonians, The (Amory), 8, 18
Probst, Marian (Cleveland Amory's
    assistant), 15, 18, 117, 194

R-D-R Farm, 196, *197,* 235
Red Lips (diving horse), *89, 90, 210*
Resorts International, 97–98, 99
Rich, Buddy, 100
Rocky, 142
Roeder, Ben, 242
Rogers, Kenny, 100
Rolling Stones, 52
Roosevelt, Theodore, 91
Royal Virginia (mare from auction),
    143, 195, 247–50

Sadat, Anwar, 198
Sally (Nim's chimpanzee companion),
    218, 223, 224, 226, 233
Schoelkopf, Bob, 94–96, 100, 171,
    174
Scout, The, 50
seals, 106, 109, 172
Sea Shepherd Conservation Society,
    106
Sewell, Anna, 109
Shakespeare, William, 126
Shiloh (diving horse)
  at Black Beauty Ranch, 122, 146,
    198, 221–22, 223, 231–32, 235
  Branigan and, 134–36, 148–49,
    174, 255
  as a diving horse, 114, 174, 211
  Gamal and, 119–21
  health of, 134–36
  move from McCook's farm, 196
  photographs of, *119, 120*
  Prince Nelson and, 141, 221
  sale of, 22, 94, 98–99, 114–15,
    116–17, 118, 139
  Sparkplug and, 181
Sinatra, Frank, 52
Skinner, B. F., 217
smegma, 86
Smith, Oscar, 91
Snow (diving horse), 174
Sparkplug (burro from the Grand
    Canyon), 128–30, 142
  arrival at Wendy's farm, 128,
    129–30, 213, 216
  Branigan's relationship with, 148,
    181, 188, 189–91
  braying of, 128–29, 147, 181
  death of, 191, 192, 193–94, 195
  Good Morning America segment and,
    132–34, 150

Sparkplug (burro from the Grand Canyon) *(continued)*
  Hot Britches' friendship with, 138, 147, 181
  ill health of, 183–91, 252
  in meadow by Branigan's home, 148–50, 255
  personality of, 146–48
  photographs of, *129, 138*
SPCA, 169–70
St. Helens, Mount, 57, 67
Standardbreds, 73
Stanley (retired New York City Park Ranger horse), 221, 222, 223, 235
Steinberg, Saul, 214
Stockbridge (Branigan's Border Collie), 69, *150,* 214, 242–43, 245, 246, 254
Super Sunday, 141–42
Swift, Jonathan, 125

Te Amo (Dale Bauersachs' horse), 249
Terrace, Herbert, 217, 218, 221
Texan (employee at Black Beauty Ranch), 225, 226
  adoption of dog, 134
  concerns about safe for gun, 130–32
  Fund's dismissal of, 213
  as part-time deputy sheriff, 131, 216
  as possible heir apparent to Cleveland, 214
  transport of Sparkplug, 127, 128, 129, 130, 132, 134, 213, 215–16
That's Incredible!, 142
Theatre Magazine, 54
Thinker, The, 142
Thoroughbreds, 72, 73, 75, 107
Those Amazing Animals, 142

thrush, 83, 84
Timex wristwatch ad, diving horse in, 100
Trapper, The, 50
Trump, Donald, 99, 260
TV Guide, 8, 10, 15
Twain, Mark, 47

Verbal Behavior (Skinner), 217
Victoria, Queen, 49

Walch, Garnet, 50
Walter (last owner of Carver diving horses), 96, 98–99, 170
Washoe (female chimpanzee), 216–17
Washoe Project, 216–17
Watson, Paul, 106
Webster, Sonora, 51
  accident during diving act, 89, 90, 171
  death of, 259
  diving career of, 52, 89, 90, 91, 171, 209
  on diving horses, 89, 91–92
  on Doc Carver, 90, 93
  A Girl and Five Brave Horses, 90, 174
  Lorena's relationship with, 176
  marriage to Al, 90, 177
  photographs of, *89, 176*
  retirement of, 90, 209
whaling, 106
Wild America show, 49, 50
Wild Hearts Can't Be Broken, 91, 177
Wilhelm II, 49
withers, 71–72
Witness, 197
Wooly Bully (burro from Death Valley), 201

Illustration Credits

29 *Diving horse, 1960:* Leon Reed

30 *Diving horse with LBJ vest:* Arthur Rickerby/Getty Images

51 *Lorena Carver at Calgary:* W.J. Oliver/Glenbow Archives, University of Calgary

53 *Steel Pier in 1933:* Atlantic City Heritage Collections, Atlantic City Free Public Library

110 *Cleveland Amory with burro:* © Barry Staver

120 *Gamal and Shiloh in field:* Andrew Holland

145 *Cynthia and Gamal in 1980:* Andrew Holland

169 *Bill Ditty removing harness:* Courtesy of Ruth Ditty

170 *Gamal, Bill, and Lorena in 1970:* Courtesy of Ruth Ditty

176 *Lorena and Sonora in the 1930s:* Atlantic City Heritage Collections, Atlantic City Free Public Library

199 *Cynthia and Calvin in 1985:* Andrew Holland

210 *Lorena with Red Lips in 1925:* Courtesy of Ruth Ditty

246 *Cynthia and King:* Andrew Holland

All other images are either courtesy of the author or are in the public domain.

A Note About the Author

Cynthia Branigan grew up in New Jersey and was educated at Franconia College and the University of Pennsylvania. She is the founder of Make Peace with Animals, Inc., and pioneered the adoption of retired racing Greyhounds worldwide. She lives in New Hope, Pennsylvania.

A Note on the Type

The text of this book was set in Garamond No. 3. It is not a true copy of any of the designs of Claude Garamond (ca. 1480–1561), but an adaptation of his types, which set the European standard for two centuries. This particular version is based on an adaptation by Morris Fuller Benton.

Composed by North Market Street Graphics
Lancaster Pennsylvania

Printed and bound by Berryville Graphics,
Berryville, Virginia

Design by Betty Lew